Safety Symbols

These symbols appear in laboratory activities.
They alert you to possible dangers and remind
you to work carefully.

General Safety Awareness Read all directions for an experiment several times. Follow the directions exactly as they are written. If you are in doubt, ask your teacher for assistance.

Physical Safety If the lab includes physical activity, use caution to avoid injuring yourself or others. Tell your teacher if there is a reason that you should not participate.

Safety Goggles Always wear safety goggles to protect your eyes in any activity involving chemicals, heating, or the possibility of broken glassware.

Lab Apron Wear a laboratory apron to protect your skin and clothing from harmful chemicals or hot materials.

Plastic Gloves Wear disposable plastic gloves to protect yourself from contact with chemicals that can be harmful. Keep your hands away from your face. Dispose of gloves according to your teacher's instructions.

Heating Use a clamp or tongs to hold hot objects. Test an object by first holding the back of your hand near it. If you feel heat, the object may be too hot to handle.

Heat-Resistant Gloves Hot plates, hot water, and hot glassware can cause burns. Never touch hot objects with your bare hands. Use an oven mitt or other hand protection.

Flames Tie back long hair and loose clothing, and put on safety goggles before using a burner. Follow instructions from your teacher for lighting and extinguishing burners.

No Flames If flammable materials are present, make sure there are no flames, sparks, or exposed sources of heat.

Electric Shock To avoid an electric shock, never use electrical equipment near water, or when the equipment or your hands are wet. Use only sockets that accept a three-prong plug. Be sure cords are untangled and cannot trip anyone. Disconnect equipment that is not in use.

Fragile Glassware Handle fragile glassware, such as thermometers, test tubes, and beakers, with care. Do not touch broken glass. Notify your teacher if glassware breaks. Never use chipped or cracked glassware.

Corrosive Chemical Avoid getting corrosive chemicals on your skin or clothing, or in your eyes. Do not inhale the vapors. Wash your hands after completing the activity.

Poison Do not let any poisonous chemical get on your skin, and do not inhale its vapor. Wash your hands after completing the activity.

Fumes When working with poisonous or irritating vapors, work in a well-ventilated area. Never test for an odor unless instructed to do so by your teacher. Avoid inhaling a vapor directly. Use a wafting motion to direct vapor toward your nose.

Sharp Object Use sharp instruments only as directed. Scissors, scalpels, pins, and knives are sharp and can cut or puncture your skin. Always direct sharp edges and points away from yourself and others.

Disposal All chemicals and other materials used in the laboratory must be disposed of safely. Follow your teacher's instructions.

Hand Washing Before leaving the lab, wash your hands thoroughly with soap or detergent, and warm water. Lather both sides of your hands and between your fingers. Rinse well.

Electricity and Magnetism

PRENTICE HALL Science Explorer

PEARSON

Prentice Hall

Boston, Massachusetts
Upper Saddle River, New Jersey

PRENTICE HALL Science Explorer

Electricity and Magnetism

Book-Specific Resources

Student Edition
StudentExpress™ with Interactive Textbook
Teacher's Edition
All-in-One Teaching Resources
Color Transparencies
Guided Reading and Study Workbook
Student Edition on Audio CD
Discovery Channel School® Video
Lab Activity Video
Consumable and Nonconsumable Materials Kits

Program Print Resources

Integrated Science Laboratory Manual
Computer Microscope Lab Manual
Inquiry Skills Activity Books
Progress Monitoring Assessments
Test Preparation Workbook
Test-Taking Tips With Transparencies
Teacher's ELL Handbook
Reading Strategies for Science Content

Differentiated Instruction Resources

Adapted Reading and Study Workbook
Adapted Tests
Differentiated Instruction Guide for Labs and Activities

Program Technology Resources

TeacherExpress™ CD-ROM
Interactive Textbooks Online
PresentationExpress™ CD-ROM
ExamView®, Computer Test Bank CD-ROM
Lab zone™ Easy Planner CD-ROM
Probeware Lab Manual With CD-ROM
Computer Microscope and Lab Manual
Materials Ordering CD-ROM
Discovery Channel School® DVD Library
Lab Activity DVD Library
Web Site at PHSchool.com

Spanish Print Resources

Spanish Student Edition
Spanish Guided Reading and Study Workbook
Spanish Teaching Guide With Tests

Acknowledgments appear on page 182, which constitutes an extension of this copyright page.

Cover
A spectacular discharge of static electricity flashes across the night sky (top). The north magnetic pole to which a compass needle points slowly moves over time (bottom).

PEARSON
Prentice Hall

ISBN 0-13-201158-1
3 4 5 6 7 8 9 10   10 09 08 07

Program Authors

Michael J. Padilla, Ph.D.
Professor of Science Education
University of Georgia
Athens, Georgia

Michael Padilla is a leader in middle school science education. He has served as an author and elected officer for the National Science Teachers Association and as a writer of the National Science Education Standards. As lead author of Science Explorer, Mike has inspired the team in developing a program that meets the needs of middle grades students, promotes science inquiry, and is aligned with the National Science Education Standards.

Ioannis Miaoulis, Ph.D.
President
Museum of Science
Boston, Massachusetts

Originally trained as a mechanical engineer, Ioannis Miaoulis is in the forefront of the national movement to increase technological literacy. As dean of the Tufts University School of Engineering, Dr. Miaoulis spearheaded the introduction of engineering into the Massachusetts curriculum. Currently he is working with school systems across the country to engage students in engineering activities and to foster discussions on the impact of science and technology on society.

Martha Cyr, Ph.D.
Director of K–12 Outreach
Worcester Polytechnic Institute
Worcester, Massachusetts

Martha Cyr is a noted expert in engineering outreach. She has over nine years of experience with programs and activities that emphasize the use of engineering principles, through hands-on projects, to excite and motivate students and teachers of mathematics and science in grades K–12. Her goal is to stimulate a continued interest in science and mathematics through engineering.

Book Author

Camille L. Wainwright, Ph.D.
Professor of Science Education
Pacific University
Forest Grove, Oregon

Contributing Writers

Edward Evans
Former Science Teacher
Hilton Central School
Hilton, New York

Mark Illingworth
Teacher
Hollis Public Schools
Hollis, New Hampshire

Thomas L. Messer
Science Teacher
Cape Cod Academy
Osterville, Massachusetts

Thomas R. Wellnitz
Science Teacher
The Paideia School
Atlanta, Georgia

Consultants

Reading Consultant

Nancy Romance, Ph.D.
Professor of Science
    Education
Florida Atlantic University
Fort Lauderdale, Florida

Mathematics Consultant

William Tate, Ph.D.
Professor of Education and
    Applied Statistics and
    Computation
Washington University
St. Louis, Missouri

Reviewers

Tufts University Content Reviewers

Faculty from Tufts University in Medford, Massachusetts, developed *Science Explorer* chapter projects and reviewed the student books.

Astier M. Almedom, Ph.D.
Department of Biology

Wayne Chudyk, Ph.D.
Department of Civil and Environmental Engineering

John L. Durant, Ph.D.
Department of Civil and Environmental Engineering

George S. Ellmore, Ph.D.
Department of Biology

David Kaplan, Ph.D.
Department of Biomedical Engineering

Samuel Kounaves, Ph.D.
Department of Chemistry

David H. Lee, Ph.D.
Department of Chemistry

Douglas Matson, Ph.D.
Department of Mechanical Engineering

Karen Panetta, Ph.D.
Department of Electrical Engineering and Computer Science

Jan A. Pechenik, Ph.D.
Department of Biology

John C. Ridge, Ph.D.
Department of Geology

William Waller, Ph.D.
Department of Astronomy

Content Reviewers

Paul Beale, Ph.D.
Department of Physics
University of Colorado
Boulder, Colorado

Jeff Bodart, Ph.D.
Chipola Junior College
Marianna, Florida

Michael Castellani, Ph.D.
Department of Chemistry
Marshall University
Huntington, West Virginia

Eugene Chiang, Ph.D.
Department of Astronomy
University of California – Berkeley
Berkeley, California

Charles C. Curtis, Ph.D.
Department of Physics
University of Arizona
Tucson, Arizona

Daniel Kirk-Davidoff, Ph.D.
Department of Meteorology
University of Maryland
College Park, Maryland

Diane T. Doser, Ph.D.
Department of Geological Sciences
University of Texas at El Paso
El Paso, Texas

R. E. Duhrkopf, Ph.D.
Department of Biology
Baylor University
Waco, Texas

Michael Hacker
Co-director, Center for Technological Literacy
Hofstra University
Hempstead, New York

Michael W. Hamburger, Ph.D.
Department of Geological Sciences
Indiana University
Bloomington, Indiana

Alice K. Hankla, Ph.D.
The Galloway School
Atlanta, Georgia

Donald C. Jackson, Ph.D.
Department of Molecular Pharmacology, Physiology, & Biotechnology
Brown University
Providence, Rhode Island

Jeremiah N. Jarrett, Ph.D.
Department of Biological Sciences
Central Connecticut State University
New Britain, Connecticut

David Lederman, Ph.D.
Department of Physics
West Virginia University
Morgantown, West Virginia

Becky Mansfield, Ph.D.
Department of Geography
Ohio State University
Columbus, Ohio

Elizabeth M. Martin, M.S.
Department of Chemistry and Biochemistry
College of Charleston
Charleston, South Carolina

Joe McCullough, Ph.D.
Department of Natural and Applied Sciences
Cabrillo College
Aptos, California

Robert J. Mellors, Ph.D.
Department of Geological Sciences
San Diego State University
San Diego, California

Joseph M. Moran, Ph.D.
American Meteorological Society
Washington, D.C.

David J. Morrissey, Ph.D.
Department of Chemistry
Michigan State University
East Lansing, Michigan

Philip A. Reed, Ph.D.
Department of Occupational & Technical Studies
Old Dominion University
Norfolk, Virginia

Scott M. Rochette, Ph.D.
Department of the Earth Sciences
State University of New York, College at Brockport
Brockport, New York

Laurence D. Rosenhein, Ph.D.
Department of Chemistry
Indiana State University
Terre Haute, Indiana

Ronald Sass, Ph.D.
Department of Biology and Chemistry
Rice University
Houston, Texas

George Schatz, Ph.D.
Department of Chemistry
Northwestern University
Evanston, Illinois

Sara Seager, Ph.D.
Carnegie Institution of Washington
Washington, D.C.

Robert M. Thornton, Ph.D.
Section of Plant Biology
University of California
Davis, California

John R. Villarreal, Ph.D.
College of Science and Engineering
The University of Texas – Pan American
Edinburg, Texas

Kenneth Welty, Ph.D.
School of Education
University of Wisconsin–Stout
Menomonie, Wisconsin

Edward J. Zalisko, Ph.D.
Department of Biology
Blackburn College
Carlinville, Illinois

Teacher Reviewers

David R. Blakely
Arlington High School
Arlington, Massachusetts

Jane E. Callery
Two Rivers Magnet Middle
School
East Hartford, Connecticut

Melissa Lynn Cook
Oakland Mills High School
Columbia, Maryland

James Fattic
Southside Middle School
Anderson, Indiana

Dan Gabel
Hoover Middle School
Rockville, Maryland

Wayne Goates
Eisenhower Middle School
Goddard, Kansas

Katherine Bobay Graser
Mint Hill Middle School
Charlotte, North Carolina

Darcy Hampton
Deal Junior High School
Washington, D.C.

Karen Kelly
Pierce Middle School
Waterford, Michigan

David Kelso
Manchester High School Central
Manchester, New Hampshire

Benigno Lopez, Jr.
Sleepy Hill Middle School
Lakeland, Florida

Angie L. Matamoros, Ph.D.
ALM Consulting, INC.
Weston, Florida

Tim McCollum
Charleston Middle School
Charleston, Illinois

Bruce A. Mellin
Brooks School
North Andover, Massachusetts

Ella Jay Parfitt
Southeast Middle School
Baltimore, Maryland

Evelyn A. Pizzarello
Louis M. Klein Middle School
Harrison, New York

Kathleen M. Poe
Fletcher Middle School
Jacksonville, Florida

Shirley Rose
Lewis and Clark Middle School
Tulsa, Oklahoma

Linda Sandersen
Greenfield Middle School
Greenfield, Wisconsin

Mary E. Solan
Southwest Middle School
Charlotte, North Carolina

Mary Stewart
University of Tulsa
Tulsa, Oklahoma

Paul Swenson
Billings West High School
Billings, Montana

Thomas Vaughn
Arlington High School
Arlington, Massachusetts

Susan C. Zibell
Central Elementary
Simsbury, Connecticut

Safety Reviewers

W. H. Breazeale, Ph.D.
Department of Chemistry
College of Charleston
Charleston, South Carolina

Ruth Hathaway, Ph.D.
Hathaway Consulting
Cape Girardeau, Missouri

Douglas Mandt, M.S.
Science Education Consultant
Edgewood, Washington

Activity Field Testers

Nicki Bibbo
Witchcraft Heights School
Salem, Massachusetts

Rose-Marie Botting
Broward County Schools
Fort Lauderdale, Florida

Colleen Campos
Laredo Middle School
Aurora, Colorado

Elizabeth Chait
W. L. Chenery Middle School
Belmont, Massachusetts

Holly Estes
Hale Middle School
Stow, Massachusetts

Laura Hapgood
Plymouth Community
Intermediate School
Plymouth, Massachusetts

Mary F. Lavin
Plymouth Community
Intermediate School
Plymouth, Massachusetts

James MacNeil, Ph.D.
Cambridge, Massachusetts

Lauren Magruder
St. Michael's Country
Day School
Newport, Rhode Island

Jeanne Maurand
Austin Preparatory School
Reading, Massachusetts

Joanne Jackson-Pelletier
Winman Junior High School
Warwick, Rhode Island

Warren Phillips
Plymouth Public Schools
Plymouth, Massachusetts

Carol Pirtle
Hale Middle School
Stow, Massachusetts

Kathleen M. Poe
Fletcher Middle School
Jacksonville, Florida

Cynthia B. Pope
Norfolk Public Schools
Norfolk, Virginia

Anne Scammell
Geneva Middle School
Geneva, New York

Karen Riley Sievers
Callanan Middle School
Des Moines, Iowa

David M. Smith
Eyer Middle School
Allentown, Pennsylvania

Gene Vitale
Parkland School
McHenry, Illinois

Contents

Electricity and Magnetism

Reference Section

VIDEO

Enhance understanding through dynamic video.

Preview Get motivated with this introduction to the chapter content.

Field Trip Explore a real-world story related to the chapter content.

Assessment Review content and take an assessment.

Web Links

Get connected to exciting Web resources in every lesson.

$SC_{\large i}$ **LINKS** NSTA Find Web links on topics relating to every section.

Active Art Interact with selected visuals from every chapter online.

Planet Diary® Explore news and natural phenomena through weekly reports.

Science News® Keep up to date with the latest science discoveries.

Interactive Textbook

Experience the complete textbook online and on CD-ROM.

Activities Practice skills and learn content.

Videos Explore content and learn important lab skills.

Audio Support Hear key terms spoken and defined.

Self-Assessment Use instant feedback to help you track your progress.

Activities

Labs
In-depth practice of inquiry skills and science concepts

At-Home Activity
Quick, engaging activities for home and family

Tech & Design
Design, build, test, and communicate

Math
Point-of-use math practice

active art
Illustrations come alive online

When Illusion Is Better Than Reality

One of the best parts of her job, says engineer Estela Hernandez, is that she gets to fly the space shuttle. "And I'm pretty good at it," she adds.

It is not the real space shuttle, but it is as close as anyone ever gets without going through astronaut training. Estela logs her shuttle hours on a flight simulator—a flight training program. The flight simulator is at the Ames Research Center at NASA (National Aeronautics and Space Administration). As a flight simulation engineer, Estela helps develop computer programs that simulate the real world of flying. So it's her job to help create the nearest thing to flying an aircraft that anyone can experience without leaving the ground.

The flight simulations may at first seem like very high-tech computer games. But they have a very serious purpose: They save lives. Estela and other engineers create flight simulations that allow pilots and astronauts to train. The pilots and astronauts make their mistakes on the ground, where no one gets hurt.

Estela flies the space shuttle—without leaving the ground.

Talking With Estela Hernandez

The Role of Computers

Estela and her fellow engineers use computers to create the illusion of flying. Because a computer can make lightning-fast calculations, it can monitor what a pilot is doing. Computers can direct the various instruments and controls to respond just as they would in a real aircraft under the same conditions. "When the pilot moves the stick," Estela says, "those inputs go back to the computer. The computer calculates how the aircraft would move, what the instruments will display, and even what the pilot sees out the window." None of the simulation would be possible without a computer.

Career Path

Estela Hernandez was born in Mexico and grew up in Valencia, California. She earned a bachelor's degree in aeronautical engineering from California Polytechnic State University in San Luis Obispo. She worked as a summer intern at NASA. After graduation, she worked at Lockheed Martin Corporation on the company's missile program. Today, Estela works as a flight simulation engineer at NASA's Ames Research Center in California. Recently, she earned a master's degree in engineering management from Santa Clara University in California.

An Unexpected Career

Estela did not set out to be a flight simulation engineer. "When I got out of high school, I wasn't sure just what I wanted to do," she says, "but I had always liked taking things apart and figuring out how they worked." Estela studied science and math for two years. Then, she took the advice of a math professor and went on to study engineering at California Polytechnic. Still, she wasn't sure what type of engineering she should choose. In the end she says, "I chose aeronautical engineering instead of mechanical engineering."

"I wasn't really sure I liked engineering until I spent a summer working for NASA," she says. She was part of a team using simulations to figure out how to refuel blimps while they are in the air. "This was really cool," she says. "Quickly, I was hooked." For the first time, she knew what career she wanted. As soon as an engineering job in flight simulation came up at NASA, Estela jumped at the chance.

The VMS can simulate the flight of a Harrier jet (above). The cab (left) contains a cockpit with the sounds and images of flight. The cab rests on a motion base that simulates the motion of flight. The out-of-the-window graphic (below) shows the Harrier pilot's view as the aircraft approaches the runway.

The Vertical Motion Simulator

Estela works on a machine called the Vertical Motion Simulator, or VMS. You can compare the VMS to a flight simulator video game that you may have played. You use the usual video game controls to steer the aircraft up, down, right, and left. You can also speed up the aircraft or slow it down. On the video game screen, you see an image of what you're flying through—the ground below and various objects visible in the sky around you. The video screen will also show such instrument readings as your speed, direction, and altitude.

However, unlike video game controls, the controls and instruments of the Vertical Motion Simulator are on an instrument panel like one in a real aircraft.

Instead of a single computer screen, you have several screens. These screens provide a view of what you would see looking out the windows of the real aircraft. The controls and instruments, the video screens, and your chair are all inside a large box, called a cab. The cab is laid out like the cockpit of the actual aircraft. Large motors move the cab around—forward and back, up and down, side to side. This movement reproduces the motion of the real aircraft as it bounces around in flight. When a tire blows, for instance, you feel your vehicle lurch.

It is this capacity for motion that makes the Vertical Motion Simulator valuable to astronauts and other pilots. "Most of the flight simulators don't have motion," she says. "They may look like the real thing, but they don't feel like the real thing."

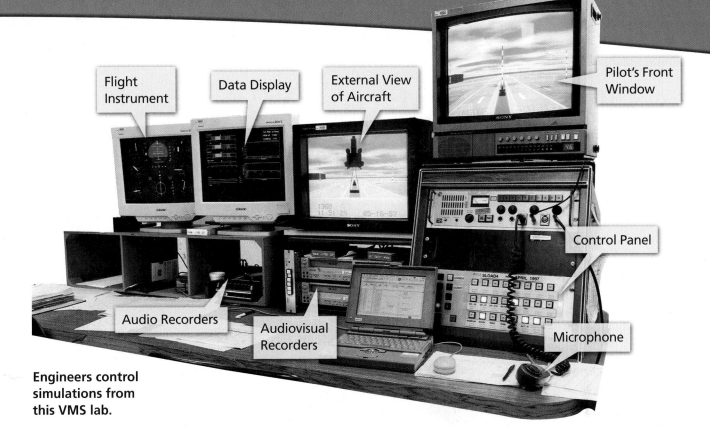

Flight Instrument

Data Display

External View of Aircraft

Pilot's Front Window

Control Panel

Audio Recorders

Audiovisual Recorders

Microphone

Engineers control simulations from this VMS lab.

Behind the illusion

Creating the illusion of flight can be as challenging and as fun as actual flying. "First, you have to know how an aircraft works," she says. "You have to understand what is being controlled." She and the other engineers who work on the VMS start with mathematical equations. These equations describe the motion of an aircraft as it flies through the air—or touches down on the ground. The engineers feed those equations into a computer. The computer can calculate just how the craft will move under different circumstances.

Estela and her co-workers must write the programming codes or instructions that tell the computer precisely what to do. Each simulation generally takes several months to develop. The engineers are responsible for the computer graphics that provide the visual images that make the simulation look so realistic. The engineers also must tell the computer how to shake the cockpit in just the right way to make it seem as though it is really moving. "We do a little bit of everything," Hernandez says, which is one of the reasons she loves what she does. "A lot of other places you are doing just one thing."

The Best Part of the Job

"Perhaps the best part of the job," she says, "is seeing how the simulation all comes together at the end to create the illusion of flying. It is very neat to write the code and then get to see how it works."

Writing in Science

Career Link Estela's job as an engineer is to develop computer programs that simulate flight. Suppose you are a simulation engineer. Plan a simulation you'd like to develop to represent driving a car, a snowmobile, a tractor, or a helicopter. In a paragraph, describe the sounds, sights, and motions you might experience in a one-minute simulation.

Go Online
PHSchool.com

For: More on this career
Visit: PHSchool.com
Web Code: cgb-4000

Chapter

1

Magnetism

Chapter Preview

The aurora borealis glows above a cabin in Manitoba, Canada. ▶

⚠ Lab zone™ Chapter **Project**

Magnetic Art

Magnetism is often used to do work, but it can also be used to create art! In this chapter project you will create a sculpture using nothing but magnetism to hold it together.

Your Goal To create a magnetic sculpture.

To complete this project, your sculpture must

● be held together *only* by magnets and objects with magnetic properties
● be at least 20 cm tall
● keep its shape for at least two hours
● follow the safety guide-lines in Appendix A

Plan It! Your teacher will suggest a variety of materials that you can use to make your sculpture. With your group, brainstorm ideas for your plan. Decide which materials can be magnetized. After obtaining your teacher's approval for your plan, make your sculpture.

What Is Magnetism?

Reading Preview

Key Concepts
- What are the properties of a magnet?
- How do magnetic poles interact?
- What is the shape of a magnetic field?

Key Terms
- magnet • magnetic pole
- magnetic force
- magnetic field
- magnetic field lines

Target Reading Skill

Using Prior Knowledge Before you read, look at the headings and visuals to see what this section is about. Then write what you know about magnetism in a graphic organizer like the one below. As you read, write what you learn.

What You Know
1. Magnets stick to refrigerators.
2.

What You Learned
1.
2.

Lab zone Discover **Activity**

What Do All Magnets Have in Common?

1. Obtain a bar magnet and a horseshoe magnet.
2. See how many paper clips you can attract to different parts of each magnet.
3. Draw a diagram showing the number and location of paper clips on each magnet.

Think It Over
Observing Where does each magnet hold the greatest number of paper clips? What similarities do you observe between the two magnets?

Imagine zooming along in a train that glides without even touching the ground. You feel no vibration and hear no noise from the steel tracks below. You can just sit back and relax as you speed toward your destination at nearly 500 kilometers per hour.

Are you dreaming? No, you are not. You are floating a few centimeters in the air on a magnetically levitating train, or maglev train. Although you have probably not ridden on such a train, they do exist. What makes them float? Believe it or not, it is magnetism that makes them float.

◀ Strong magnets move this Japanese maglev train.

Properties of Magnets

When you think of magnets, you might think about the objects that hold notes to your refrigerator. But magnets can also be found in many other everyday items such as wallets, kitchen cabinets, and security tags at a store. A **magnet** is any material that attracts iron and materials that contain iron.

Magnets have many modern uses, but they are not new. More than 2,000 years ago, people living in the ancient Greek city of Magnesia (in what is now Turkey) discovered an unusual kind of rock. This kind of rock contained a mineral called magnetite. Both the word *magnetite* and the word *magnet* come from the name Magnesia. Rocks containing magnetite attracted materials that contained iron. They also attracted or repelled other magnetic rocks. The attraction or repulsion of magnetic materials is called magnetism.

About a thousand years ago, people in other parts of the world discovered another property of magnetic rocks. If they allowed such a rock to swing freely from a string, one part of the rock would always point in the same direction. That direction was toward the North Star, Polaris. This star is also called the leading star, or lodestar. For this reason, magnetic rocks are known as lodestones.

Magnets have the same properties as magnetic rocks. **Magnets attract iron and materials that contain iron. Magnets attract or repel other magnets. In addition, one part of a magnet will always point north when allowed to swing freely.**

 Reading Checkpoint What mineral found in rocks can attract materials containing iron?

FIGURE 1
A Natural Magnet
Some magnets are found in nature. This rock attracts iron nails because it contains the magnetic mineral called magnetite.

FIGURE 2
Modern Magnets
Magnets come in a variety of shapes and sizes, but they share certain characteristics.
Inferring *What substance might the scissors, paper clips, and spoon have in common?*

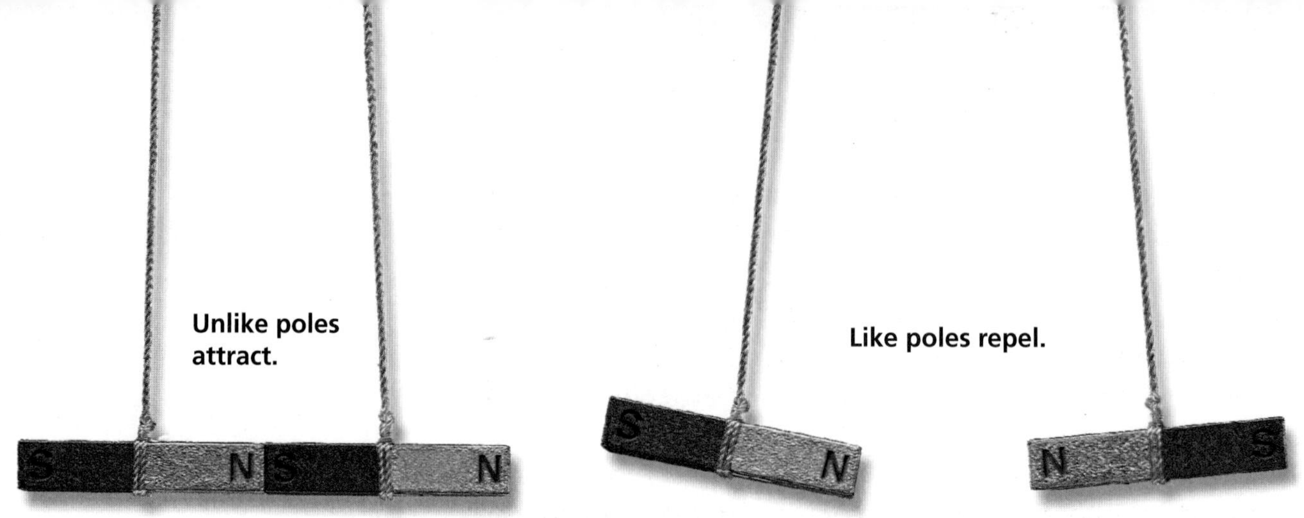

Unlike poles attract.

Like poles repel.

FIGURE 3
Attraction and Repulsion
Two bar magnets suspended by strings are brought near each other. Unlike poles attract each other; like poles repel each other.
Predicting *What would happen if two south poles were brought near one another?*

Magnetic Poles

The magnets in your everyday life have the same properties as magnetic rocks because they are made to have them. Recall that one end of a magnet always points north. Any magnet, no matter what its shape, has two ends, each one called a **magnetic pole.** The magnetic effect of a magnet is strongest at the poles. The pole of a magnet that points north is labeled the north pole. The other pole is labeled the south pole. A magnet always has a pair of poles, a north pole and a south pole.

Magnetic Interactions What happens if you bring two magnets together? The answer depends on how you hold the poles of the magnets. If you bring the north pole of one magnet near the south pole of another, the two unlike poles attract one another. However, if you bring two north poles together, the like poles move away from each other. The same is true if two south poles are brought together. **Magnetic poles that are unlike attract each other, and magnetic poles that are alike repel each other.** Figure 3 shows how two bar magnets interact.

Magnetic Force The attraction or repulsion between magnetic poles is **magnetic force.** A force is a push or a pull that can cause an object to move. A magnetic force is produced when magnetic poles interact. Any material that exerts a magnetic force is considered to be a magnet.

The maglev train you read about earlier depends on magnetic force to move. Magnets in the bottom of the train and in the guideway on the ground have like poles facing each other. Because like poles repel, the two magnets move away from each other. The result is that the train car is lifted up, or levitated. Other magnets make the train move forward.

 Reading Checkpoint **What does every magnet have in common?**

Magnetic Fields

A magnetic force is strongest at the poles of a magnet, but it is not limited to the poles. Magnetic forces are exerted all around a magnet. The area of magnetic force around a magnet is known as its **magnetic field.** Because of magnetic fields, magnets can interact without even touching.

Figure 4 shows the magnetic field of a bar magnet. Notice the red lines, called magnetic field lines, around the magnet. **Magnetic field lines** are invisible lines that map out the magnetic field around a magnet. **Magnetic field lines spread out from one pole, curve around the magnet, and return to the other pole.** The lines form complete loops from pole to pole and never cross. Arrows are used to indicate the direction of the magnetic field lines—always leaving the north pole and entering the south pole.

The distance between magnetic field lines indicates the strength of a magnetic field. The closer together the lines are, the stronger the field. A magnet's magnetic field lines are closest together at the poles.

Reading Checkpoint Where is the magnetic field strongest?

Go **O**nline
active art

For: Magnetic Field Lines activity
Visit: PHSchool.com
Web Code: cgp-4011

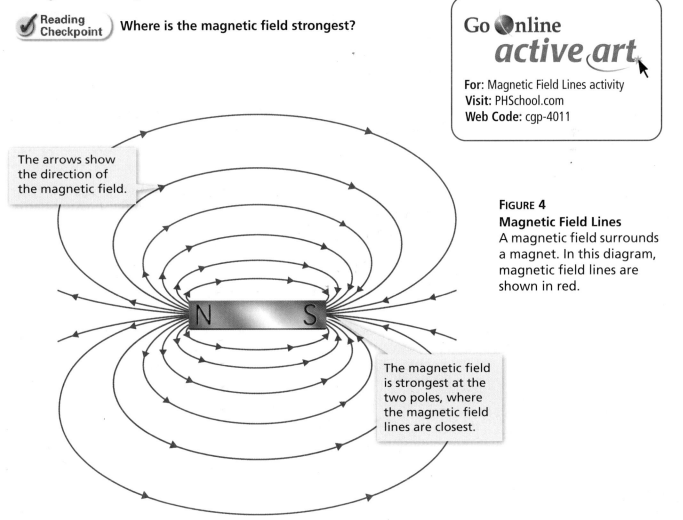

The arrows show the direction of the magnetic field.

The magnetic field is strongest at the two poles, where the magnetic field lines are closest.

FIGURE 4
Magnetic Field Lines
A magnetic field surrounds a magnet. In this diagram, magnetic field lines are shown in red.

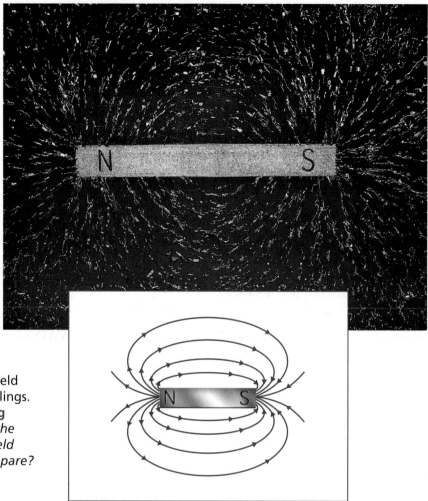

FIGURE 5
A Single Magnetic Field
A bar magnet's magnetic field
is mapped out using iron filings.
Comparing and Contrasting
*How do the iron filings in the
photo and the magnetic field
lines in the illustration compare?*

A Single Magnetic Field Although you cannot see a magnetic field, you can see its effects. The photograph in Figure 5 shows iron filings sprinkled on a sheet of plastic that covers one magnet. The magnetic forces of the magnet act on the iron filings and align them along the invisible magnetic field lines. The result is that the iron filings form a pattern similar to the magnetic field lines shown in the diagram in Figure 5.

Combined Magnetic Fields When the magnetic fields of two or more magnets overlap, the result is a combined field. Figure 6 shows the magnetic field produced when the poles of two bar magnets are brought near each other. Compare the combined field of two like poles to that of two unlike poles. Depending on which poles are near each other, the magnetic field lines are different. The fields from the like poles repel each other. But the fields from unlike poles attract each other. They combine to form a strong field between the two poles.

Reading Checkpoint What happens when the magnetic fields of two or more magnets overlap?

FIGURE 6
Combined Magnetic Fields
The magnetic field of a single bar
magnet is altered when another bar
magnet is brought near it.

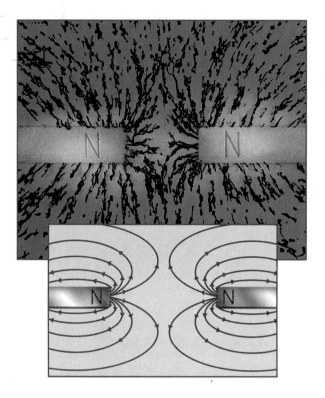

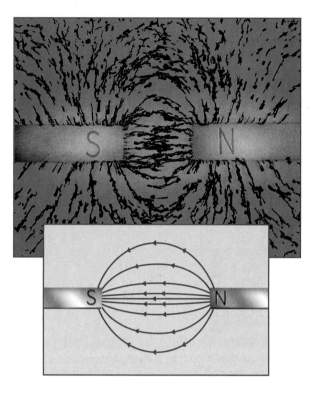

Section **1** **Assessment**

 Target Reading Skill Using Prior
Knowledge Review your graphic organizer
and revise it based on what you just learned in
the section.

Reviewing Key Concepts

1. **a. Reviewing** What is a magnet?
   b. Summarizing What are three properties of
   a magnet?
   c. Predicting What will happen to a bar
   magnet that is allowed to swing freely?
2. **a. Describing** What area of a magnet has the
   strongest magnetic effect?
   b. Explaining How does a magnet's north
   pole behave when brought near another
   north pole? Near a magnet's south pole?
   c. Relating Cause and Effect How can the
   behavior of two magnets show the
   presence of a magnetic force?

3. **a. Defining** What is a magnetic field?
   b. Interpreting Diagrams Look at Figure 4. What
   is the shape of the magnetic field?

Lab zone **At-Home Activity**

Magnetic Helpers Explain the properties of
magnets to a member of your family. Then
make a list of objects around your home that
are most likely to contain or use one or more
magnets. For example, magnets are used to
hold some cabinet doors closed. Have your
family member make a separate list. Compare
the two lists and explain to your family
member why each object is or is not likely to
contain or use magnets.

Detecting Fake Coins

Problem

How can you use a magnet to tell the difference between real and fake coins?

Skills Focus

predicting, observing, developing hypotheses

Materials

- various coins   • craft stick   • tape
- metric ruler   • pencil   • protractor
- coin-size steel washers
- small bar magnet, about 2 cm wide
- thin, stiff cardboard, about 25 cm × 30 cm

Procedure

1. Use a pencil to label the front, back, top, and bottom of the piece of cardboard.

2. Draw a line lengthwise down the middle of both sides of the cardboard.

3. On the back of the cardboard, draw a line parallel to the first and about 2 cm to the right.

4. Place a magnet, aligned vertically, about a third of the way down the line you drew in Step 3. Tape the magnet in place.

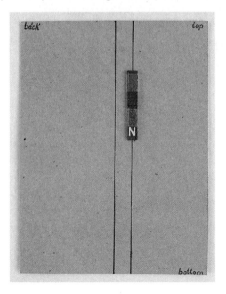

5. Place a craft stick on the front of the cardboard. The stick's upper end should be about 1 cm to the left of the center line and about 8 cm from the bottom of the cardboard.

6. Tape the stick at an angle, as shown in the photograph on the following page.

7. Prop the cardboard against something that will hold it at an angle of about 45°. Predict what will happen when you slide a coin down the front of the cardboard.

8. Place a coin on the center line and slide the coin down the front of the cardboard. (*Hint*: If the coin gets stuck, slowly increase the angle.)

9. Predict what will happen when you slide a steel washer.

10. Test your prediction by sliding a washer down the cardboard. Again, if the washer gets stuck, slowly increase the angle and try again.

11. Once you have reached an angle at which the objects slide easily, send down a randomly mixed group of coins and washers one at a time.

Analyze and Conclude

1. **Predicting** What was your prediction from Step 7? Explain your reasoning.

2. **Predicting** What was your prediction from Step 9? Explain your reasoning.

3. **Observing** Describe how observations made during the lab either supported or did not support your predictions.

4. **Developing Hypotheses** What is the role of the magnet in this lab?

5. **Developing Hypotheses** What is the role of the craft stick?

6. **Drawing Conclusions** What can you conclude about the metals from which the coins are made? About the metals in the washers?

7. **Controlling Variables** Why does the steepness of the cardboard affect how the coin-separating device works?

8. **Predicting** Some Canadian coins contain metals that are attracted to magnets. Would this device be useful in Canada to detect fake coins? Explain your answer.

9. **Communicating** Write a brochure that explains how the device could be used to separate real coins from fake coins and what advantages it might have for vending machine owners.

More to Explore

Go to a store that has vending machines. Find out who owns the vending machines. Ask the owners if they have a problem with counterfeit coins (sometimes called "slugs"). Ask how they or the makers of the vending machines solve the problem. How is their solution related to the device you built in this lab?

Inside a Magnet

Reading Preview

Key Concepts
- How can an atom behave like a magnet?
- How are magnetic domains arranged in a magnetic material?
- How can magnets be changed?

Key Terms
- atom • element • nucleus
- proton • neutron • electron
- magnetic domain
- ferromagnetic material
- temporary magnet
- permanent magnet

Target Reading Skill

Asking Questions Before you read, preview the red headings. In a graphic organizer like the one below, ask a *what* or *how* question for each heading. As you read, write the answers to your questions.

Inside an Atom

Question	Answer
What are the three particles that make up an atom?	The three particles that make up an atom are . . .

Lab zone · Discover Activity

How Can Materials Become Magnetic?

1. Fill a clear plastic tube about two-thirds full with iron filings.
2. Observe the arrangement of the filings.
3. Rub the tube lengthwise about 30 times in the same direction with one end of a strong magnet.
4. Again, observe the arrangement of the filings.

Think It Over
Drawing Conclusions What can you conclude from your observations?

You've probably noticed that if you bring a magnet near the door of your refrigerator, it clings. But what happens if you bring a piece of paper near the same refrigerator door? Nothing. You have to use a magnet to hold the paper against the door. Materials such as paper, plastic, rubber, and glass do not have magnetic properties. They will not cling to magnets and certain metals. Why are some materials magnetic while others are not?

Only certain materials will ▶ cling to the refrigerator using magnetism.

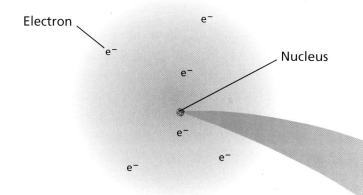

Electron

e⁻

e⁻

Nucleus

e⁻

e⁻

e⁻

e⁻

FIGURE 7
Structure of an Atom
An atom contains neutrons and positively charged protons in its nucleus. Negatively charged electrons move randomly throughout the atom.

Proton   Neutron

The Atom

The magnetic properties of a material depend on the structure of its atoms. Because materials take up space and have mass, they are classified as matter. All matter is made up of atoms. An **atom** is the smallest particle of an element. An **element** is one of about 100 basic substances that make up all matter. The structure and composition of the atoms that make up a particular element make that element different from any other element.

Structure of an Atom Although atoms can differ, they have some characteristics in common. Every atom has a center region and an outer region. The center region of an atom is called a **nucleus.** Inside the nucleus two kinds of particles may be found: protons and neutrons. A **proton** is a particle that carries a positive charge. A **neutron** is a particle that does not carry a charge.

The outer region of an atom is mainly empty space. However, particles called electrons usually exist there. An **electron** is a particle that carries a negative charge. Electrons move randomly throughout the atom. They are much smaller than neutrons and protons. Look at Figure 7 to see the structure of an atom.

Electron Spin Each electron in an atom has a property called electron spin, so it behaves as if it were spinning. **A spinning electron produces a magnetic field that makes the electron behave like a tiny magnet in an atom.**

In most atoms, electrons form pairs that spin in opposite directions. Opposite spins produce opposite magnetic fields that cancel. Therefore, most atoms have weak magnetic properties. But some atoms contain electrons that are not paired. These atoms tend to have strong magnetic properties.

Reading Checkpoint **Why are most materials not magnetic?**

Magnetic Domains

The magnetic fields of the atoms in most materials point in random directions. The result is that the magnetic fields cancel one another almost entirely. The magnetic force is so weak that you cannot usually detect it.

In certain materials, however, the magnetic fields of many atoms are aligned with one another. A grouping of atoms that have their magnetic fields aligned is known as a **magnetic domain.** The entire domain acts like a bar magnet with a north pole and a south pole.

Alignment of Domains The direction in which the domains point determines if the material is magnetized or not magnetized. In a material that is not magnetized, the magnetic domains point in random directions, as shown in Figure 8. Therefore, the magnetic fields of some domains cancel the magnetic fields of other domains. The result is that the material is not a magnet.

Figure 8 has a diagram showing the arrangement of the domains in a magnetized material. You can see that most of the domains are pointing in the same direction. **In a magnetized material, all or most of the magnetic domains are arranged in the same direction.** In other words, the magnetic fields of the domains are aligned. If you did the Discover Activity at the beginning of this section you aligned the magnetic domains of the iron filings.

Reading Checkpoint What is the arrangement of the magnetic domains in a material that is not magnetized?

FIGURE 8
Magnetic Domains
The arrows represent the magnetic domains of a material. The arrows point toward the north pole of each magnetic domain.
Comparing and Contrasting *How does the arrangement of domains differ between magnetized iron and unmagnetized iron?*

Unmagnetized Iron

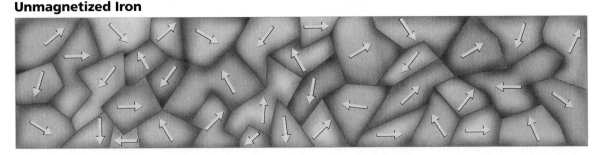

Magnetized Iron

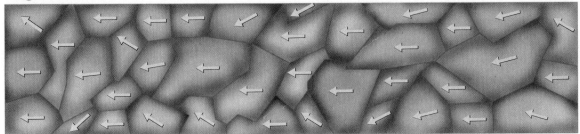

Neodymium Magnets

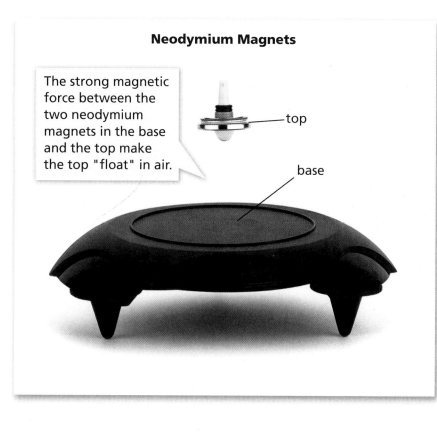

The strong magnetic force between the two neodymium magnets in the base and the top make the top "float" in air.

top

base

Ferrite Magnets

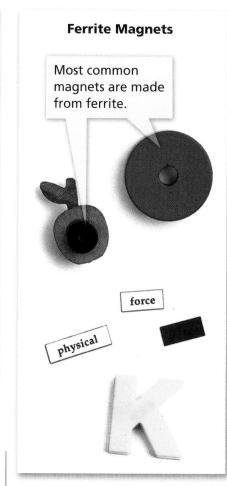

Most common magnets are made from ferrite.

force

physical

FIGURE 9
Magnets of Different Materials
Modern magnets come in a variety of shapes and are made from many different materials.

Magnetic Materials A material can be a strong magnet if its magnetic domains align. A material that shows strong magnetic properties is said to be a **ferromagnetic material**. The word *ferromagnetic* comes from the Latin *ferrum*, which means "iron." So a ferromagnetic material behaves like a piece of iron when it is placed in a magnetic field. In nature, iron, nickel, cobalt, and gadolinium are common ferromagnetic materials. Others include the rare elements samarium and neodymium, which can be made into extremely strong magnets as you can see in Figure 9.

Some magnets are made from several different metals. A combination of several metals is called an alloy. For example, the magnetic alloy alnico is made of <u>al</u>uminum, <u>ni</u>ckel, iron, and <u>co</u>balt. Powerful magnets are also made of alloys of platinum and cobalt, and alloys of cobalt and neodymium.

Today, the most commonly used magnets are not made from alloys, but rather from a material called ferrite. Ferrite is a mixture of substances that contain ferromagnetic elements. Ferrite is a brittle material that chips easily, like some dishes. However, ferrite magnets are usually stronger and less expensive than metal magnets of similar size. Figure 9 shows some ferrite magnets.

 Reading Checkpoint **What are some common ferromagnetic materials found in nature?**

Go Online
SciLINKS NSTA

For: Links on magnetic materials
Visit: www.SciLinks.org
Web Code: scn-1412

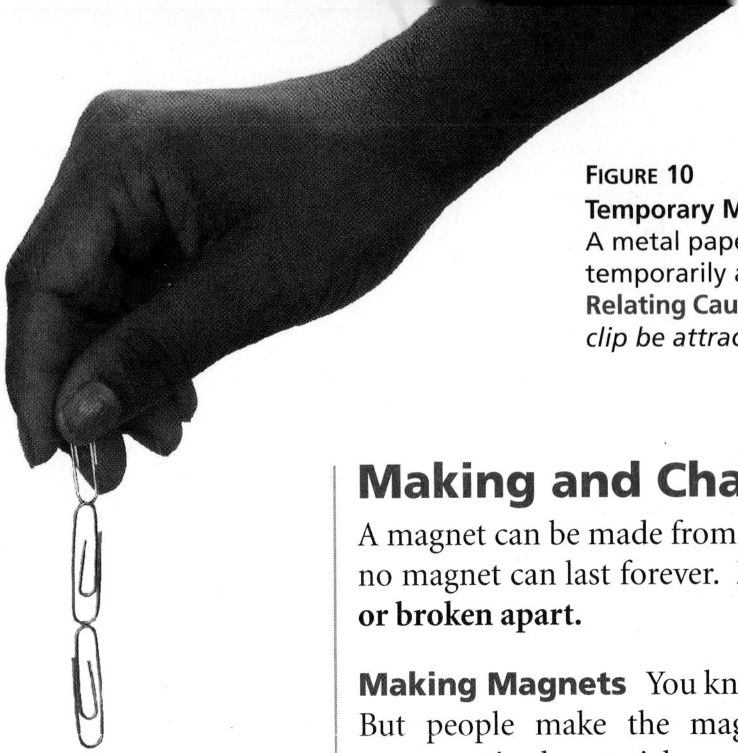

FIGURE 10
Temporary Magnets
A metal paper clip can be magnetized and temporarily attract another paper clip.
Relating Cause and Effect *How can a paper clip be attracted to another paper clip?*

Making and Changing Magnets

A magnet can be made from ferromagnetic material. However, no magnet can last forever. **Magnets can be made, destroyed, or broken apart.**

Making Magnets You know that magnetite exists in nature. But people make the magnets you use every day. Some unmagnetized materials can be magnetized. A magnet can be made by placing an unmagnetized ferromagnetic material in a strong magnetic field or by rubbing the material with one pole of a magnet.

Suppose, for example, that you want to magnetize a steel paper clip. Steel contains iron. So you can magnetize the paper clip by rubbing in one direction with one pole of a magnet. The magnetic field of the magnet causes some domains in the paper clip to line up in the same direction as the domains in the magnet. The more domains that line up, the more magnetized the paper clip becomes.

Some materials, such as the steel in a paper clip or pure iron, are easy to magnetize, but lose their magnetism quickly. A magnet made from a material that easily loses its magnetism is called a **temporary magnet**. Other materials, such as those in strong magnets, are hard to magnetize, but tend to stay magnetized. A magnet made from a material that keeps its magnetism for a long time is called a **permanent magnet**.

Destroying Magnets Like a temporary magnet, a permanent magnet can also become unmagnetized. One way for a magnet to become unmagnetized is to drop it or strike it hard. If a magnet is hit hard, its domains can be knocked out of alignment. Heating a magnet will also destroy its magnetism. When an object is heated, its particles vibrate faster and more randomly. These movements make it more difficult for all the domains to stay lined up. Above a certain temperature, every ferromagnetic material loses its magnetic properties. The temperature depends on the material.

Breaking Magnets What happens if you break a magnet in two? Do you have a north pole in one hand and a south pole in the other? The answer is no—you have two smaller magnets. Each smaller magnet has its own north pole and south pole. If you break those two halves again, you have four magnets.

Now that you know about domains, you can understand why breaking a magnet in half does not result in two pieces that are individual poles. Within the original magnet shown in Figure 11, many north and south poles are facing each other. Many of the magnet's domains are lined up in one direction. This produces a strong magnetic force at the magnet's north and south poles. If the magnet is cut in half, the domains in the two halves will still be lined up in the same way. So the shorter pieces will still have strong ends made up of many north or south poles.

 Reading Checkpoint **What is a temporary magnet?**

FIGURE 11
Magnet Pieces
Each piece of a magnet retains its magnetic properties after it is cut in half.

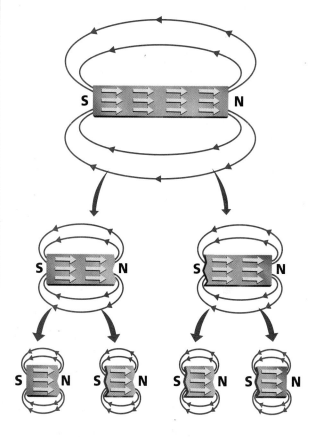

Section 2 Assessment

Target Reading Skill **Asking Questions** Work with a partner to check the answers in your graphic organizer.

Reviewing Key Concepts

1. a. Listing What particles are found in an atom?
   b. Identifying Which particle is responsible for a material's magnetic properties?
   c. Relating Cause and Effect How is a magnetic field produced in an atom?
2. a. Defining What is a magnetic domain?
   b. Explaining How are domains arranged in materials that are magnetized and in ones that are not?
   c. Applying Concepts What happens to the domains in iron filings that line up with the magnetic field of a bar magnet?

3. a. Reviewing How can magnets be changed?
   b. Comparing and Contrasting How are temporary and permanent magnets alike? How are they different?

Writing in Science

Writing Dialogue You are discussing magnets with another person. That person thinks that breaking a magnet will destroy the magnet's magnetic properties. Write a conversation you might have with the other person as you try to explain why the person's idea is incorrect.

Design and Build a Magnetic Paper Clip Holder

Problem

Many objects that you use in your daily life contain magnets. Can you design and build a magnetic paper clip holder?

Skills Focus

designing the solution, evaluating the design, troubleshooting

Materials

- 2 bar magnets
- masking tape
- container of 150 regular size paper clips
- an assortment of types, shapes, and sizes of magnets, including two bar magnets
- modeling clay, string, and other materials approved by your teacher

Procedure

PART 1 Research and Investigate

1. Copy the data table into your notebook.

2. Place one pole of a bar magnet into a container of paper clips. Slowly lift the magnet and count how many paper clips are attached to it. Record the number of paper clips in your data table. Return the paper clips to the container.

3. Repeat Step 2 two more times.

4. Calculate the average number of paper clips you lifted in the three trials.

Data Table	
Type of magnet	Number of paper clips

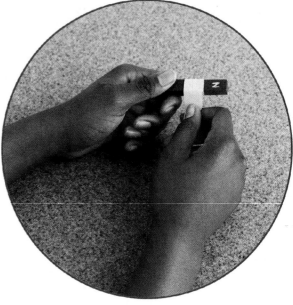

5. Use the other pole of the bar magnet and repeat Step 2.

6. Repeat Step 2 again using the poles of each of the other magnets to pick up the paper clips.

7. Repeat Step 2 using 3 or 4 different combinations of magnets. For example, you can tape two magnets together, as shown in the photo.

PART 2 Design and Build

8. Examine your data. Use it to design a magnetic paper clip holder that
   - holds at least 150 paper clips
   - allows easy access to the paper clips (Hint: The holder could sit on a desk or hang suspended from an object)
   - is made of materials approved by your teacher
   - is built following the Safety Guidelines in Appendix A

9. Draw a sketch of your paper clip holder and include a list of materials you'll need. Obtain your teacher's approval of your design. Then build your holder.

PART 3 Evaluate and Redesign

10. Test your holder. Does the device meet the criteria listed in Step 8? Compare the design and performance of your holder with the holders of some of your classmates.

11. Based on what you learned, redesign your holder. After you receive your teacher's approval, build and test your redesigned holder.

Analyze and Conclude

1. **Inferring** Why did you test each magnet three times in Part 1?

2. **Drawing Conclusions** What conclusions did you draw from the data you collected in Part 1?

3. **Designing a Solution** How did you use the data you collected to design your paper clip holder?

4. **Troubleshooting** Describe one problem you faced while designing or building your holder. How did you solve the problem?

5. **Working With Design Constraints** What limitations did the criteria of holding at least 150 paper clips place on your design? How did you solve those limitations?

6. **Evaluating the Impact on Society** Describe how a device that uses magnets affects your life on a daily basis.

Communicate

Write a letter to a friend that describes how you combined magnets to build a practical paper clip holder.

Go Online
PHSchool.com

For: Data sharing
Visit: PHSchool.com
Web Code: cgd-4034

Magnetic Earth

Reading Preview

Key Concepts
- How is Earth like a bar magnet?
- What are the effects of Earth's magnetic field?

Key Terms
- compass • magnetic declination
- Van Allen belts • solar wind
- magnetosphere • aurora

Target Reading Skill

Building Vocabulary Using a word in a sentence helps you think about how best to explain the word. After you read the section, reread the paragraphs that contain definitions of Key Terms. Use all the information you have learned to write a meaningful sentence using the Key Term.

Lab zone Discover **Activity**

Can You Use a Needle to Make a Compass?

1. ✂ Magnetize a large needle by rubbing it several times in the same direction with one end of a strong bar magnet. Push the needle through a ball of foam or tape it to a small piece of cork.
2. Place a drop of dishwashing soap in a bowl of water. Then float the foam or cork in the water. Adjust the needle until it floats horizontally.
3. Allow the needle to stop moving. Note the direction it points.
4. Use a local map to determine the direction in which it points.

Think It Over

Observing In what direction did the needle point? If you repeat the activity, will it still point in the same direction? What does this tell you about Earth?

When Christopher Columbus sighted land in 1492, he didn't know what he had found. He was trying to find a shortcut from Europe to India. Where he landed, however, was on an island in the Caribbean Sea just south of the present-day United States. He had no idea that such an island even existed.

In spite of his error, Columbus had successfully followed a course west to the Americas without the help of an accurate map. Instead, Columbus used a compass for navigation. A **compass** is a device that has a magnetized needle that spins freely. A compass needle usually points north. As you read, you'll find out why.

◀ Columbus navigated across the Atlantic Ocean using a compass similar to one of these.

FIGURE 12
Earth's Magnetic Field
The magnetic field lines show the shape of Earth's magnetic field.
Observing *What magnetic properties does Earth have?*

Geographic north pole

Magnetic pole

Earth's magnetic field

Magnetic pole

Geographic south pole

Earth as a Magnet

In the late 1500s, the English physician Sir William Gilbert became interested in compasses. He spoke with several navigators and experimented with his own compass. Gilbert confirmed that a compass always points in the same direction, no matter where it is. But no one knew why.

Gilbert hypothesized that a compass behaves as it does because Earth acts as a giant magnet. Although many educated people of his time laughed at this idea, Gilbert turned out to be correct. **Just like a bar magnet, Earth has a magnetic field surrounding it and two magnetic poles.**

The fact that Earth has a magnetic field explains why a compass works as it does. The poles of the magnetized needle on the compass align themselves with Earth's magnetic field.

Earth's Core Gilbert thought that Earth's center, or core, contains magnetic rock. Scientists now think that this is not the case, since the material inside Earth's core is too hot to be solid. Also, the temperature is too high for the material to be magnetic. Earth's magnetism is still not completely understood. But scientists do know that the circulation of molten material in Earth's core is related to Earth's magnetism.

Earth's Magnetic Poles You know that Earth rotates on its axis, around the geographic poles. But Earth also has magnetic poles. These magnetic poles are located on Earth's surface where the magnetic force is strongest. As you can see in Figure 12, the magnetic poles are not in the same place as the geographic poles. For example, the magnetic pole in the Northern Hemisphere is located in northern Canada about 1,250 kilometers from the geographic North Pole.

Discovery
CHANNEL
SCHOOL

Magnetism

▶ Video Preview
▶ Video Field Trip
Video Assessment

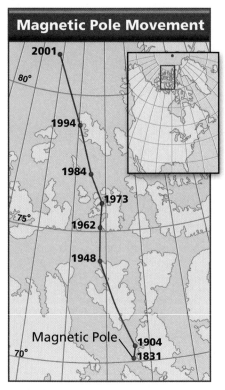

Magnetic Pole Movement

2001
80°
1994
1984
1973
75°
1962
1948

Magnetic Pole
70°
1904
1831

FIGURE 13
The location of Earth's magnetic poles does not stay the same.

Magnetic Declination If you use a compass, you have to account for the fact that Earth's geographic and magnetic poles are different. Suppose you could draw a line between you and the geographic North Pole. The direction of this line is geographic north. Then imagine a second line drawn between you and the magnetic pole in the Northern Hemisphere. The angle between these two lines is the angle between geographic north and the north to which a compass needle points. This angle is known as **magnetic declination**. So, magnetic declination differs depending on your location on Earth.

The magnetic declination of a location on Earth today is not the same as it was 10 years ago. The magnetic declination of a location changes. Earth's magnetic poles do not stay in one place as the geographic poles do. Figure 13 shows how the location of Earth's magnetic pole in the Northern Hemisphere has drifted over time.

Earth's Magnetic Field

You learned that a material such as iron can be made into a magnet by a strong magnetic field. **Since Earth produces a strong magnetic field, Earth itself can make magnets out of ferromagnetic materials.**

Earth as a Magnet Maker Suppose you leave an iron bar lying in a north-south direction for many years. Earth's magnetic field may attract the domains strongly enough to cause them to line up in the same direction. When the domains in the iron bar align, the bar becomes a magnet. This can happen to some everyday objects. So even though no one has tried to make metal objects such as file cabinets in your school into magnets, Earth might have done so anyway!

Math Analyzing Data

Movement of Earth's Magnetic Poles

Earth's magnetic poles move slowly over time. The data in the table show the position of Earth's magnetic north pole in specific years.

1. **Interpreting Data** What is the trend in the speed of the pole's movement?

2. **Calculating** What is the total distance the pole has traveled over the time shown?

3. **Predicting** Using this data, predict the average speed of the pole's movement between 2001 and 2010. Explain.

	Magnetic North Pole Movement	
Year of Reading	Distance Moved Since Previous Reading (km)	Average Speed (km/yr)
1948	420	9.5
1962	150	10.7
1973	120	10.9
1984	120	10.9
1994	180	18.0
2001	287	41.0

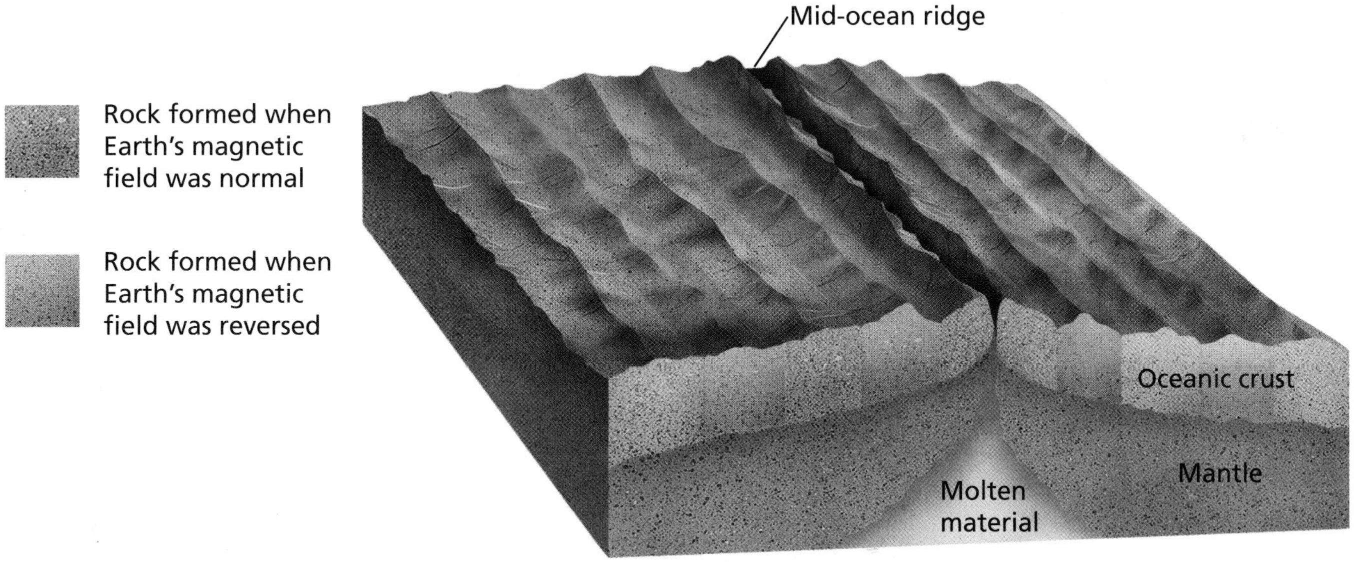

Mid-ocean ridge

 Rock formed when Earth's magnetic field was normal

Rock formed when Earth's magnetic field was reversed

Oceanic crust

Mantle

Molten material

FIGURE 14
Earth's Magnetic Stripes
When molten material hardens into the rock of the ocean floor, the direction of Earth's magnetic field at that time is permanently recorded. **Applying Concepts** *How can scientists use this rock record to study changes in Earth's magnetic field?*

Earth Leaves a Record Earth's magnetic field also acts on rocks that contain magnetic material, such as rock on the ocean floor. Rock is produced on the ocean floor from molten material that seeps up through a long crack in the ocean floor known as a mid-ocean ridge. When the rock is molten, the iron it contains lines up in the direction of Earth's magnetic field. As the rock cools and hardens, the iron is locked in place. This creates a permanent record of the magnetic field.

As scientists studied such rock, they discovered that the direction and strength of Earth's magnetic field have changed over time. Earth's magnetic field has completely reversed direction every million years or so.

The different colored layers in Figure 14 indicate the directions of Earth's magnetic field over time. Notice that the patterns of bands on either side of the ridge are mirror images. This is because the sea floor spreads apart from the mid-ocean ridge. So rocks farther from the ridge are older than rocks near the ridge. Scientists can determine when the rock was formed by looking at the rock's magnetic record.

Why does Earth's magnetic field change direction? No one knows. Scientists hypothesize that changes in the motion of molten material in Earth's core may cause changes in Earth's magnetic field. But scientists cannot explain why changes in the molten material take place.

Reading Checkpoint **What evidence shows that Earth's magnetic field changes?**

Lab zone Skills Activity

Measuring
1. Use a local map to locate geographic north relative to your school. Mark the direction on the floor with tape or chalk.
2. Use a compass to find magnetic north. Again mark the direction.
3. Use a protractor to measure the number of degrees between the two marks.

Compare the directions of magnetic and geographic north. Is magnetic north to the east or west of geographic north?

The Magnetosphere

Earth's magnetic field extends into space. Space is not empty. It contains electrically charged particles. **Earth's magnetic field affects the movements of electrically charged particles in space.** Those charged particles also affect Earth's magnetic field.

Between 1,000 and 25,000 kilometers above Earth's surface are two doughnut-shaped regions called the **Van Allen belts.** They are named after their discoverer, J. A. Van Allen. These regions contain electrons and protons traveling at very high speeds. At one time it was feared that these particles would be dangerous for spacecraft passing through them, but this has not been the case.

Solar Wind Other electrically charged particles in space come from the sun. Earth and the other objects in our solar system experience a solar wind. The **solar wind** is a stream of electrically charged particles flowing at high speeds from the sun. The solar wind pushes against Earth's magnetic field and surrounds the field, as shown in Figure 15. The region of Earth's magnetic field shaped by the solar wind is called the **magnetosphere.** The solar wind constantly reshapes the magnetosphere as Earth rotates on its axis.

Although most particles in the solar wind cannot penetrate Earth's magnetic field, some particles do. They follow Earth's magnetic field lines to the magnetic poles. At the poles, the magnetic field lines dip down to Earth's surface.

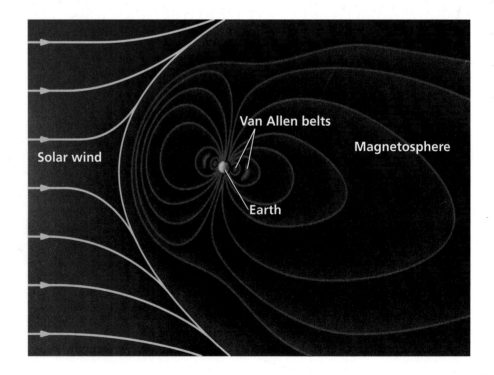

FIGURE 15
Earth's Magnetosphere
The solar wind causes Earth's magnetic field to stretch out on the side of Earth not facing the sun.
Relating Cause and Effect *What shapes the magnetosphere?*

Solar wind
Van Allen belts
Magnetosphere
Earth

FIGURE 16
Aurora
A band of colored light called
an aurora occasionally appears
in the night sky near the
magnetic poles.

Auroras When high-speed, charged particles get close to Earth's surface, they interact with atoms in the atmosphere. This causes some of the atoms to give off light. The result is one of Earth's most spectacular displays—a curtain of shimmering bright light in the atmosphere. A glowing region in the atmosphere caused by charged particles from the sun is called an **aurora**. In the Northern Hemisphere, an aurora is called the Northern Lights, or aurora borealis. In the Southern Hemisphere, it is called the Southern Lights, or aurora australis.

Reading Checkpoint: **What causes an aurora?**

Go Online
PHSchool.com

For: More on Earth's magnetic field
Visit: PHSchool.com
Web Code: cgd-4013

Section 3 Assessment

Target Reading Skill Building Vocabulary Use your sentences to help answer the questions.

Reviewing Key Concepts

1. a. **Reviewing** How are Earth and a bar magnet similar?
   b. **Describing** How do Earth's magnetic properties explain how a compass works?
   c. **Interpreting Diagrams** Look at Figure 12. How do the positions of the geographic and magnetic poles compare?
2. a. **Identifying** What are two effects of Earth's magnetic field?
   b. **Explaining** How can scientists use rocks to learn about Earth's magnetic field?
   c. **Relating Cause and Effect** What causes the part of Earth's magnetic field called the magnetosphere to exist?

Lab zone At-Home **Activity**

House Compass With a family member, explore your home with a compass. Use the compass to discover magnetic fields in your house. Try metal objects that have been in the same position over a long period of time. Explain to your family member why the compass needle moves away from north near some objects.

1 What Is Magnetism?

Key Concepts

- Magnets attract iron and similar materials that contain iron. They attract or repel other magnets. In addition, one part of a magnet will always point north when allowed to swing freely.

- Magnetic poles that are unlike attract each other and magnetic poles that are alike repel each other.

- Magnetic field lines spread out from one pole, curve around the magnet, and return to the other pole.

Key Terms

magnet
magnetic pole

magnetic force
magnetic field
magnetic field lines

2 Inside a Magnet

Key Concepts

- A spinning electron produces a magnetic field that makes the electron behave like a tiny magnet in an atom.

- In a magnetized material, all or most of the magnetic domains are arranged in the same direction.

- Magnets can be made, destroyed, or broken apart.

Key Terms

atom
element
nucleus
proton
neutron
electron

magnetic domain
ferromagnetic
  material
temporary magnet
permanent magnet

3 Magnetic Earth

Key Concepts

- Just like a bar magnet, Earth has a magnetic field surrounding it and two magnetic poles.

- Since Earth produces a strong magnetic field, Earth itself can make magnets out of ferromagnetic materials.

- Earth's magnetic field affects the movements of electrically charged particles in space.

Key Terms

compass
magnetic declination
Van Allen belts

solar wind
magnetosphere
aurora

Review and Assessment

Organizing Information

Concept Mapping Copy the concept map about magnetism onto a separate sheet of paper. Then complete it and add a title. (For more on concept maps, see the Skills Handbook.)

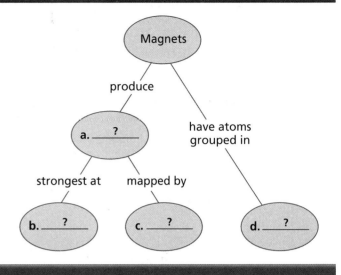

Magnets

produce

have atoms grouped in

a. _____?_____

strongest at   mapped by

b. _____?_____   c. _____?_____   d. _____?_____

Reviewing Key Terms

Choose the letter of the best answer.

1. The area of a magnet where the magnetic force is strongest is a
   a. magnetic pole.
   b. magnetic field.
   c. magnetic field line.
   d. magnetosphere.

2. The negatively charged particles within atoms are
   a. electrons.   b. nuclei.
   c. protons.   d. orbits.

3. An example of a ferromagnetic material is
   a. plastic.
   b. copper.
   c. wood.
   d. iron.

4. A compass works because its magnetic needle
   a. contains atoms.
   b. contains charged particles.
   c. repels magnets.
   d. spins freely.

5. A stream of electrically charged particles flowing from the sun is called the
   a. Van Allen belt.
   b. magnetosphere.
   c. solar wind.
   d. magnetic field.

If the statement is true, write *true*. If it is false, change the underlined word or words to make the statement true.

6. <u>Magnetic field lines</u> map out the magnetic field around a magnet.

7. In an atom, the <u>electrons</u> and protons are located in the nucleus.

8. A <u>ferromagnetic material</u> is a material like iron that has strong magnetic properties.

9. A magnet that keeps its magnetism for a long time is called a <u>temporary magnet</u>.

10. The region of Earth's magnetic field shaped by the solar wind is called the <u>aurora</u>.

Writing in Science

Research Report You are a geologist reporting about Earth's magnetic field. In your report, explain what causes the field and give information on how scientists study it.

Discovery CHANNEL **SCHOOL**

Magnetism
Video Preview
Video Field Trip
▶ Video Assessment

Review and Assessment

Checking Concepts

11. Explain how magnetic field lines are used to represent the field of a magnet. Draw a diagram that shows magnetic field lines around a magnet.

12. Describe the structure of an atom.

13. How do the atoms differ in materials that can be used as magnets and materials that cannot?

14. Describe the magnetic domains in a magnetized material.

15. Explain why you are not left with one north pole and one south pole if you break a magnet in half. Draw a diagram to support your answer.

16. How does a material become a magnet?

17. How does Earth act like a magnet?

18. What is an aurora? How is it produced?

Thinking Critically

19. **Applying Concepts** Examine the diagram below. Is the magnetic pole on the left a north or south pole? Are the two poles like or unlike?

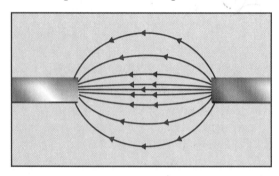

20. **Applying Concepts** The north pole of a bar magnet is held next to one end of an iron rod. Is the other end of the iron rod a north pole or a south pole? Why?

21. **Inferring** A compass points north until a bar magnet is brought next to it. The compass needle is then attracted or repelled by the magnet. What inference can you make about the strengths of the magnetic fields of Earth and the bar magnet?

22. **Problem Solving** Cassia borrowed her brother's magnet. When she returned it, it was barely magnetic. What might Cassia have done to the magnet?

23. **Drawing Conclusions** Why might an inexperienced explorer get lost using a compass?

24. **Relating Cause and Effect** What might happen to a metal pair of scissors if rubbed in one direction with the north pole of a magnet?

Applying Skills

Use the illustration to answer Questions 25–27.

The illustration shows two pairs of magnets.

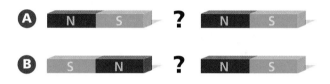

25. **Interpreting Diagrams** Which pair of magnets will have a force of attraction between them? Which pair will have a force of repulsion between them? Explain your choices.

26. **Predicting** Suppose the left-side magnet in pair A traded places with the left-side magnet in pair B. Use magnetic field lines to make a sketch to show how the new pairs would look. Predict if the pairs will attract or repel. Explain.

27. **Problem Solving** If the poles of the magents were not identified, how could you identify them without using a compass?

Lab zone ▸ Chapter **Project**

Performance Assessment Present your sculpture to the class. Use a diagram of your sculpture to show the materials you used to create it and to show how the materials are connected to each other. Explain how you included any materials that were not originally magnetic.

Standardized Test Prep

Use the diagram below to answer Question 3.

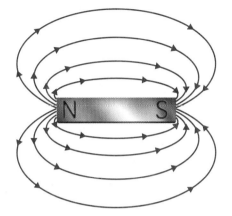

3. If the bar magnet in the above diagram were cut in half, which diagram below *best* represents the magnetic field of the two new pieces?

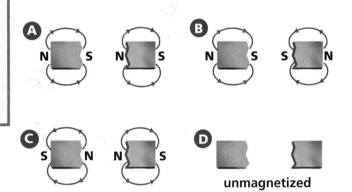

Choose the letter of the best answer.

1. Maglev trains use magnets to elevate trains so that they never touch the tracks. The poles of the magnets on the trains facing the poles of the magnets on the tracks must be
   A the same, so they attract each other.
   B the same, so they repel each other.
   C opposites, so they repel each other.
   D opposites, so they attract each other.

2. In lab, Claudio rubs the north pole of a bar magnet against a wooden coffee stirrer, iron nail, and plastic spoon. After rubbing each item for 2 minutes, Claudio tries to pick up one steel paper clip using each object. The variable tested in this experiment was
   F the magnetic strength of the bar magnet.
   G time.
   H the magnetic properties of selected materials.
   J the amount of rubbing.

4. Which of the following statements *best* describes why compasses point north?
   F Compasses, like all magnets, always point to the geographic North Pole.
   G The magnetized compass needle aligns itself with Earth's magnetic field.
   H Compass needles point toward the sun.
   J The compass needle is repelled by Earth's geographic South Pole.

Constructed Response

5. A bar magnet picks up one paper clip. A second paper clip clings to the first paper clip but does not directly touch the magnet. Explain why the second paper clip clings to the first without touching the bar magnet.

Chapter

2

Electricity

Interactive Textbook

Electric lights sparkle in New York City at night. ▶

Lab zone™ Chapter **Project**

Cause for Alarm

In this chapter, you will learn about electric charges and how they are involved in electricity. You will also learn about types of circuits and how to use electric current safely. As you work on this chapter project, you will choose an event, such as the opening or closing of a door or window, and design a circuit that alerts you when the event happens.

Your Goal To construct an alarm circuit that will light a bulb in response to some event

For your project to be complete, your circuit must

- be powered by one or two D-cells
- have a switch that detects your chosen event
- turn on a light when the switch is closed
- follow the safety guidelines in Appendix A

Plan It! Brainstorm with your classmates about ways to make two pieces of a conductor come in contact. Then, design a detector switch to complete a circuit when the event happens. Submit the design for approval. When your teacher has approved your design, build the alarm circuit and demonstrate it to the class.

Electric Charge and Static Electricity

Reading Preview

Key Concepts
- How do electric charges interact?
- What is an electric field?
- How does static electricity build up and transfer?

Key Terms
- electric force • electric field
- static electricity
- conservation of charge
- friction • conduction
- induction • static discharge

Target Reading Skill

Previewing Visuals Before you read, preview Figure 4. Then write two questions that you have about the diagram in a graphic organizer like the one below. As you read, answer your questions.

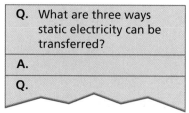

Transferring Static Electricity

Q.	What are three ways static electricity can be transferred?
A.	
Q.	

Lab zone Discover **Activity**

Can You Move a Can Without Touching It?

1. Place an empty aluminum can on its side on the floor.
2. Blow up a balloon. Then rub the balloon back and forth on your hair several times.
3. Hold the balloon about 2 to 3 centimeters away from the can.
4. Slowly move the balloon farther away from the can. Observe what happens.
5. Move the balloon to the other side of the can and observe what happens.

Think It Over

Inferring What happens to the can? What can you infer from your observation?

You're in a hurry to get dressed for school, but you can't find one of your socks. You quickly head for the pile of clean laundry. You've gone through everything, but where's your matching sock? The dryer couldn't have really destroyed it, could it? Oh no, there it is. It's sticking to the back of your blanket. What makes clothes and blankets stick together? The explanation has to do with tiny electric charges.

Why do these clothes stick together? ▶

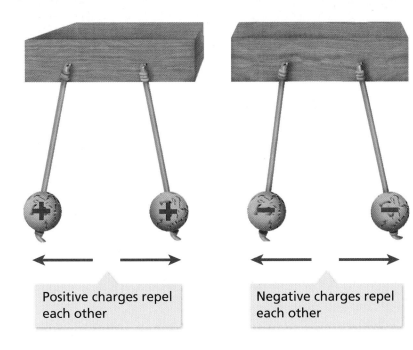

| Positive charges repel each other | Negative charges repel each other | Positive and negative charges attract each other |

Electric Charge

Recall that the charged parts of atoms are electrons and protons. When two protons come close together, they push one another apart. In other words, the protons repel each other. But if a proton and an electron come close together, they attract one another.

Why do protons repel protons but attract electrons? The reason is that they have different types of electric charge. Electric charge is a property of electrons and protons. Protons and electrons have opposite charges. The charge on a proton is called positive (+), and the charge on a electron is called negative (−). The names *positive* and *negative* were given to charges by Benjamin Franklin in the 1700s.

The two types of electric charges interact in specific ways, as you see in Figure 1. **Charges that are the same repel each other. Charges that are different attract each other.** Does this sound familiar to you? This rule is the same as the rule for interactions between magnetic poles. Recall that magnetic poles that are alike repel each other, and magnetic poles that are different attract each other. This interaction between magnetic poles is called magnetism. The interaction between electric charges is called electricity.

There is one important difference between electric charges and magnetic poles. Recall that magnetic poles cannot exist alone. Whenever there is a south pole, there is always a north pole. In contrast, electric charges can exist alone. In other words, a negative charge can exist without a positive charge.

Reading Checkpoint What is one important difference between magnetism and electricity?

FIGURE 1
Repel or Attract?
The two types of charge, positive and negative, react to one another in specific ways.
Interpreting Diagrams *Which combinations of charges repel each other?*

Lab zone Skills **Activity**

Drawing Conclusions

1. Tear tissue paper into small pieces, or use a hole punch to cut circles.
2. Run a plastic comb through your hair several times.
3. Place the comb close to but not touching, the tissue paper pieces. W do you observe?

What can you conclude about the electric charges on the comb and the tissue paper?

FIGURE 2

Electric Charges and Fields
The lines in each diagram represent an electric field. The stronger the field, the closer together the lines are.

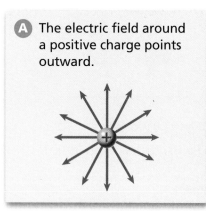

A The electric field around a positive charge points outward.

B The electric field around a negative charge points inward.

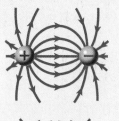

C The electric fields around charged particles are combined when they are brought near each other.

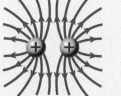

Electric Force

You may think of force as a push or pull on an object. For example, the force of gravity pulls objects toward the ground. You have learned that magnetic force is the attraction or repulsion between magnetic poles. In electricity, **electric force** is the attraction or repulsion between electric charges.

Electric Field Just as magnetic poles exert their forces over a distance, so do electric charges. Recall that a magnetic field extends around a magnet. Similarly, an **electric field** extends around a charged object. **An electric field is a region around a charged object where the object's electric force is exerted on other charged objects.**

When one charged object is placed in the electric field of another charged object, it is either pushed or pulled. It is pushed away if the two objects have the same charge. It is pulled toward the other charged object if their charges are different.

Electric Field Around a Single Charge An electric field is invisible, just like a magnetic field. You may recall using magnetic field lines to represent a magnetic field. In a similar way, you can use electric field lines to represent the electric field. Electric field lines are drawn with arrows to show the direction of the electric force. The electric force always points away from positive charges, as shown in Figure 2A. Notice in Figure 2B that the electric force always points toward negative charges.

The strength of an electric field is related to the distance from the charged object. The greater the distance, the weaker the electric field is. The strength of an electric field is represented by how close the electric field lines are to each other. The electric field is strongest where the lines are closest together. Since the strength of the electric field is greatest near the charged object, that's where the lines appear closest together. Farther from the charged object, the lines appear more spread out because the magnetic field is weaker.

Electric Field Around Multiple Charges When there are two or more charges, the shape of the electric field of each charge is altered. The electric fields of each individual charge combine by repelling or attracting. Figure 2C shows the interaction of the electric fields from two pairs of charges.

Reading Checkpoint What is electric force?

Static Electricity

Most objects normally have no overall charge, which means that they are neutral. Each atom has an equal number of protons and electrons. So each positive charge is balanced by a negative charge. As a result, there is no overall electric force on an atom.

Some objects, however, can become charged. Protons are bound tightly in the center of an atom, but electrons can sometimes leave their atoms. In materials such as silver, copper, gold, and aluminum, some electrons are held loosely by the atoms. These electrons can move to other atoms. As you see in Figure 3, an uncharged object becomes charged by gaining or losing electrons. If an object loses electrons, it is left with more protons than electrons. Therefore, the object has an overall positive charge. If an object gains electrons, it has more electrons than protons and has an overall negative charge.

The buildup of charges on an object is called **static electricity.** *Static* means "not moving or changing." **In static electricity, charges build up on an object, but they do not flow continuously.**

Go Online

SciLINKS

For: Links on static electricity
Visit: www.SciLinks.org
Web Code: scn-1421

FIGURE 3
Charging by Friction
Rubbing two objects together may produce a buildup of static electricity.
Relating Cause and Effect *In what two ways can an uncharged object become charged?*

An uncharged balloon does not attract the girl's hair.

Rubbing the balloon allows more electrons to move onto the balloon. The balloon gains a negative charge.

The negative charges of the balloon attract the positive charges in the girl's hair.

Sparks Are Flying

Lightning is the result of static electricity. You can make your own lightning.

1. Cut a strip 3 cm wide from the middle of a foam plate. Fold the strip to form a W. Tape it to the center of an aluminum pie plate as a handle.

2. Rub a second foam plate on your hair. Place it upside down on a table.

3. Use the handle to pick up the pie plate. Hold the pie plate about 30 cm over the foam plate and drop it.

4. Now, very slowly, touch the tip of your finger to the pie plate. Be careful not to touch the foam plate. Then take your finger away.

5. Use the handle to pick up the pie plate again. Slowly touch the pie plate again.

Inferring What did you observe each time you touched the pie plate? How can you explain your observations?

Transferring Charge

An object becomes charged only when electrons are transferred from one location to another. Charges are neither created nor destroyed. This is a rule known as the law of **conservation of charge.** If one object gives up electrons, another object gains those electrons. **There are three methods by which charges can be transferred to build up static electricity: charging by friction, by conduction, and by induction.**

Charging by Friction When two uncharged objects rub together, some electrons from one object can move onto the other object. The object that gains electrons becomes negatively charged, and the object that loses electrons becomes positively charged. Charging by **friction** is the transfer of electrons from one uncharged object to another by rubbing. In Figure 4, when the girl's socks rub the carpet, electrons move from the carpet onto her sock. This causes an overall negative charge on the sock. Clothing that sticks together when it is taken out of the dryer is another example of charging by friction.

Charging by Conduction When a charged object touches another object, electrons can be transferred between the objects. Electrons transfer from the object that has the more negative charge to the one that has the more positive charge. For example, a positively charged object will gain electrons when it touches an uncharged object. Charging by **conduction** is the transfer of electrons from a charged object to another object by direct contact. In Figure 4, charges are transferred from the girl's feet to the rest of her body because of charging by conduction.

Charging by Induction In charging by friction and by conduction, electrons are transferred when objects touch one another. In charging by induction, however, objects do not touch when the charges transfer. Charging by **induction** is the movement of electrons to one part of an object that is caused by the electric field of a second object. The electric field around the charged object attracts or repels electrons in the second object. In Figure 4, for example, the negative charges in the girl's fingertip produce an electric field that repels the electrons on the surface of the doorknob. The electrons on the doorknob move away from the finger. This movement produces an induced positive charge on the doorknob.

 **Reading Checkpoint** What is the difference between charging by induction and charging by conduction?

FIGURE 4

Transferring Electrons

Static electricity involves the transfer of electrons from one object to another. Electrons can be transferred by friction, conduction, or induction.

Interpreting Photos *How can charges on the carpet induce a charge on the doorknob?*

Transfer of electrons

A Charging by Friction
Electrons are rubbed from the carpet to the girl's sock. The charges are distributed evenly over the sock.

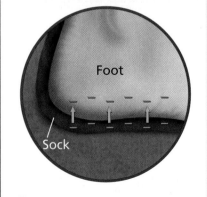

B Charging by Conduction
When the negatively charged sock touches the skin, electrons are transferred by direct contact. Electrons are then distributed throughout the girl's body.

Foot

Sock

C Charging by Induction
Electrons on the girl's fingertip produce an electric field that repels negative charges and attracts positive charges on the doorknob. An overall positive charge is induced on the edge of the doorknob.

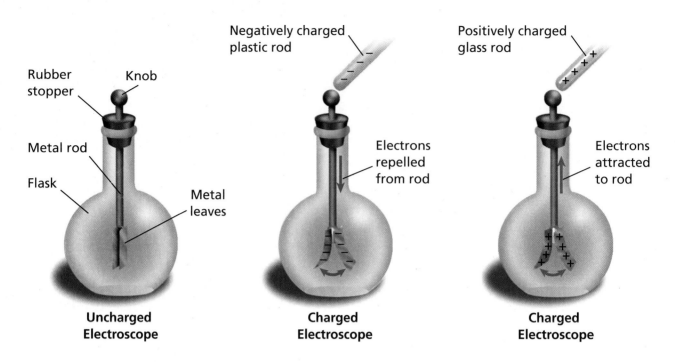

Rubber stopper — Knob

Metal rod

Flask

Metal leaves

Uncharged Electroscope

Negatively charged plastic rod

Electrons repelled from rod

Charged Electroscope

Positively charged glass rod

Electrons attracted to rod

Charged Electroscope

FIGURE 5
An Electroscope
An electroscope can be used to detect the presence of a charge, but it does not tell you whether the charge is positive or negative.
Relating Cause and Effect *Why do the leaves of the electroscope move apart when a charged object touches the knob?*

Electricity

Video Preview
▶ Video Field Trip
Video Assessment

Detecting Charge Electric charge is invisible, but it can be detected by an instrument called an electroscope. A typical electroscope, shown in Figure 5, consists of a metal rod with a knob at the top and two thin metal leaves at the bottom. When the electroscope is uncharged, its metal leaves hang straight down. When a charged object touches the knob, electric charge travels by conduction into or out of the leaves. Since the charge on both leaves is the same, the leaves repel each other and spread apart. The leaves move apart in response to either negative charge or positive charge. Therefore, you cannot use an electroscope to determine the type of charge.

Static Discharge

Charges that build up as static electricity on an object don't stay there forever. Electrons tend to move, returning the object to its neutral condition. Consider what happens when two objects with opposite charges touch one another. **When a negatively charged object and a positively charged object are brought together, electrons transfer until both objects have the same charge.** The loss of static electricity as electric charges transfer from one object to another is called **static discharge**.

Often, a static discharge produces a spark. As electrons transfer between objects, they heat the air around the path they travel until it glows. The glowing air is the spark you see. The tiny spark you may have seen when you touch a doorknob or metal object is an example of static discharge.

Lightning is a dramatic example of static discharge. You can think of lightning as a huge spark. During thunderstorms, air swirls violently. Water droplets within the clouds become electrically charged. To restore a neutral condition in the clouds, electrons move from areas of negative charge to areas of positive charge and produce an intense spark. You see that spark as lightning.

Some lightning reaches Earth because negative charges at the bottom of storm clouds may cause the surface of Earth to become positively charged by induction. Electrons jump between the cloud and Earth's surface, producing a giant spark as they travel through the air. This is possible because of charging by conduction.

 Reading Checkpoint How is lightning formed?

Electric discharge

FIGURE 6
Static Discharge
Lightning is a spectacular discharge of static electricity. Lightning can occur within a cloud, between two clouds, or between a cloud and Earth.

Section 1 Assessment

Target Reading Skill Previewing Visuals Refer to your questions and answers about Figure 4 to help you answer Question 3 below.

Reviewing Key Concepts

1. a. **Identifying** What are the two types of electric charge?
   b. **Explaining** How do objects with the same charge interact? How do objects with opposite charges interact?
   c. **Comparing and Contrasting** How are electric charges similar to magnetic poles? How are they different?
2. a. **Defining** What is an electric field?
   b. **Interpreting Diagrams** What do the lines represent in an electric field diagram?
3. a. **Reviewing** What is static electricity?
   b. **Describing** How is static electricity transferred during charging by conduction?
   c. **Applying Concepts** What role does induction play when lightning strikes Earth?

Lab zone At-Home **Activity**

TV Attraction Rub a balloon against your hair and bring the balloon near one of your arms. Observe the hair on your arm; then put down the balloon. Then bring your other arm near the front of a television screen that is turned on. Ask a family member to explain why the hairs on your arms are attracted to the balloon and to the screen. Explain that this is evidence that there is static electricity present on both the balloon and the screen.

The Versorium

Problem

A versorium is a device that was first described in 1600 by Sir William Gilbert. Why does a versorium turn?

Skills Focus

observing, predicting, classifying

Materials

- foam cup • plastic foam plate • pencil
- aluminum foil • wool fabric • paper
- scissors

Procedure

PART 1 Aluminum Foil Versorium

1. Cut a piece of aluminum foil approximately 3 cm by 10 cm.

2. Make a tent out of the foil strip by gently folding it in half in both directions.

3. Push a pencil up through the bottom of an inverted cup. **CAUTION:** *Avoid pushing the sharpened pencil against your skin.* Balance the center point of the foil tent on the point of the pencil as shown.

4. Make a copy of the data table.

5. Predict what will happen if you bring a foam plate near the foil tent. Record your prediction in the data table.

6. Predict what will happen if you rub the foam plate with wool fabric and then bring the plate near the foil tent. Record your prediction.

7. Predict what will happen if you bring the rubbed wool near the foil tent. Again record your prediction.

8. Test each of your three predictions and record your observations in the data table.

PART 2 Paper Tent Versorium

9. What might happen if you used a paper tent versorium instead of aluminum foil? Record your prediction for each of the three tests.

10. Test your prediction and record your observations in the data table.

Data Table			
	Unrubbed Foam Plate	Rubbed Foam Plate	Rubbed Wool Fabric
Aluminum Tent: Prediction			
Aluminum Tent: Observation			
Paper Tent: Prediction			
Paper Tent: Observation			

Analyze and Conclude

1. **Inferring** At the beginning of the lab, is the foil negatively charged, positively charged, or uncharged? Use your observations to explain your answer.

2. **Predicting** Refer to the predictions you recorded in Steps 5, 6, and 7. Explain the reasoning behind those predictions.

3. **Observing** Did the behavior of the foil match each of your predictions in Steps 5, 6, and 7? Refer to your observations to explain your answer.

4. **Classifying** Did the effect of the foam plate differ in Steps 5 and 6? If so, identify which process—charging by friction, by conduction, or by induction—produced that change.

5. **Classifying** In Step 7, which process—charging by friction, by conduction, or by induction—explains the behavior of the foil when you brought the rubbed wool near it? Explain.

6. **Predicting** Explain the reasoning for your prediction about the paper tent versorium in Part B.

7. **Observing** Did the behavior of the paper tent match your prediction in Step 9? Refer to your observations to explain your answer.

8. **Drawing Conclusions** Were the procedures and results in Part 2 generally similar to those in Part 1? Explain your answer with reference to charging by friction, by conduction, or by induction.

9. **Controlling Variables** During this lab, why is it important to avoid touching the foam plate or the wool with other objects before testing them with the versorium?

10. **Communicating** Another student who did this lab says that the versorium can show whether an object has a positive or negative charge. Write an e-mail to that student giving your reasons for agreeing or disagreeing.

Design an Experiment

What other materials besides foam or wool might have an effect on the versorium? What other materials could you use to make the versorium tent? Design an experiment to test specific materials and see how they respond. *Obtain your teacher's permission before carrying out your investigation.*

Section 2

Electric Current

Reading Preview

Key Concepts
- How is an electric current produced?
- How are conductors different from insulators?
- What causes electric charges to flow in a circuit?
- How does resistance affect current?

Key Terms
- electric current
- electric circuit • conductor
- insulator • voltage
- voltage source • resistance

Target Reading Skill

Outlining As you read, make an outline about electric current. Use the red headings for the main ideas and the blue headings for the supporting ideas.

Lab zone Discover Activity

How Can Current Be Measured?

1. Obtain four pieces of wire with the insulation removed from both ends. Each piece should be about 25 cm long.
2. Wrap one of the wires four times around a compass as shown. You may use tape to keep the wire in place.
3. Build a circuit using the remaining wire, wrapped compass, two bulbs, and a D-cell as shown. Adjust the compass position so that the wire is aligned directly over the compass needle.
4. Make sure the compass is level. If it is not, place it on a piece of modeling clay so that the needle swings freely.
5. Observe the compass needle as you complete the circuit. Record the number of degrees the needle moves.
6. Repeat the activity using only one bulb, and again with no bulb. Record the number of degrees the needle moves.

Think It Over

Inferring Based on your observations of the compass, when did the compass needle move the most? How can you explain your observations?

Thousands of tomatoes ride along a conveyer belt through a giant machine. The conveyer belt carries the tomatoes through a cleaning station, a sorter, and into a lane to be packaged. You might be wondering what a huge conveyer belt of tomatoes could possibly have to do with electricity. Like the tomatoes, electric charges can be made to move in a confined path.

▼ Tomatoes moving on a conveyer belt

Flow of Electric Charges

Lightning releases a large amount of electrical energy. However, the electric charge from lightning can't be used to power your TV, clock radio, video game, or kitchen lights because it only lasts for an instant. These electric devices need electric charges that flow continuously. They require electric current.

What Is Electric Current? Recall that static electric charges do not flow continuously. However, when electric charges are made to flow through a wire or similar material, they produce an electric current. **Electric current** is the continuous flow of electric charges through a material. The amount of charge that passes through the wire in a unit of time is the rate of electric current. The unit for the rate of current is the ampere, named for André Marie Ampère, an early investigator of electricity. The name of the unit is often shortened to *amp* or *A*. The number of amps describes the amount of charge flowing past a given point each second.

FIGURE 7
Representing an Electric Current
Tomatoes moving on a conveyer belt are similar to charges moving in a wire, or electric current.
Interpreting Photos *Which characteristics of electric current are represented in the illustrations?*

Tomatoes on a conveyer belt are similar to electric current in a wire. Both the tomatoes and the current move in a confined path.

If the tomatoes move faster, more tomatoes pass the worker every second. Similarly, if current is increased in a wire, more charges pass by a point on the wire every second.

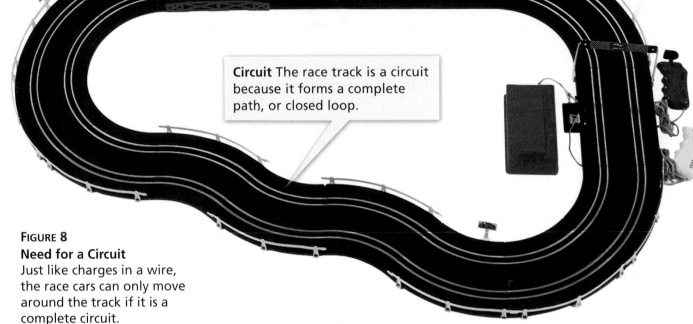

Circuit The race track is a circuit because it forms a complete path, or closed loop.

FIGURE 8
Need for a Circuit
Just like charges in a wire, the race cars can only move around the track if it is a complete circuit.

Current in a Circuit Electric current does not automatically exist in a material. Current requires a specific path to follow. **To produce electric current, charges must flow continuously from one place to another.** Current requires an electric circuit. An **electric circuit** is a complete, unbroken path through which electric charges can flow.

The cars on the racetrack in Figure 8 are like the charges in an electric circuit. If the racetrack forms a complete loop, the cars can move around the track continuously. However, if a piece of the racetrack is missing, the cars are unable to move around the loop. Similarly, if an electric circuit is complete, charges can flow continuously. If an electric circuit is broken, charges will not flow.

Electric circuits are all around you. All electrical devices, from toasters to radios to electric guitars and televisions, contain electric circuits. You will learn more about the characteristics of electric circuits in Section 4.

✓ **Reading Checkpoint** What is an electric circuit?

Conductors and Insulators

Charges flow easily through a circuit made of metal wires. But would charges flow in wires made of plastic? The answer is no. Electric charges do not flow easily through every material. **A conductor transfers electric charge well. An insulator does not transfer electric charge well.** Figure 9 shows materials that are good conductors and materials that are insulators.

Conductors Metals, such as silver, copper, aluminum, and iron, are good conductors. A **conductor** is a material through which charge can flow easily. In a conductor, atoms contain electrons that are bound loosely. These electrons, called conduction electrons, are able to move throughout the conductor. As these electrons flow through a conductor, they form an electric current. Conductors are used to carry electric charge.

Did you ever wonder why a light goes on the instant you flip the switch? How do the electrons get to your lamp from the electric company so fast? The answer is that electrons are not sent to your house when you flip a switch. They are already present inside the conductors that make up the circuit. When you flip the switch, electrons at one end of the wire are pulled, while those at the other end are pushed. The result is a continuous flow of electrons through all parts of the circuit as soon as the circuit is completed.

Insulators A material through which charges cannot flow easily is called an **insulator**. The electrons in an insulator are bound tightly to their atoms and do not move easily. Rubber, glass, sand, plastic, and wood are good insulators. Insulators are used to stop the flow of charges.

The rubber coating on an appliance cord is an example of an insulator. A cord carries charges from an electrical outlet to an appliance. So why don't you get a shock when you touch a cord? The inner wire is the conductor for the current. The rubber coating around the wire is an insulator. The cord allows charge to continue to flow to the appliance, but stops it from flowing into your hand and shocking you.

 **Reading Checkpoint** Why don't you get a shock from touching an extension cord?

Go Online
PHSchool.com

For: More on electric current
Visit: PHSchool.com
Web Code: cgd-4022

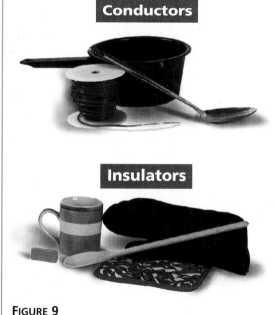

Conductors

Insulators

FIGURE 9
Conductors and Insulators
Charges easily move through conductors. In contrast, charges do not move easily through insulators. **Classifying** *In which category do metals belong?*

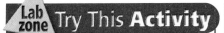
Down the Tubes

Use water to model voltage.

1. Set up a funnel, tubing, beaker, and ring stand as shown.

2. Have a partner start a stopwatch as you pour 200 mL of water into the funnel.

3. Stop the stopwatch when all of the water has flowed into the beaker.

4. Repeat steps 2 and 3 setting the funnel at different heights.

Making Models How did your model represent voltage? How did changing the height affect the model's "voltage"?

Voltage

Imagine you are on a roller coaster at an amusement park. Strapped in your seat, you wait anxiously as your car climbs to the top of the hill. Then, whoosh! Your car speeds down the steel track. Believe it or not, electric charges flow in much the same way as your roller coaster car moves on the track.

Charges Need Energy to Flow The roller coaster cars need energy to give you an exciting ride, but they have no energy when you first climb aboard. A motor provides energy to move a chain attached to the cars. The moving chain pulls the cars to the top of the hill. As they climb, the cars gain potential energy. Potential energy is the energy an object has as a result of its position, or height. The higher up the hill the chain carries the cars, the more potential energy the cars gain. Then, after reaching the hilltop, the cars rush down the hill. As they do, they move from a place of high potential energy—the hilltop—to a place of low potential energy—the bottom of the hill. It is the difference in potential energy between the hilltop and the bottom of the hill that allows the cars to speed down the hill.

In a similar way, charges in an electric circuit flow because of a difference in electrical potential energy. Think of the charges that make up the electric current as being like the roller coaster cars. The circuit is like the steel track. An energy source, such as a battery, is like the roller coaster motor. The battery provides the potential energy difference for the circuit. However, its potential energy is not related to height, as in the roller coaster. Instead it is related to the charges inside the battery.

Voltage Just as the roller coaster creates a difference in potential energy between two places, so does an electric circuit. The difference in electrical potential energy between two places in a circuit is called **voltage,** or potential difference. The unit of measure of voltage is the volt (V). **Voltage causes a current in an electric circuit.** You can think of voltage as the amount of force pushing an electric current.

Voltage Sources At the amusement park, if there were no way of pulling the roller coaster cars to the top of the first hill, there would be no ride. Recall that the ride has a source of energy, a motor. The motor moves the chain that takes the cars to the top of the hill. Once the cars reach the top of any hill, they gain a high potential energy.

An electric circuit also requires a source of energy, such as a battery, to maintain a voltage. A **voltage source** is a device that creates a potential difference in an electric circuit. Batteries and generators are examples of voltage sources. A voltage source has two terminals. The voltage between the terminals causes charges to move around the circuit.

 Reading Checkpoint What does a voltage source do?

FIGURE 10
Voltage

Voltage in a circuit is similar to the difference in potential energy on a roller coaster. **Interpreting Diagrams** *From where do the cars get their energy?*

The difference in potential energy between the top and bottom of the roller coaster's hill is like the voltage in an electric circuit.

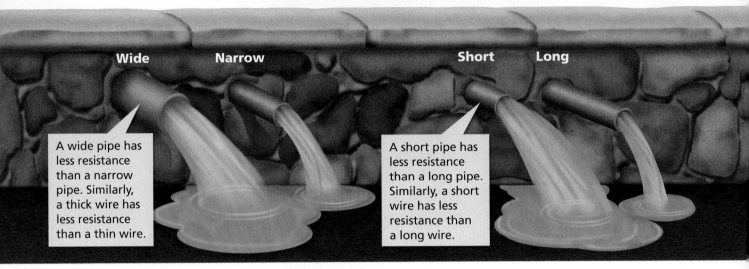

Wide   **Narrow**   **Short**   **Long**

A wide pipe has less resistance than a narrow pipe. Similarly, a thick wire has less resistance than a thin wire.

A short pipe has less resistance than a long pipe. Similarly, a short wire has less resistance than a long wire.

Figure 11
Resistance
Two factors that affect the resistance of water flowing in a pipe are diameter and length. The diameter and length of a wire also affect resistance in a circuit.
Inferring *If you reduce the resistance in a circuit, will there be more or less current?*

Resistance

In the example of the roller coaster, you only learned how the height difference, or "voltage," affected the cars' speed. But other factors affect how fast the cars move. For instance, if the roller coaster cars have rusty wheels, their speed will decrease because the wheels do not turn as well. Current in a circuit works in a similar way.

Current Depends on Resistance The amount of current that exists in a circuit depends on more than just the voltage. Current also depends on the resistance of the material. **Resistance** is the measure of how difficult it is for charges to flow through a material. **The greater the resistance, the less current there is for a given voltage.** The unit of measure of resistance is the ohm (Ω). The ohm is named for Georg Ohm, a German physicist who investigated resistance.

Factors That Determine Resistance There are four factors that determine the resistance of a wire, or any object. The first factor is the material from which the wire is made. Some materials, such as insulators, have electrons that are tightly held to their atoms. Insulators have a high resistance because it is difficult for charges to move. Other materials, such as conductors, have electrons that are loosely held to their atoms. Conductors have a low resistance because charges can move through them easily.

The second factor is length. Long wires have more resistance than short wires. The resistance of current in a wire can be compared to the resistance of water flowing through a pipe. Suppose water is being released from a reservoir held by a dam. As shown in Figure 11, less water flows from the reservoir through the long pipe than through the short pipe. The water in the long pipe slows down because it bumps into more of the pipe's inner wall.

Diameter is the third factor. In Figure 11, the pipe with the small diameter has less water flowing through it than the pipe with the large diameter. In the small-diameter pipe, there is less area through which the water can flow. Similarly, thin wires have more resistance than thick wires.

The fourth factor that determines the resistance of a wire is the temperature of the wire. The electrical resistance of most materials increases as temperature increases. As the temperature of most materials decreases, resistance decreases as well.

Path of Least Resistance Perhaps you have heard it said that someone is taking the "path of least resistance." This means that the person is doing something in the easiest way possible. In a similar way, if electric charge can flow through either of two paths, more of the charge will flow through the path with lower resistance.

Have you seen a bird perched on an uninsulated electric fence? The bird doesn't get hurt because charges flow through the path of least resistance. Since the bird's body offers more resistance than the wire, charges flow directly through the wire without harming the bird.

FIGURE 12
Which Path?
Charges flow through the wire, not the bird, because the wire offers less resistance.

 Reading Checkpoint　**What is the "path of least resistance"?**

Section 2 Assessment

Target Reading Skill Outlining Use your outline to help you answer the questions below.

Reviewing Key Concepts

1. a. Reviewing What happens when an electric current is produced?
　b. Comparing and Contrasting Contrast electric current and static electricity.
　c. Relating Cause and Effect Explain why electric current cannot exist if an electric circuit is broken.

2. a. Defining Define *conductor* and *insulator*.
　b. Listing List materials that make good conductors. List materials that are insulators.
　c. Applying Concepts If a copper wire in a working electric circuit is replaced by a piece of rubber tubing, will there be a current in the circuit? Explain.

3. a. Listing What are two examples of voltage sources?

　b. Explaining How does voltage cause charges to flow in a circuit?
　c. Predicting The electrical potential energy at one point in a circuit is greater than the electrical potential energy at another point. Will there be a current between the two points? Explain.

4. a. Reviewing What is resistance?
　b. Summarizing What are four factors that determine resistance?

Writing in Science

Analogies An analogy can help people understand new information by comparing it to something familiar. Write a paragraph that compares an electric circuit to skiing down a slope and riding the chairlift to the top.

Constructing a Dimmer Switch

Problem

What materials can be used to make a dimmer switch?

Skills Focus

predicting, observing

Materials

- D-cell
- masking tape
- flashlight bulb in a socket
- thick lead from mechanical pencil
- uninsulated copper wire, the same length as the pencil lead
- rubber tubing, the same length as the pencil lead
- 1 wire, 10–15 cm long
- 2 wires, 20–30 cm long
- 2 alligator clips

Procedure

1. To make a device that can dim a light bulb, construct the circuit shown in the photo on the opposite page. To begin, attach wires to the ends of the D-cell.

2. Connect the other end of one of the wires to the bulb in a socket. Attach a wire with an alligator clip to the other side of the socket.

3. Attach an alligator clip to the other wire.

4. The pencil lead will serve as a resistor that can be varied—a variable resistor. Attach one alligator clip firmly to the tip of the pencil lead. Be sure the clip makes good contact with the lead. (*Note*: Pencil "lead" is actually graphite, a form of the element carbon.)

5. Predict how the brightness of the bulb will change as you slide the other alligator clip back and forth along the lead. Test your prediction.

6. What will happen to the brightness of the bulb if you replace the lead with a piece of uninsulated copper wire? Adapt your pencil-lead investigation to test the copper wire.

7. Predict what will happen to the brightness of the bulb if you replace the pencil lead with a piece of rubber tubing. Adapt your pencil-lead investigation to test the rubber tubing.

Analyze and Conclude

1. **Controlling Variables** What variable did you manipulate by sliding the alligator clip along the pencil lead in Step 5?

2. **Observing** What happened to the brightness of the bulb when you slid the alligator clip along the pencil lead?

3. **Predicting** Explain your reasoning in making predictions about the brightness of the bulb in Steps 6 and 7. Were your predictions supported by your observations?

4. **Interpreting Data** Do you think that pencil lead has more or less resistance than copper? Do you think it has more or less resistance than rubber? Use your observations to explain your answers.

5. **Drawing Conclusions** Which material tested in this lab would make the best dimmer switch? Explain your answer.

6. **Communicating** Suppose you want to sell your dimmer switch to the owner of a theater. Write a product information sheet that describes your device and explains how it works.

More to Explore

The volume controls on some car radios and television sets contain resistors that can be varied, called rheostats. The sliding volume controls on a sound mixing board are rheostats as well. Homes and theaters may use rheostats to adjust lighting. Where else in your house would rheostats be useful? (*Hint*: Look for applications where you want to adjust a device gradually rather than just turn it on or off.)

Batteries

Reading Preview

Key Concepts
- What was the first battery made of?
- How does an electrochemical cell work?

Key Terms
- chemical energy
- chemical reaction
- electrochemical cell
- electrode • electrolyte
- terminal • battery
- wet cell • dry cell

Target Reading Skill

Building Vocabulary After you read the section, reread the paragraphs that contain definitions of Key Terms. Use the information you have learned to write a definition of each Key Term in your own words.

Lab zone Discover **Activity**

Can You Make Electricity Using a Penny?

1. Clean a penny with vinegar. Wash your hands.
2. Cut a 2-cm × 2-cm square from a paper towel and a similar square from aluminum foil.
3. Stir salt into a glass of warm water until the salt begins to sink to the bottom. Then soak the paper square in the salt water.
4. Put the penny on your desktop. Place the wet paper square on top of it. Then place the piece of aluminum foil on top of the paper.
5. Set a voltmeter to read DC volts. Touch the red lead to the penny and the black lead to the foil. Observe the reading on the voltmeter.

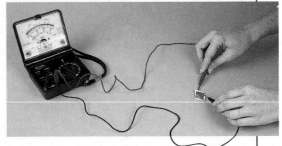

Think It Over
Observing What happened to the voltmeter? What type of device did you construct?

Using a headlamp for light ▼

When you finally step into camp, barely enough light is left to see the trees in front of you. But you must still set up your tent. You need more light. There are no generators or electric lines nearby. Where can you find enough electrical energy to produce some light? Fortunately, your headlamp contains a battery that provides electrical energy to its bulb. In this section, you'll find out how a battery produces electrical energy.

The First Battery

Energy can be transformed from one form into another. For example, batteries transform chemical energy into electrical energy. **Chemical energy** is energy stored in chemical compounds.

Luigi Galvani The research that led to the development of the battery came about by accident. In the 1780s, an Italian physician named Luigi Galvani was studying the anatomy, or body structure, of a frog. He was using a brass hook to hold a leg muscle in place. As he touched one end of the hook to an iron railing, he noticed that the frog's leg twitched. Galvani hypothesized that there was some kind of "animal electricity" present only in living tissue. This hypothesis was later proven to be incorrect. However, Galvani's observations and hypothesis led to further research.

Alessandro Volta An Italian scientist named Alessandro Volta developed a different hypothesis to account for Galvani's observations. Volta argued that the electrical effect Galvani observed was actually a result of a chemical reaction. A **chemical reaction** is a process in which substances change into new substances with different properties. In this case, Volta hypothesized that a chemical reaction occurred between the two different metals (the iron railing and the brass hook) and the salty fluids in the frog's leg muscle.

To confirm his hypothesis, Volta placed a piece of paper that had been soaked in salt water in between a piece of zinc and a piece of silver. Volta found that if he connected wires to the silver and zinc, current was produced. Then he repeated the layers: zinc, paper, silver, zinc, and so on. When he added more layers, a greater current was produced. If you did the Discover activity, you did something similar to what Volta did.

Volta built the first electric battery by layering zinc, paper soaked in salt water, and silver. In 1800, he made his discovery public. Although his battery was much weaker than those made today, it produced a current for a relatively long period of time. Volta's battery was the basis of more powerful modern batteries.

 Reading Checkpoint What is a chemical reaction?

FIGURE 13
The First Battery
Alessandro Volta demonstrates the first battery. **Interpreting Diagrams** *What materials made up Volta's battery?*

+

Zinc
Paper soaked in salt water
Silver

−

FIGURE 14

An Electrochemical Cell
An electrochemical cell can make a complete circuit.

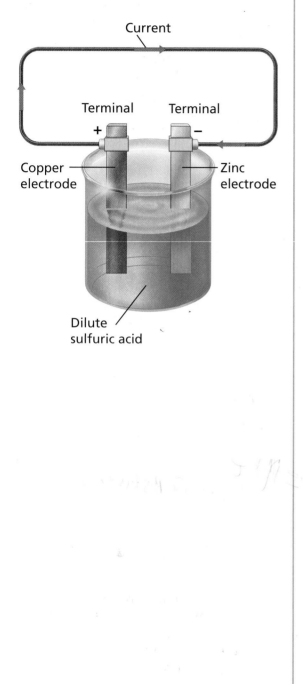

Electrochemical Cells

In Volta's setup, each pair of zinc and silver layers separated by paper soaked in salt water acted as an electrochemical cell. An **electrochemical cell** is a device that transforms chemical energy into electrical energy. An electrochemical cell consists of two different metals called **electrodes,** which are immersed in a substance called an electrolyte. An **electrolyte** is a substance that conducts electric current. Volta used silver and zinc as electrodes and salt water as his electrolyte.

A Simple Cell In the cell in Figure 14, the electrolyte is dilute sulfuric acid. Dilute means that the sulfuric acid has been mixed with water. One of the electrodes in this cell is made of copper and the other is made of zinc. The part of an electrode above the surface of the electrolyte is called a **terminal**. The terminals are used to connect the cell to a circuit.

Chemical reactions occur between the electrolyte and the electrodes in an electrochemical cell. These reactions cause one electrode to become negatively charged and the other electrode to become positively charged. Because the electrodes have opposite charges, there is a voltage between them. Recall that voltage causes charges to flow. If the terminals are connected by a wire, charge will flow from one terminal to the other. In other words, the electrochemical cell produces an electric current in the wire. Charges flow back through the electrolyte to make a complete circuit.

Batteries Several electrochemical cells can be stacked together to form a battery. A **battery** is a combination of two or more electrochemical cells in a series. Today, single cells are often referred to as "batteries." So the "batteries" you use in your flashlight are technically cells rather than batteries.

In a battery, two or more electrochemical cells are connected in series. This means the positive terminal of one cell is connected to the negative terminal of the next. The voltage of the battery is the sum of the voltages of the cells. You connect two cells in this way inside a flashlight. The total voltage of a battery is found by adding the voltages of the individual cells.

Reading Checkpoint What is a battery?

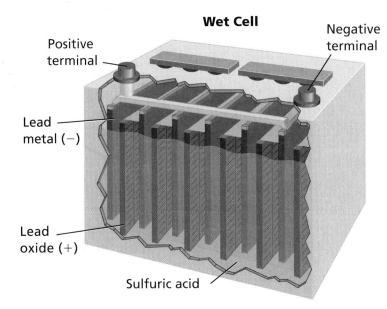

Wet Cell

Positive terminal

Negative terminal

Lead metal (−)

Lead oxide (+)

Sulfuric acid

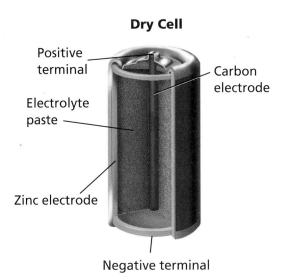

Dry Cell

Positive terminal

Carbon electrode

Electrolyte paste

Zinc electrode

Negative terminal

FIGURE 15
Wet and Dry Cells
The wet electrolyte in the car battery on the left is sulfuric acid. The diagram on the right shows the parts of a typical dry cell. The electrolyte is not really dry — it is a paste.

Wet Cells There are two kinds of electrochemical cells: wet cells and dry cells. An electrochemical cell in which the electrolyte is a liquid is a **wet cell**. Volta's battery consisted of wet cells because the electrolyte was salt water. The 12-volt automobile battery in Figure 15 consists of six wet cells. In this case, the electrolyte is sulfuric acid.

Dry Cells Flashlights and many other devices use dry cells. A **dry cell** is an electrochemical cell in which the electrolyte is a paste. Figure 15 shows the parts of a dry cell.

Section 3 Assessment

Target Reading Skill Building Vocabulary Use your definitions to help answer the questions.

Reviewing Key Concepts

1. a. **Describing** Describe the parts of Volta's battery and how they were arranged.
   b. **Explaining** What happened when Volta connected the parts of his cells in a circuit?
   c. **Relating Cause and Effect** What caused the event in Question b to happen?
   d. **Explaining** Explain how Volta used Galvani's observations to develop a relationship between chemical energy and electrical energy.

2. a. **Listing** What are the parts of an electrochemical cell?
   b. **Summarizing** Summarize how the parts of a cell interact to produce a current.
   c. **Predicting** Would a current be produced if both terminals had the same charge? Explain your answer.

Lab zone At-Home Activity

Reviving Old Cells Test a flashlight with two old D-cells and observe its brightness. Then ask a family member to remove the D-cells and place them in direct sunlight to warm up. After an hour or more, use the cells to test the flashlight. Compare the brightness of the bulb in the two tests. Explain what your observations indicate about the chemical reactions in the battery.

Build a Flashlight

Problem

How can you use a battery to build a working flashlight?

Skills Focus

making models, observing, inferring

Materials

- one cardboard tube
- one D-cell
- flashlight bulb
- aluminum foil
- paper cup
- duct tape
- scissors
- 2 lengths of wire, about 10 cm each, with the insulation stripped off about 2 cm at each end
- 1 length of wire, 15–20 cm, with the insulation stripped off each end

Procedure

1. Check that the D-cell fits inside the cardboard tube. Make two holes in the side of the tube about 2–3 cm apart. The holes should be near the middle of the tube.

2. Use duct tape to connect a 10-cm wire to each terminal of the battery. Touch the other ends of the wires to a flashlight bulb in order to find where to connect them. (*Hint*: Most bulbs have a bottom contact and a side contact. If there is no obvious side contact, try touching the metal on the side of the base.)

3. Line a paper cup with aluminum foil. Use a pencil to poke a hole in the bottom of the paper cup. The hole should be slightly smaller than the bulb, but large enough to allow the base of the bulb through.

4. Insert the base of the light bulb through the hole. Be sure the bulb fits securely.

5. Pass the long wire through one of the holes in the tube. Tape it to the inside of the tube, leaving about 2 cm outside the tube. The other end should reach the end of the tube.

6. Place the battery in the tube. Pass the wire attached to the bottom of the battery through the other hole in the tube. (Make sure the two wires outside the tube can touch.)

7. Make a sling from duct tape to hold the battery inside the tube.

8. Attach the wires from the end of the tube to the contact points on the bulb.

9. Tape the cup on top of the tube, keeping all connections tight.

10. Touch the two free ends of the wires together to see if the bulb lights. If it doesn't, check to be sure all connections are taped together securely.

Analyze and Conclude

1. **Inferring** What is the purpose of lining the cup with aluminum foil?

2. **Drawing Conclusions** Does it matter which way the battery is placed in the tube? Explain.

3. **Making Models** Why does the bulb have to be connected at two points in order for it to light?

4. **Drawing Conclusions** How could you make your flashlight brighter? How could you make it more rugged?

5. **Observing** Compare your flashlight to a manufactured one. Explain the differences.

6. **Communicating** Write an advertisement for your flashlight. In your ad, list the features of your flashlight and explain why a consumer should buy it.

Design an Experiment

People use different types of flashlights for different purposes. Some are narrow and flexible while others are wide and sturdy. Compare several different flashlights. Describe the flashlights. Note the type and number of batteries required, the type of switch used, and any other features that you observe. Suggest useful applications for each flashlight. Then design a new flashlight based on a need that you observe.

Electric Circuits

Reading Preview

Key Concepts
- What is Ohm's law?
- What are the basic features of an electric circuit?
- How many paths can currents take in series and parallel circuits?

Key Terms
- Ohm's law • series circuit
- ammeter • parallel circuit
- voltmeter

Target Reading Skill

Comparing and Contrasting
As you read, compare and contrast series circuits and parallel circuits in a Venn diagram like the one below. Write the similarities in the space where the circles overlap and the differences on the left and right sides.

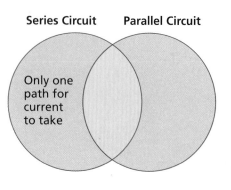

Series Circuit   Parallel Circuit

Only one path for current to take

Lab zone Discover **Activity**

Do the Lights Keep Shining?

1. Construct both of the circuits shown using a battery, several insulated wires, and two light bulbs for each circuit.
2. Connect all wires and observe the light bulbs.
3. Now unscrew one bulb in each circuit. Observe the remaining bulbs.

Think It Over
Observing What happened to the remaining light bulbs when you unscrewed one bulb? How can you account for your observations?

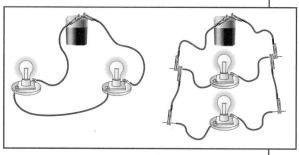

It's a cool, clear night as you stroll along the river with your family. The city is brightly lit, and the river water sparkles with reflected light. In addition to the lights at the top of the lamp-posts, a string of lights borders the river path. They make a striking view.

As you walk, you notice that a few of the lights in the string are burned out. The rest of the lights, however, burn brightly. If one bulb is burned out, how can the rest of the lights continue to shine? The answer depends on how the electric circuit is designed.

Although most lights are shining, some lights are burned out. ▶

Ohm's Law

To understand electric circuits, you need to understand how current, voltage, and resistance are related to one another. In the 1800s, Georg Ohm performed experiments that demonstrated how those three factors are related. Ohm experimented with many substances while studying electrical resistance. He analyzed different types of wire in order to determine the characteristics that affect a wire's resistance.

Ohm's Results   Ohm set up a circuit with a voltage between two points on a conductor. He measured the resistance of the conductor and the current between those points. Then he varied the voltage and took new measurements.

Ohm found that if the factors that affect resistance are held constant, the resistance of most conductors does not depend on the voltage across them. Changing the voltage in a circuit changes the current, but will not change the resistance. Ohm concluded that conductors and most other devices have a constant resistance regardless of the applied voltage.

Calculating With Ohm's Law   The relationship between resistance, voltage, and current is summed up in **Ohm's law. Ohm's law says that the resistance is equal to the voltage divided by the current.**

This relationship can be represented by the equation below:

$$\text{Resistance} = \frac{\text{Voltage}}{\text{Current}}$$

The units are ohms (Ω) = volts (V) ÷ amps (A). You can rearrange Ohm's law as follows:

$$\text{Voltage} = \text{Current} \times \text{Resistance}$$

You can use the formula to see how changes in resistance, voltage, and current are related. For example, what happens to current if voltage is doubled without changing the resistance? For a constant resistance, if voltage is doubled, current is doubled as well.

Figure 16
Measuring Factors in a Circuit
You can use a meter to measure voltage, current, and resistance. *Measuring What units are used to measure current and voltage?*

Decimals

When calculating voltage, you often use decimals. When you multiply two decimals, the number of decimal places in the product is the sum of the number of decimal places in each decimal you multiply.

If a circuit has a resistance of 30.5 ohms and a current of 0.05 amps, what is its voltage?

$$30.5 \text{ ohms} \times \frac{0.05 \text{ amps}}{1.525 \text{ volts}}$$

Practice Problems   Use Ohm's law to calculate the voltage of a circuit with a resistance of 15.2 ohms and a current of 0.10 amps.

Calculating Resistance

The brake light on an automobile is connected to a 12-volt battery. If the resulting current is 0.40 amps, what is the resistance of the brake light?

1 Read and Understand
What information are you given?

Battery Voltage = 12 V
Current = 0.40 A

2 Plan and Solve
What quantity are you trying to calculate?

The resistance of the brake light.

What formula contains the given quantities and the unknown quantity?

$$\text{Resistance} = \frac{\text{Voltage}}{\text{Current}}$$

Perform the calculation.

$$\text{Resistance} = \frac{12\ V}{0.40\ A} = 30\ \Omega$$

3 Look Back and Check
Does the answer make sense?

The answer makes sense because you are dividing the voltage by a decimal. The answer should be greater than either number in the fraction, which it is.

1. In a circuit, there is a 0.5-A current in the bulb. The voltage across the bulb is 4.0 V. What is the bulb's resistance?

2. A waffle iron has a 12-A current. If the resistance of the coils is 10 Ω, what must the voltage be?

Features of a Circuit

All electric circuits have the same basic features. **First, circuits have devices that are run by electrical energy.** A radio, a computer, a light bulb, and a refrigerator are all devices that transform electrical energy into another form of energy. A light bulb, for example, transforms electrical energy into electromagnetic energy by giving off light. The light bulb also produces thermal energy by giving off heat. By making fan blades rotate, electric fans transform electrical energy to mechanical energy. Devices such as light bulbs and fans resist the flow of electric current. They are therefore represented as resistors in a circuit.

Second, a circuit has a source of electrical energy. Batteries, generators, and electric plants all supply energy to circuits. Recall that energy is the ability to do work. The source of electrical energy makes charges move around a circuit, allowing the device to do work.

Third, electric circuits are connected by conducting wires. The conducting wires complete the path of the current. They allow charges to flow from the energy source to the device that runs on electric current and back to the energy source. A switch is often included in a circuit to control the current in the circuit. Using a switch, you can turn a device on or off by closing or opening the circuit.

Notice that all the parts of a circuit are shown in Figure 17. Each part shown in the photograph is represented in the diagram by a simple symbol. Arrows indicate the direction of current. The + and – on the battery indicate the positive and negative terminals.

✔ **Reading Checkpoint** What is the function of conducting wires in a circuit?

FIGURE 17

Diagraming a Circuit
Simple symbols make it easy to diagram a circuit. The resistor represents the device that is being run by the current. Resistors include light bulbs, appliances, and huge machines.
Interpreting Diagrams *Which symbol is used to represent a battery?*

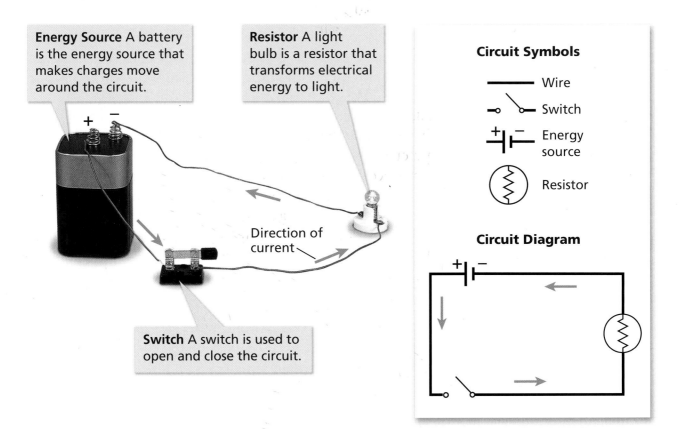

Energy Source A battery is the energy source that makes charges move around the circuit.

Resistor A light bulb is a resistor that transforms electrical energy to light.

Direction of current

Switch A switch is used to open and close the circuit.

Circuit Symbols

Wire
Switch
Energy source
Resistor

Circuit Diagram

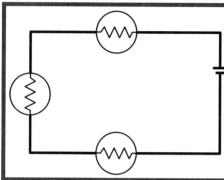

FIGURE 18

A Series Circuit
A series circuit provides only one path for the flow of electrons. **Predicting** *What will happen in a series circuit if one bulb burns out?*

Go Online

active art

For: Series and Parallel Circuits Activity
Visit: PHSchool.com
Web Code: cgp-4023

Series Circuits

If all the parts of an electric circuit are connected one after another along one path, the circuit is called a **series circuit.** Figure 18 illustrates a series circuit. **In a series circuit, there is only one path for the current to take.** For example, a switch and two light bulbs connected by a single wire are in series with each other.

One Path A series circuit is very simple to design and build, but it has some disadvantages. What happens if a light bulb in a series circuit burns out? A burned-out bulb is a break in the circuit, and there is no other path for the current to take. So if one light goes out, the other lights go out as well.

Resistors in a Series Circuit Another disadvantage of a series circuit is that the light bulbs in the circuit become dimmer as more bulbs are added. Why does that happen? A light bulb is a type of resistor. Think about what happens to the overall resistance of a series circuit as you add more bulbs. The resistance increases. Remember that for a constant voltage, if resistance increases, current decreases. So as light bulbs are added to a series circuit, the current decreases. The result is that the bulbs burn less brightly.

Measuring Current An **ammeter** is a device used to measure current. If you want to measure the current through some device in a circuit, the ammeter should be connected in series with that device.

 Reading Checkpoint How does resistance change as you add bulbs to a series circuit?

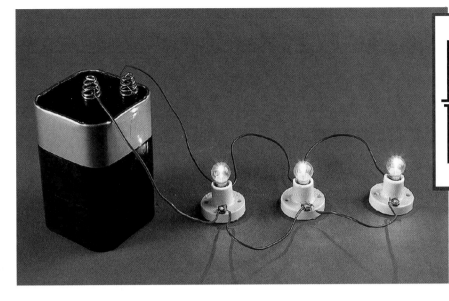

Parallel Circuits

As you gaze at a string of lights, you observe that some bulbs burn brightly, but others are burned out. Your observation tells you that these bulbs are connected in a parallel circuit. In a **parallel circuit,** the different parts of the circuit are on separate branches. Figure 19 shows a parallel circuit. **In a parallel circuit, there are several paths for current to take.** Each bulb is connected by a separate path from the battery and back to the battery.

Several Paths What happens if a light burns out in a parallel circuit? If there is a break in one branch, charges can still move through the other branches. So if one bulb goes out, the others remain lit. Switches can be added to each branch to turn lights on and off without affecting the other branches.

Resistors in a Parallel Circuit What happens to the resistance of a parallel circuit when you add a branch? The overall resistance actually decreases. To understand why this happens, consider blowing through a single straw. The straw resists the flow of air so that only a certain amount of air comes out. However, if you use two straws, twice as much air can flow. The more straws you have, the more paths the air has to follow. The air encounters less resistance. As new branches are added to a parallel circuit, the electric current has more paths to follow, so the overall resistance decreases.

Remember that for a given voltage, if resistance decreases, current increases. The additional current travels along each new branch without affecting the original branches. So as you add branches to a parallel circuit, the brightness of the light bulbs does not change.

Measuring Voltage A **voltmeter** is a device used to measure voltage, or electrical potential energy difference. When you measure the voltage of a device, the voltmeter and the device should be wired as a parallel circuit.

Household Circuits Would you want the circuits in your home to be series circuits? Of course not. With a series circuit, all the electrical devices in your home would stop working every time a switch was turned off or a light bulb burned out. Instead, the circuits in your home are parallel circuits.

Electrical energy enters a home through heavy-duty wires. These heavy-duty wires have very low resistance. Parallel branches extend out from the heavy-duty wires to wall sockets, and then to appliances and lights in each room. Switches are installed to control one branch of the circuit at a time. The voltage in most household circuits is 120 volts.

FIGURE 20
Household Circuits
Homes and businesses are wired with parallel circuits. That means that other appliances will stay on if the bulb in one light burns out.

Reading Checkpoint The wiring in your house forms what kind of circuit?

Section 4 Assessment

Target Reading Skill Comparing and Contrasting Use the information in your Venn diagram about series and parallel circuits to help you answer Question 3.

Reviewing Key Concepts

1. **a. Reviewing** What three related electrical factors did Georg Ohm investigate?
   b. Explaining What did Ohm discover about the relationship between these three factors?
   c. Predicting In a circuit with a constant resistance, what will happen to the current if the voltage is multiplied four times?

2. **a. Listing** List three basic features of an electric circuit.
   b. Interpreting Diagrams Use Figure 17 to show how each feature is represented in a circuit diagram.
   c. Applying Concepts Draw a diagram of a circuit that includes one resistor. The resistor is located between the switch and the positive terminal of the energy source.

3. **a. Comparing and Contrasting** Compare and contrast series and parallel circuits.
   b. Relating Cause and Effect If you remove one bulb from a string of lights, all the remaining lights will go out. Are the lights in a series circuit or parallel circuit? Explain.

Math Practice

4. **Calculating Resistance** The current through a resistor of unknown value is 0.025 A when it is connected to a 10.0-V source. What is the value of the resistor?

5. **Calculating Resistance** Suppose that the voltage remains the same as in Question 4, and the current changes to 0.031 A. What is the new value of the resistor?

5 Electric Power

Reading Preview

Key Concepts
• How do you calculate electric power?
• What factors are used to determine how people pay for electrical energy?

Key Term
• power

Target Reading Skill
Asking Questions Before you read, preview the red headings. In a graphic organizer like the one below, ask a *what* or *how* question for each heading. As you read, write the answer to your questions.

Electric Power

Question	Answer
What is electric power?	Electric power is . . .

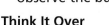

Lab zone Discover Activity

How Can You Make a Bulb Burn More Brightly?

1. Attach a light bulb in its socket to a hand generator as shown.
2. Slowly crank the generator. Observe the brightness of the bulb.
3. Crank the generator a little faster and again observe the bulb.
4. Crank the generator quickly and observe the bulb once more.

Think It Over
Posing Questions How does the speed at which you crank the generator affect the brightness of the bulb? What questions do you need to ask to explain how the rate of generating electrical energy is related to the brightness of the bulb?

Your band is auditioning for the school dance. The drummer pounds away on his snares and cymbals. The lead guitar lays down some rockin' riffs. Deep-toned plucks from your electric bass guitar maintain the beat. The judges enjoy what they hear but say they couldn't hear your bass guitar very well. "Turn up the power of your amplfier," one of them suggests. You know that means increase the volume, but what does that have to do with power?

◄ Powering up a performance

FIGURE 21

FIGURE 21
Power Ratings
Consumers can use power rating information in buying and using appliances. **Interpreting Diagrams** *Which four appliances listed here use the most power?*

Power Ratings for Appliances

Appliance	Power (Watts)
Stove	6,000
Hair dryer	1,200
Microwave	1,000
Refrigerator	500
Computer	150
TV	150
Clock radio	12

6,000 Watts

150 Watts

1,200 Watts

12 Watts

Electric Power

An electrical appliance transforms electrical energy into another form. This energy transformation enables the appliance to perform its function. Hair dryers transform electrical energy to thermal energy to dry your hair. An amplifier that a guitar player uses transforms electrical energy into sound. A washing machine transforms electrical energy to mechanical energy to wash your clothes. The rate at which energy is transformed from one form to another is known as **power.** The unit of power is the watt (W).

Power Ratings You are already familiar with different amounts of electric power. The power rating of a bright light bulb, for example, might be 100 W. The power rating of a dimmer bulb might be 60 W. The bright bulb transforms (or uses) electrical energy at a faster rate than the dimmer bulb.

The appliances in your home vary greatly in their power ratings. New appliances are sold with labels that show the power rating for each product. Look at the table in Figure 21 to see some typical power ratings. Do any of these ratings surprise you?

Lab zone Skills **Activity**

Observing

Study the back or bottom of some electrical appliances around your home. Make a chart of their power ratings. Do you see any relationship between the power rating and whether or not the appliance produces heat?

Calculating Power The power of a light bulb or appliance depends on two factors: voltage and current. **You can calculate power by multiplying voltage by current.**

For: Links on electric power
Visit: www.SciLinks.org
Web Code: scn-1425

$$Power = Voltage \times Current$$

The units are watts (W) = volts (V) × amperes (A). Using the symbols P for power, V for voltage, and I for current, this equation can be rewritten

$$P = VI$$

 Reading Checkpoint How can you calculate power if you know the voltage and current?

Calculating Power

A household light bulb has about 0.5 amps of current in it. Since the standard household voltage is 120 volts, what is the power rating for this bulb?

1 **Read and Understand**
What information are you given?
Current = 0.5 A
Voltage = 120 V

2 **Plan and Solve**
What quantity are you trying to calculate?
The power of the light bulb = ?

What formula contains the given quantities and the unknown quantity?
Power = Voltage × Current

Perform the calculation.
Power = 120 V × 0.5 A
Power = 60 W

3 **Look Back and Check**
Does your answer make sense?
The answer is reasonable, because 60 W is a common rating for household light bulbs.

Math **Practice**

1. A flashlight bulb uses two 1.5-V batteries in series to create a current of 0.5 A. What is the power rating of the bulb?

2. A hair dryer has a power rating of 1,200 W and uses a standard voltage of 120 V. What is the current through the hair dryer?

Paying for Electrical Energy

The electric bill that comes to your home charges for energy use, not power. Energy use depends on both power and time. Different appliances transform electrical energy at different rates. And you use some appliances more than others. **The total amount of energy used by an appliance is equal to the power of the appliance multiplied by the amount of time the appliance is used.**

$$\text{Energy} = \text{Power} \times \text{Time}$$

Electric power is usually measured in thousands of watts, or kilowatts (kW), and time is measured in hours. The unit of electrical energy is the kilowatt-hour (kWh).

$$\text{Kilowatt-hours} = \text{Kilowatts} \times \text{Hours}$$

Ten 100-watt light bulbs turned on for one hour use 1,000 watt-hours, or 1 kilowatt-hour, of energy.

The amount of electrical energy used in your home is measured by a meter. As more lights and appliances are turned on, you can observe a dial on the meter turning more rapidly. The electric company uses the meter to keep track of the number of kilowatt-hours used. You pay a few cents for each kilowatt-hour.

FIGURE 22
The Cost of Electrical Energy
Electric bills are based on the amount of time various appliances are used. For any type of appliance, energy guides help consumers make the most efficient purchase.

Section 5 Assessment

Target Reading Skill Asking Questions Use the answers to the questions about headings to help you answer the questions below.

Reviewing Key Concepts

1. **a. Defining** What is electric power?
   b. Calculating What formula can you use to calculate power?
   c. Making Generalizations Is it correct to say the bigger the electrical device, the greater its power rating? Use Figure 21 to explain your answer.
2. **a. Reviewing** When utility companies calculate a consumer's electric bill, do they consider power or energy use? Explain.

   b. Explaining If the power rating of an appliance is known, how can you find the amount of energy it uses?
   c. Interpreting Tables Which appliance in Figure 21 has the greatest power rating? How can some appliances with lower power ratings cost more to use over a month?

Math Practice

3. **Calculating Power** An electric water heater that uses 40 kW runs for 5.0 hours. What is its power?
4. **Calculating Power** What is the power of the same water heater if it was run for 20 hours?

Electrical Safety

Reading Preview

Key Concepts
• What measures help protect people from electrical shocks and short circuits?

Key Terms
• short circuit • grounded
• third prong • fuse
• circuit breaker

Target Reading Skill

Using Prior Knowledge Before you read, write what you know about electrical safety in a graphic organizer like the one below. As you read, write what you learn.

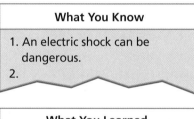

What You Know
1. An electric shock can be dangerous.
2.

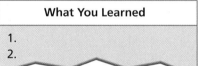

What You Learned
1.
2.

How Can You Blow a Fuse?

1. Begin by constructing the circuit shown using a D-cell, a light bulb, and two alligator clips.
2. Pull a steel fiber out of a piece of steel wool. Wrap the ends of the steel fiber around the alligator clips.
3. Complete the circuit and observe the steel fiber and the bulb.

Think It Over
Developing Hypotheses Write a hypothesis to explain your observations.

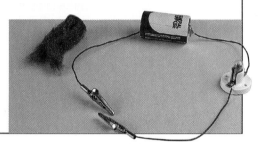

The ice storm has ended, but it has left a great deal of destruction in its wake. Trees have been stripped of their branches, and a thick coating of ice covers the countryside. Perhaps the greatest danger is from the downed high-voltage electric wires. Residents are being warned to stay far away from them. What makes these high-voltage wires so dangerous?

Personal Safety

You may have noticed high-voltage wires hanging from poles beside the highway. These wires form a circuit to and from the electric plant. The wires carry electric current from the electric plant to the customer. If these wires are damaged, they can cause serious injury. Potential dangers include short circuits, electric shocks, and ungrounded wires.

Short Circuits If someone touches a downed electric wire, the person's body can form a short circuit between the wire and the ground. A short circuit can also occur in your home if you touch frayed wires. A **short circuit** is a connection that allows current to take the path of least resistance. For example, the electric charge can flow through the person rather than through the wire to the power plant. The unintended path usually has less resistance than the intended path. Therefore, the current can be very high. The shock that the person receives may be fatal.

Electrical Equipment and Fires

If electrical equipment is not properly used and maintained, it can cause fires. The circle graph shows the percentage of fires caused by different types of electrical equipment.

1. **Reading Graphs** What determines the size of each wedge in the graph?

2. **Reading Graphs** What percentage of fires are caused by appliances?

3. **Interpreting Data** Which category of equipment is responsible for most fires? Which category is responsible for the fewest fires?

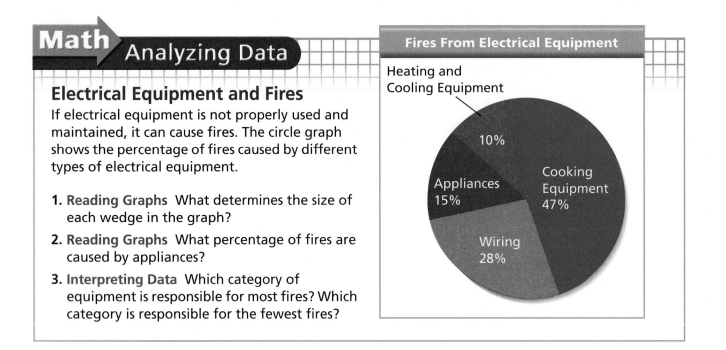

Fires From Electrical Equipment

Heating and Cooling Equipment 10%

Cooking Equipment 47%

Appliances 15%

Wiring 28%

The ground prong connects the metal shell of an appliance to the ground wire of a building.

FIGURE 23
Grounding
A third prong protects against a short circuit by directing current into Earth.

Electric Shocks Electrical signals in the human body control breathing, heartbeat, and muscle movement. If your body receives an electric current from an outside source, it can result in a shock that interferes with your body's electrical signals.

The shock you feel from static discharge after walking across a carpet is very different from the shock that could come from touching a fallen high-voltage wire. The severity of an electric shock depends on the current. A current of less than 0.01 A is almost unnoticeable. But a current greater than 0.2 A can be dangerous, causing burns or even stopping your heart.

Grounding Earth plays an important role in electrical safety. **One way to protect people from electric shock and other electrical danger is to provide an alternate path for electric current.** Most buildings have a wire that connects all the electric circuits to the ground, or Earth. A circuit is electrically **grounded** when charges are able to flow directly from the circuit into Earth in the event of a short circuit.

One method of grounding is to use a third prong on a plug. Two flat prongs of a plug connect an appliance to the household circuit. The **third prong,** which is round, connects any metal pieces of the appliance to the ground wire of the building. If a short circuit occurs in the appliance, the electric charge will flow directly into Earth. Any person who touches the device will be protected.

Reading Checkpoint What is the function of a third prong?

Breaking a Circuit

If you use too many appliances at once, a circuit's current can become dangerously high and heat the wires that carry it. Overloading a circuit can result in a fire. **In order to prevent circuits from overheating, devices called fuses and circuit breakers are added to circuits.**

A **fuse** is a device that contains a thin strip of metal that will melt if there is too much current through it. When the strip of metal "blows," or melts, it breaks the circuit. The breaking of the circuit stops the current. Fuses are commonly found in cars and older buildings. Figure 24 shows how a fuse works.

A disadvantage of using a fuse is that once it burns out, it must be replaced. To avoid the task of replacing fuses, circuits in new buildings are protected by devices called circuit breakers. A **circuit breaker** is a reusable safety switch that breaks the circuit when the current gets too high. In some circuit breakers, a high current causes a small metal band to heat up. As the band heats up it bends away from wires in the circuit, disrupting the current.

It's easy to reset the circuit breaker. By pulling the switch back, you reconnect the metal band to the wires. However, the appliances that are causing the high current in the circuit need to be turned off first.

FIGURE 24
A Fuse
When a circuit becomes overloaded, a fuse stops the current. **Interpreting Diagrams** *How does a fuse work?*

A low current travels through the thin strip of metal to complete a circuit.

If too much current is in the thin strip of metal, it will melt and break the circuit.

Reading Checkpoint What is the difference between a fuse and a circuit breaker?

Section 6 Assessment

Target Reading Skill Using Prior Knowledge Review your graphic organizer about electrical safety and revise it based on what you have just learned in the section.

Reviewing Key Concepts

1. a. **Defining** What are grounded electric circuits? What are fuses and circuit breakers?
   b. **Explaining** Explain how grounding, fuses, and circuit breakers protect people from electrical shocks and short circuits.
   c. **Predicting** Without a fuse or circuit breaker, what might happen in a house with an overloaded electric circuit? Explain your answer.

Lab zone **At-Home Activity**

Checking Circuits Along with members of your family, find out whether the circuits in your home are protected by fuses or circuit breakers. **CAUTION:** *Be careful not to touch the wiring during your inspection.* How many circuits are there in your home? Make a diagram showing the outlets and appliances on each circuit. Explain the role of fuses and circuit breakers. Ask your family members if they are aware of these devices in other circuits, such as in a car.

1 Electric Charge and Static Electricity

Key Ideas

- Charges that are the same repel each other. Charges that are different attract each other.

- An electric field is a region around a charged object where the object's electric force interacts with other charged objects.

- Static electricity charge builds up on an object but does not flow continuously.

- Static electricity is transferred through charging by friction, by conduction, and by induction.

- When negatively and positively charged objects are brought together, electrons transfer until both objects have the same charge.

Key Terms
- electric force • electric field
- static electricity • conservation of charge
- friction • conduction • induction
- static discharge

2 Electric Current

Key Ideas

- To produce electric current, charges must flow continuously from one place to another.

- A conductor transfers electric charge well. An insulator does not transfer electric charge well.

- Voltage causes a current in an electric circuit.

- The greater the resistance, the less current there is for a given voltage.

Key Terms
- electric current • electric circuit • conductor
- insulator • voltage • voltage source
- resistance

3 Batteries

Key Ideas

- Volta built the first battery by layering zinc, paper soaked in salt water, and silver.

- Chemical reactions in an electrochemical cell cause one electrode to become negatively charged and the other electrode to become positively charged.

Key Terms
- chemical energy • chemical reaction
- electrochemical cell • electrode • electrolyte
- terminal • battery • wet cell • dry cell

4 Electric Circuits

Key Ideas

- Ohm's law says that the resistance is equal to the voltage divided by the current.

$$\text{Resistance} = \text{Voltage} \div \text{Current}$$

- Circuits have a source of electrical energy and devices that are run by electrical energy. Circuits are connected by conducting wires.

- In a series circuit, there is only one path for the current to take. In a parallel circuit, there are several paths for the current to taket.

Key Terms
- Ohm's law • series circuit • ammeter
- parallel circuit • voltmeter

5 Electric Power

Key Ideas

- You can calculate power by multiplying voltage by current.

$$\text{Energy} = \text{Power} \times \text{Time}$$

- The total amount of energy used by an appliance is equal to its power multiplied by the amount of time it is used.

Key Term
- power

6 Electrical Safety

Key Ideas

- One way to protect people from electric shock and other electrical danger is to provide an alternate path for electric current.

- In order to prevent circuits from overheating, devices called fuses and circuit breakers are added to circuits.

Key Terms
- short circuit • grounded • third prong
- fuse • circuit breaker

Review and Assessment

Go Online
PHSchool.com
For: Self-Assessment
Visit: PHSchool.com
Web Code: cga-4020

Organizing Information

Concept Mapping Copy the concept map about devices that prevent circuits from overheating. Then complete the concept map. (For more information on concept maps, see the Skills Handbook.)

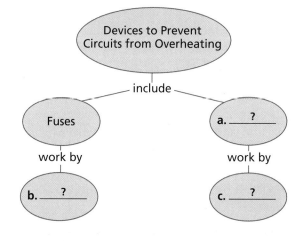

Devices to Prevent Circuits from Overheating

include

Fuses   a. _____?_____

work by   work by

b. _____?_____   c. _____?_____

Reviewing Key Terms

Choose the letter of the best answer.

1. The attraction or repulsion between electric charges is called a(n)
   a. electric field.
   b. electric force.
   c. electron.
   d. static electricity.

2. The potential difference that causes charges to move in a circuit is called
   a. current.
   b. electric discharge.
   c. resistance.
   d. voltage.

3. A combination of two or more electrical cells in a series is called a(n)
   a. wet cell.
   b. dry cell.
   c. battery.
   d. electrode.

4. A device that measures electric current is a(n)
   a. ammeter.
   b. battery.
   c. resistor.
   d. voltmeter.

5. Connecting a circuit to Earth as a safety precaution is called
   a. a short circuit.   b. an insulator.
   c. grounding.   d. static discharge.

If the statement is true, write *true*. If it is false, change the underlined word or words to make the statement true.

6. <u>Conduction</u> is the process of charging an object without touching it.

7. Electrical resistance is low in a good <u>conductor</u>.

8. An <u>electrolyte</u> is an attachment point used to connect a cell or battery to a circuit.

9. In a <u>series circuit</u>, all parts of the circuit are connected in a single path.

10. <u>Power</u> is the rate at which energy is transformed from one form to another.

Writing in Science

Descriptive Paragraph Describe the journey of an electron in a lightning bolt. Begin at the thundercloud and follow the path of the electron until the lightning bolt strikes the ground.

Discovery CHANNEL SCHOOL

Electricity
Video Preview
Video Field Trip
▶ Video Assessment

Review and Assessment

Checking Concepts

11. Describe the three ways in which an object can become charged.
12. What units are used to measure voltage, current, and resistance?
13. Explain how the components of an electrochemical cell produce voltage.
14. What is Ohm's law?
15. What would happen if the circuits in your school building were series circuits? Explain.
16. Which glows more brightly—a 100-W bulb or a 75-W bulb? Explain your answer.
17. What is a short circuit?

Thinking Critically

18. **Classifying** Identify each of the following statements as characteristic of series circuits, parallel circuits, or both:
    a. Current = Voltage ÷ Resistance
    b. Total resistance increases as more light bulbs are added.
    c. Total resistance decreases as more branches are added.
    d. Current in each part of the circuit is the same.
    e. A break in any part of the circuit will cause current to stop.
19. **Interpreting Diagrams** Is the electroscope shown below charged or uncharged? Explain.

20. **Applying Concepts** Explain why the third prong of a plug should not be removed.
21. **Comparing and Contrasting** Compare and contrast wet cells and dry cells.

Math Practice

22. **Calculating Resistance** A toaster is plugged into a 120-volt socket. If it has a current of 0.25 amps in its coils, what is the resistance of the toaster? Show your work.
23. **Calculating Power** The voltage of a car battery is 12 volts. When the car is started, the battery produces a 40-amp current. How much power does it take to start the car?

Applying Skills

Use the diagram below for Questions 24–27.

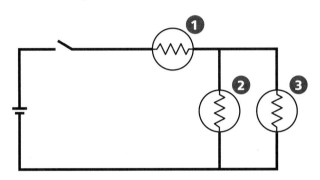

24. **Classifying** Is the circuit in the illustration a series or parallel circuit? Explain.
25. **Controlling Variables** Would the other bulbs continue to shine if you removed bulb 1? Would they shine if you removed bulb 2 instead? Explain your reasoning.
26. **Predicting** Will any of the bulbs be lit if you open the switch? Explain.
27. **Making Models** Redraw the circuit diagram to include a switch that controls only Bulb 3.

Lab zone Chapter **Project**

Performance Assessment Prepare a description and circuit diagram for your display. If any parts of your alarm circuit are not visible, draw a second diagram showing how all the parts are assembled. Then present your alarm to your class and explain how it could be used. Include a description of the reliability of your switch.

Standardized Test Prep

Choose the letter of the best answer.

1. Which of the following is a reusable device that protects a circuit from becoming overheated?
   A a circuit breaker
   B a third prong
   C a fuse
   D an electroscope

2. You want to build a device that can conduct current but that will be safe if touched by a person. Which of the following pairs of materials could you use?
   F glass for the conductor and rubber for the insulator
   G copper for the insulator and silver for the conductor
   H sand for the conductor and plastic for the insulator
   J plastic for the insulator and silver for the conductor

3. The graph shows the cost of using three household appliances. Which of the following is a valid interpretation of the graph?

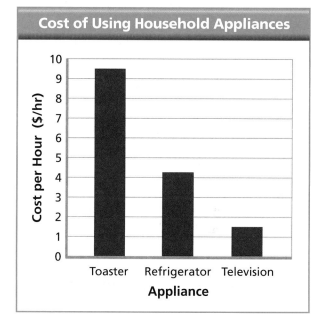

   A A toaster has high voltage.
   B It costs more per hour to run a refrigerator than a television.
   C During a month, a family pays more to run a toaster than a refrigerator.
   D A toaster uses more current than any other appliance.

4. An electrochemical cell has one copper nail and one zinc nail. When the nails are placed in vinegar, the light bulb lights up. What conclusion can be made?
   F No chemical reaction occurred.
   G Vinegar is an electrolyte.
   H All electrochemical cells contain vinegar.
   J The zinc nail reacted with the vinegar but the copper nail did not.

Constructed Response

5. Explain why people should never touch a high-voltage wire that has blown down in a storm. In your explanation, use the words *electric shock* and *short circuit*.

Interactive Textbook

To deliver the mail, this letter carrier rides ▶ a machine that uses electromagnetism.

Lab zone™ Chapter **Project**

Electrical Energy Audit

In this chapter, you will discover how electrical energy is generated. You will also study how electrical energy is used in motors and other devices.

Your Goal To analyze how you use electrical energy at home and to determine how much electrical energy your family uses

To complete the project, you must
- list the appliances in your home that use electrical energy
- record the power rating in kilowatts of each appliance or calculate it using Ohm's law
- record how long each appliance is used during an average week
- calculate how much electrical energy is used by each appliance using the formula Energy = Power × Time
- follow the safety guidelines in Appendix A

Plan It! Begin by listing the appliances in your home. Then prepare a data table to keep track of your observations. Include columns for the name of the appliance, its primary use, its energy source, and the number of hours it is used each day. After collecting data for a full week, calculate the amount of time each appliance was used and the amount of electrical energy each appliance consumed.

What Is Electromagnetism?

Reading Preview

Key Concepts
- How is an electric current related to a magnetic field?
- What are some characteristics of a magnetic field produced by a current?
- What are the characteristics of an electromagnet?

Key Terms
- electromagnetism
- solenoid
- electromagnet

Target Reading Skill

Identifying Main Ideas As you read the Solenoid section, write the main idea—the biggest or most important idea—in a graphic organizer like the one below. Then write three supporting details. The supporting details further explain the main idea.

Main Idea

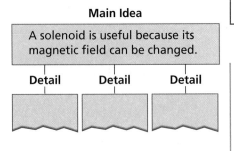

A solenoid is useful because its magnetic field can be changed.

Detail	Detail	Detail

Lab zone Discover Activity

Are Magnetic Fields Limited to Magnets?

1. Obtain two wires with the insulation removed from both ends. Each wire should be 20 to 30 cm long.
2. Connect one end of each wire to a socket containing a small light bulb.
3. Connect the other end of one of those wires to a D-cell battery.
4. Place three compasses near the wire at different positions. Before you continue, note the direction in which each of the compasses is pointing.
5. Center the wire over the compasses. Make sure the compass needles are free to turn.
6. Touch the free end of the remaining wire to the battery. Observe the compasses as charges flow through the wire. Move the wire away from the battery, and then touch it to the battery again. Watch the compasses.

Think It Over
Inferring What happened to the compasses when charges flowed through the wire? What can you infer about electricity and magnetism?

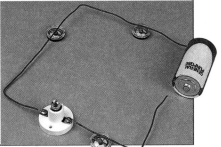

In 1820, the Danish scientist Hans Christian Oersted (UR sted) was teaching a class at the University of Copenhagen. During his lecture he produced a current in a wire, just like the current in the wires of your appliances at home. When he brought a compass near the wire, he observed that the compass needle changed direction.

Oersted was surprised. He could have assumed that something was wrong with his equipment and ignored what he saw. Instead, he investigated further. He set up several compasses around a wire. Oersted discovered that whenever he produced a current in the wire, the compass needles lined up around the wire in the shape of a circle.

Oersted's discovery showed that magnetism and electricity are related. But just how are they related?

FIGURE 1
Currents and Magnetic Fields
Current in a wire affects nearby compasses.

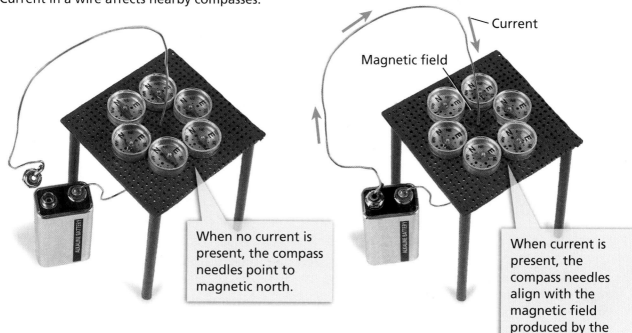

Current

Magnetic field

When no current is present, the compass needles point to magnetic north.

When current is present, the compass needles align with the magnetic field produced by the current in the wire.

Electric Current and Magnetism

Wherever there is electricity, there is magnetism. **An electric current produces a magnetic field.** This relationship between electricity and magnetism is called **electromagnetism.**

You can't see electromagnetism, but you can use a compass and an electric current to observe its effect on objects. A compass needle normally points north because it aligns itself with Earth's magnetic field. It will point in a different direction only if another magnetic field is present. For example, look at the compasses shown in the photo on the left in Figure 1. They surround a straight wire that has no current. Because there is no current, the wire has no magnetic field. Therefore, the compasses align with Earth's magnetic field and point north.

In the photo on the right in Figure 1, the wire has a current. Notice that in this case the compasses no longer point north. The needles of the compasses change direction because a magnetic field is produced around a wire that has a current. The needles of the compasses align with the magnetic field that the current produces.

In Figure 2, iron filings surround a wire that has a current. You can see that the filings form a pattern. They map out the magnetic field produced by the current in the wire.

 Reading Checkpoint What can produce a magnetic field?

FIGURE 2
A Magnetic Field Map
Iron filings show the magnetic field lines around a wire with a current. **Observing** *What is the shape of the field lines?*

FIGURE 3

Controlling a Magnetic Field
Both the direction and strength of a
magnetic field produced by a current can
be controlled.

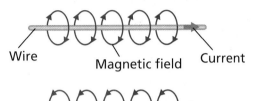

A Reversing the direction of the
current reverses the direction
of the magnetic field.

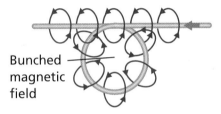

Wire   Magnetic field   Current

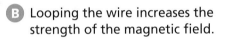

B Looping the wire increases the
strength of the magnetic field.

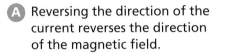

Bunched
magnetic
field

FIGURE 4

Magnetic Field Around a Solenoid
The magnetic field around a solenoid
resembles that of a bar magnet.
Comparing and Contrasting *How is a
solenoid different from a bar magnet?*

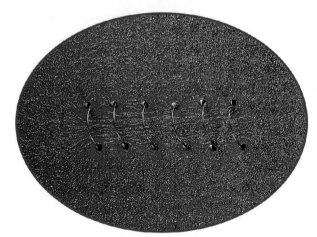

Solenoids

The magnetic field produced by a current has three distinct characteristics. The field can be turned on or off, have its direction reversed, or have its strength changed. Unlike Earth's magnetic field, you can turn a magnetic field produced by a current on or off. To do so you simply turn the current on or off. In addition, you can change the direction of the magnetic field by reversing the direction of the current. When the current reverses, the magnetic field reverses also, as shown in Figure 3A.

You can also change the strength of a magnetic field produced by a current. The magnetic field around a wire with a current forms a cylinder around the wire. If the wire is twisted into a loop, the magnetic field lines become bunched up inside the loop, as shown in Figure 3B. If the wire is bent into a second loop, the concentration of magnetic field lines within the loops is twice as great. So, the strength of the magnetic field increases as the number of loops, or coils, increases.

By winding a wire with a current into many loops you strengthen the magnetic field in the center of the coil. A coil of wire with a current is called a **solenoid.** The two ends of a solenoid act like magnetic poles. In Figure 4 you can see that the iron filings around a solenoid line up much as they would around a bar magnet. However, in a solenoid, the north and south poles change with the direction of the current.

Reading Checkpoint What happens to the magnetic field lines in a twisted loop of wire?

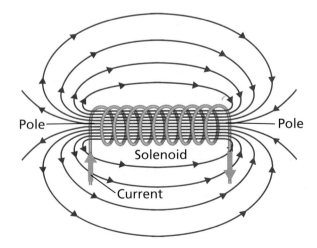

Pole   Pole
Solenoid
Current

FIGURE 5
How a Doorbell Works
A doorbell rings as the magnetic field
of an electromagnet changes.

Closed Circuit
Pressing the button closes the circuit of
the doorbell. Closing the circuit turns on
the electromagnet in the doorbell.

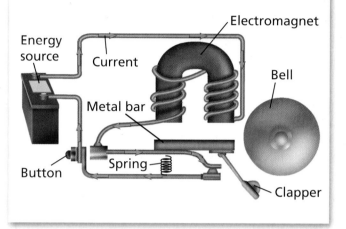

Open Circuit
The electromagnet attracts a metal bar, and the
clapper strikes the bell. At the same time, the
circuit opens, turning off the electromagnet.
The spring returns the metal bar to its resting
position.

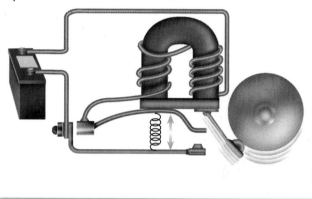

Electromagnets

If you place a ferromagnetic material such as iron inside a solenoid, the strength of the magnetic field increases. The increase in strength occurs because the ferromagnetic material becomes a magnet.

What Is an Electromagnet? A solenoid with a ferromagnetic core is called an **electromagnet.** The magnetic field of an electromagnet is produced by both the current in the wire and the magnetized core. The overall magnetic field of an electromagnet can be hundreds or thousands of times stronger than the magnetic field produced by the current alone. **An electromagnet is a strong magnet that can be turned on and off.**

You can increase the strength of an electromagnet in a number of ways. First, you can increase the current in the solenoid; second, you can add more loops of wire to the solenoid. Third, you can wind the coils of the solenoid closer together. Finally, you can increase the strength of an electromagnet by using a stronger ferromagnetic material for the core.

Common Electromagnets Electromagnets are very common. You probably use many every day. Electromagnets are used to record information onto audiotapes, videotapes, computer hard drives, and credit cards. In addition, many devices, such as the doorbell shown in Figure 5, use electromagnets.

Lab zone Try This Activity

On/Off
1. Your teacher will give you a piece of insulated copper wire. Tightly wrap it around a nail 10–12 times.
2. Tape one end of the wire to a battery terminal.
3. Touch the other end of the wire to the other battery terminal and dip the nail into a container of paper clips. Slowly lift the nail above the container.
4. Pull the wire away from the battery terminal and observe what happens.

Inferring Why did the paper clips drop when you pulled the wire away from the battery terminal?

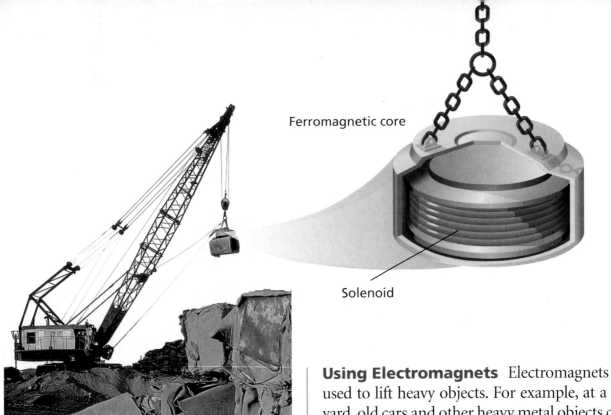

Ferromagnetic core

Solenoid

FIGURE 6
Electromagnets at Work
These heavy loads can be lifted easily
because of powerful electromagnets.

Using Electromagnets Electromagnets are
used to lift heavy objects. For example, at a junk-
yard, old cars and other heavy metal objects can be
moved by a strong electromagnet on a crane. To
lift the object a switch is turned on in the crane so
that a current is produced in the electromagnet.
The current forms a strong magnetic field that
attracts metal objects. When the object needs to be
dropped, the switch is turned off and the object
falls from the magnet.

Section 1 Assessment

Target Reading Skill Identifying Main Ideas
Use your graphic organizer to help you answer
Question 2 below.

Reviewing Key Concepts

1. a. **Identifying** Who discovered that electricity
   and magnetism are related?
   b. **Explaining** What is the relationship between
   an electric current and a magnetic field?
   c. **Relating Cause and Effect** How can a
   magnetic field be produced around a wire?
2. a. **Defining** What is a solenoid?
   b. **Explaining** What are the three characteristics
   of a magnetic field produced by a current?
   c. **Applying Concepts** How could you increase
   the strength of a solenoid?

3. a. **Reviewing** What makes an electromagnet
   stronger than a solenoid?
   b. **Describing** What are four ways to make an
   electromagnet stronger?

Writing in Science

Product Description Suppose you are an
inventor who just built a device that will lift
heavy objects using an electromagnet. Write
a description for your product brochure that
explains how the magnet can move heavy
objects.

Electricity, Magnetism, and Motion

Reading Preview

Key Concepts
- How can electrical energy be transformed into mechanical energy?
- How does a galvanometer work?
- What does an electric motor do?

Key Terms
- energy • electrical energy
- mechanical energy
- galvanometer • electric motor

Target Reading Skill

Outlining As you read, make an outline about the section that you can use for review. Use the red headings for the main ideas and the blue headings for the supporting ideas.

Electricity, Magnetism, and Motion
I. Electrical Energy and Motion
A. Types of Energy
B.
II. Galvanometers
III. Electric Motors
A.

Lab zone Discover **Activity**

How Does a Magnet Move a Wire?

1. Make an electromagnet by winding insulated copper wire around a steel nail. Leave 30–40 cm of wire at each end of the electromagnet.
2. Pile up some books. Place a ruler between the top two books.
3. Hang the electromagnet over the ruler so that it hangs free.
4. Complete the circuit by connecting the electromagnet to a switch and a battery.
5. Place a horseshoe magnet near the electromagnet. Then close the switch briefly and observe what happens to the electromagnet.
6. Reverse the wires connected to the battery and repeat Step 5.

Think It Over

Inferring What happened to the electromagnet when you closed the switch? Was anything different when you reversed the wires? How can you use electricity to produce motion?

What do you think about when you hear the word *electricity?* You may think about the bright lights of a big city, the lightning during a thunderstorm, or the music from your stereo in the morning. You might think about how useful electricity is. For example, if you are familiar with electric motors like the one in a blender, then you already know about an important use of electricity. Electricity can produce motion.

Electricity makes the blades spin. ▶

FIGURE 7
Producing Motion
The magnetic field of a permanent magnet interacts with the magnetic field produced by a current.
Relating Cause and Effect
How does the direction of the current affect the motion of the wire?

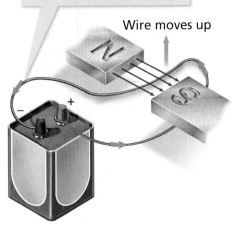

The wire moves when current is present.

Wire moves down

When the current is reversed, the wire moves in the opposite direction.

Wire moves up

Electrical Energy and Motion

As you know, magnetic force can produce motion. Magnets can move together or move apart, depending on how their poles are arranged. You also know that an electric current in a wire produces a magnetic field similar to that of a permanent magnet. So a magnet can move a wire with a current, just as it would move another magnet.

In Figure 7 you can see how a wire placed in the magnetic field of two permanent magnets can move. With current in the wire, the magnetic field of the wire interacts with the magnetic field of the permanent magnets. The wire moves down. If the current is reversed, the wire moves up. The direction in which the wire moves depends on the direction of the current.

Types of Energy When electricity and magnetism interact, something can move—in this case, a wire moved. The ability to move an object over a distance is called **energy.** The energy associated with electric currents is called **electrical energy.** And the energy an object has due to its movement or position is called **mechanical energy.**

Energy Transformation Energy can be transformed from one form into another. **When a wire with a current is placed in a magnetic field, electrical energy is transformed into mechanical energy.** This happens when the magnetic field produced by the current causes the wire to move.

Reading Checkpoint What is mechanical energy?

Galvanometers

The wire shown in Figure 7 that moves in the magnetic field is straight. But what happens if you place a loop with a current in a magnetic field? Look at Figure 8. The current in one side of the loop is in the opposite direction than the current in the other side of the loop. Because the direction of the current determines the direction in which the wire moves, the two sides of the loop move in opposite directions. Once each side has moved as far up or down as it can go, it will stop moving. As a result, the loop can rotate a half turn.

The rotation of a wire loop in a magnetic field is the basis of a galvanometer. A **galvanometer** is a device that measures small currents. In a galvanometer, an electromagnet is suspended between opposite poles of two permanent magnets. The electromagnet's coil is attached to a pointer, as shown in Figure 9. When a current is in the electromagnet's coil, a magnetic field is produced. This field interacts with the permanent magnet's field, causing the loops of wire and the pointer to rotate. **An electric current is used to turn the pointer of a galvanometer.** The distance the loops and the pointer rotate depends on the amount of current in the wire.

A galvanometer has a scale that is marked to show how much the pointer turns for a known current. An unknown current can then be measured using the galvanometer. So galvanometers are very useful in everyday life. For example, electricians use them in their work and drivers of cars use them to know when to stop for fuel.

 Reading Checkpoint Where are galvanometers used?

FIGURE 8
How a Galvanometer Works
Current is in different directions in each side of the wire loop, so one side of the loop moves down as the other side moves up. This causes the loop to rotate.

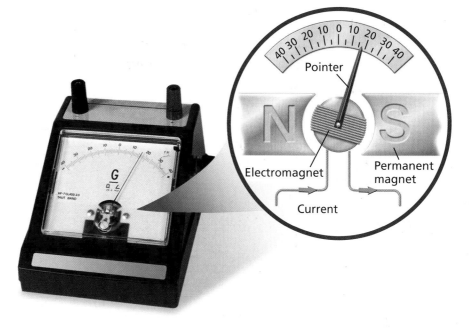

FIGURE 9
Inside a Galvanometer
An electromagnet turns the pointer to indicate the amount of current present. The amount of current can be read on the scale.

Electric Motors

The electromagnet in the magnetic field of a galvanometer cannot rotate more than half a turn. But suppose you could make it rotate continuously. Instead of moving a pointer, the electromagnet could turn a rod, or axle. The axle could then turn something else, such as the blades of a fan or a blender. Such a device would be what is called an electric motor. An **electric motor** is a device that uses an electric current to turn an axle. **An electric motor transforms electrical energy into mechanical energy.**

How a Motor Works How can you make a loop of wire continue to spin? Recall that the direction in which the loop moves in a magnetic field depends on the direction of the current in the loop. In a motor, current is reversed just as the loop, or armature, gets to the vertical position. This reverses the direction of the movement of both sides of the loop. The side of the loop that moved up on the left now moves down on the right. The side of the loop that moved down on the right now moves up on the left. The current reverses after each half turn so that the loop spins continuously in the same direction. You can see how a motor works in Figure 10.

FIGURE 10
An Electric Motor
A loop of wire in a motor spins continuously because the current reverses every half turn.
Observing *What part of an electric motor must be attached directly to the energy source?*

1 Brushes
The brushes that touch the commutator conduct current to the armature. The brushes do not move.

2 Armature
The current is in opposite directions on each side of the armature causing one side to move up while the other side moves down.

3 Commutator
The commutator rotates with the armature. The direction of current reverses with each half turn so the armature spins continuously.

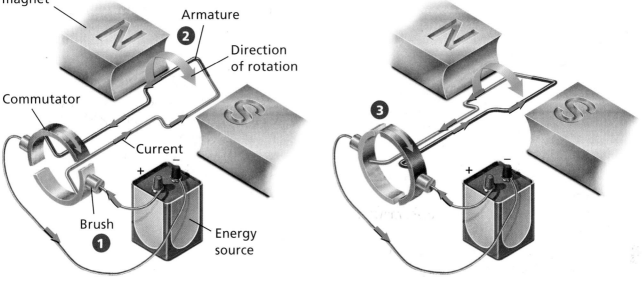

Parts of a Motor Notice that the armature in Figure 10 is only one loop of wire. However, practical armatures, like the one shown in Figure 11, have dozens or hundreds of wire loops wrapped around a ferromagnetic core. Using many loops increases the strength of the motor and allows it to rotate more smoothly. Large electric motors also use electromagnets instead of permanent magnets to increase the strength of the magnetic field.

A commutator repeatedly reverses the flow of current through the armature. A commutator is a ring split in half. Each half is attached to one end of the armature. When the armature rotates, the commutator rotates as well. As it moves, the commutator slides past two contact points called brushes. Each half of the commutator is connected to the current source by one of the brushes. As the armature rotates, each part of the commutator contacts one brush and then the other. Because the brushes conduct the current, changing brushes reverses the direction of the current in the armature. The reversing of the direction of the current causes the armature to spin continuously.

Armature

FIGURE 11

Inside a Motor
The armature inside this motor contains hundreds of loops of copper wire wrapped around a ferromagnetic core.
Applying Concepts *How does a motor transform energy?*

Reading Checkpoint **How can the strength of a motor be increased?**

Section 2 Assessment

Target Reading Skill **Outlining** Use the information in your outline about electricity, magnetism, and motion to help you answer the questions below.

Reviewing Key Concepts

1. **a. Identifying** What is energy?
   b. Applying Concepts What energy transformation occurs when a wire with a current is placed in a magnetic field?
   c. Predicting If a wire with a current moved upward in a magnetic field, how would it move when the direction of the current reversed?

2. **a. Reviewing** What does a galvanometer measure?
   b. Describing What energy transformation occurs in a galvanometer?
   c. Relating Cause and Effect What causes the pointer to move in a galvanometer?

3. **a. Defining** What is an electric motor?
   b. Classifying What type of energy transformation occurs in a motor?
   c. Relating Cause and Effect What does the commutator do in an electric motor?

Writing in Science

Make a List Make a list of at least ten motor-operated devices in your community. Beside each device, describe the motion produced by the motor.

Magnetic Resonance Imaging

Imagine powerful magnets and electromagnetic energy scanning you from head to toe. Science fiction? No, it's magnetic resonance imaging (MRI.) MRI is a safe and painless way of looking inside the body. The technology uses large electromagnets, radio waves, and computers to make a three-dimensional model of the body.

Hydrogen, Magnets, and Radio Waves

Different types of body tissue contain different amounts of hydrogen atoms. The MRI machine uses the magnetic properties of hydrogen atoms to create images. The main electromagnet of an MRI machine creates a strong magnetic field that causes the magnetic fields of the hydrogen atoms in a body to align. Three weaker magnetic coils—the X-coil, the Y-coil, and the Z-coil—specify an area, or "slice," of the body to be imaged. Short pulses of radio waves knock the hydrogen atoms out of alignment. When the radio wave pulses are stopped, the atoms realign. As they do, they release energy in the form of radio signals. The signals are collected and sent to a computer that translates them into images.

Main Electromagnet
The main electromagnet produces an even, strong magnetic field around the patient.

Y-Coil

Radio-frequency Coil
This coil applies short radio pulses to knock the hydrogen atoms in a person's body out of alignment. It also acts as an antenna, receiving radio signals from the realigning atoms.

X-Coil

Z-Coil

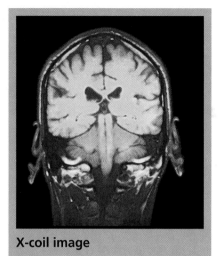

X-coil image

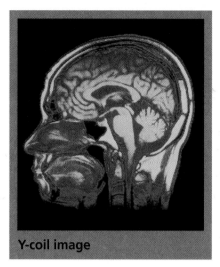

Y-coil image

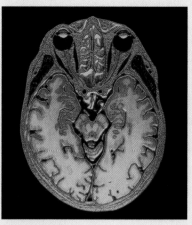

Z-coil image

X-coil
The X-coil magnet scans from front to back.

Y-coil
The Y-coil magnet scans from side to side.

Z-coil
The Z-coil magnet scans from top to bottom.

Seeing Inside the Body

MRI has advantages over X-ray scanning. MRI is safer because it doesn't use radiation. Also, unlike an X-ray machine, MRI shows soft tissues clearly. Therefore, MRI is used to examine ligaments and parts of organs, such as the brain and circulatory system.

Why isn't MRI used more often? There are many answers. An MRI machine is costly to build and use. Very large people cannot fit inside the machine. People with a pacemaker or with some types of metallic implants in their bodies cannot have MRI. In addition, some people find this procedure uncomfortable because the machine is noisy and they must lie very still inside it for a long time.

Weigh the Impact

1. Identify the Need
MRI is not used in every medical situation. What factors might a doctor consider before ordering an MRI test?

2. Research
Explore the latest MRI technology on the Internet. Focus on how MRI technology is being improved for children.

3. Write
Use your research to create a pamphlet for children describing an MRI test. Include facts about how MRI technology is improving.

For: More on magnetic resonance imaging
Visit: PHSchool.com
Web Code: cgh-4030

Building an Electric Motor

Problem

Electric trolley cars, food blenders, garage door openers, and computer disk drives are only some of the everyday devices that have electric motors. How does an electric motor operate?

Skills Focus

classifying, inferring, drawing conclusions

Materials

- D-cell
- 2 large paper clips
- permanent disk magnet
- 3 balls of clay
- empty film canister
- pliers
- sandpaper
- 2 insulated wires, approximately 15 cm each
- enamel-coated wire, 22–24 gauge, approximately 1 meter

Procedure ✂

1. Wrap about 1 meter of enamel-coated wire around a film canister to produce a wire coil. Leave approximately 5 cm free at each end.

2. Remove the film canister and wrap the two free ends three or four times around the wire coil to keep the coil from unwinding.

3. Use sandpaper to scrape off all the enamel from about 2 or 3 centimeters of one end of the wire coil.

4. Use sandpaper to scrape off one side of the enamel from about 2 or 3 centimeters of the other end of the wire. See the illustration below.

5. Bend two paper clips as shown in the photo on the next page.

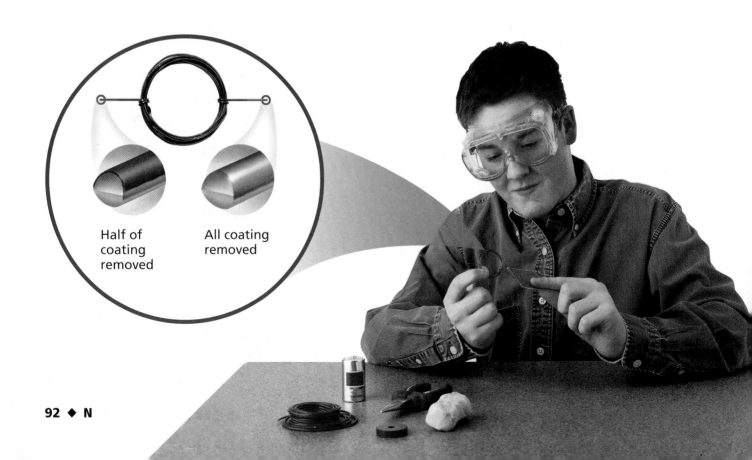

Half of coating removed

All coating removed

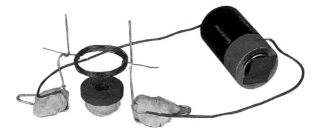

6. Place the free ends of the wire coil on the paper clips. Make sure the coil is perfectly balanced. Adjust the paper clips and wire so that the coil can rotate freely.

7. Use clay to hold a permanent magnet in place directly below the wire coil. The coil needs to be able to rotate without hitting the magnet.

8. Remove the insulation from the ends of two 15-cm insulated wires. Use these wires to connect the paper clips to a D-cell.

9. Give the coil a gentle push to start it turning. If it does not spin or stops spinning after a few seconds, check the following:
   • Are the paper clips in good contact with the D-cell?
   • Will the coil spin in the opposite direction?
   • Will the coil work on someone else's apparatus?

Analyze and Conclude

1. **Observing** Describe the movement of the wire coil when your setup was complete and working.

2. **Classifying** Which part of your setup contained a permanent magnet? Describe the location of the magnetic field produced by that magnet.

3. **Inferring** What was the effect of removing all the insulation from one end of the wire coil but only half from the other end?

4. **Inferring** Explain how a magnetic field is produced when the motor is connected to the D-cell.

5. **Drawing Conclusions** How do magnetism and electricity interact to cause the wire coil to rotate?

6. **Communicating** Your motor produced motion, but it does not yet do useful work. Think of an object your motor might cause to move. Consider how you could modify the motor to move that object. Write a procedure for changing your motor to carry out the task.

Design an Experiment

You have built a simple electric motor. List three factors that may affect the motion of the coil. Design an experiment to test one of those factors. *Obtain your teacher's permission before carrying out your investigation.*

Electricity From Magnetism

Reading Preview

Key Concepts
- How can an electric current be produced in a conductor?
- How does a generator work?
- What is the function of a transformer?

Key Terms
- electromagnetic induction
- direct current
- alternating current
- electric generator
- transformer
- step-up transformer
- step-down transformer

Target Reading Skill

Previewing Visuals When you preview, you look ahead at the material to be read. Preview Figure 13. Then write two questions that you have about the diagram in a graphic organizer like the one below. As you read, answer your questions.

Generators

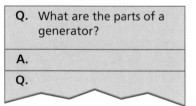

Q. What are the parts of a generator?
A.
Q.

Lab zone Discover **Activity**

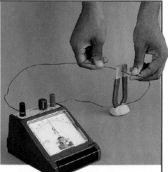

Can You Produce Current Without a Battery?

1. Obtain one meter of wire with the insulation removed from both ends.
2. Connect the wire to the terminals of a galvanometer or a sensitive multimeter.
3. Hold the wire between the poles of a strong horseshoe magnet. Observe the meter.
4. Move the wire up and down between the poles. Observe the meter.
5. Move the wire faster, and again observe the meter.

Think It Over

Developing Hypotheses In which steps does the meter indicate a current? Propose a hypothesis to explain why a current is present. Try using an "If . . . then . . ." statement.

An electric motor uses electrical energy to produce motion. Is the reverse true? Can motion produce electrical energy? In 1831, scientists found out that moving a wire in a magnetic field can cause an electric current. That discovery has allowed electrical energy to be supplied to homes, schools, and businesses all over the world.

Induction of Electric Current

Before you can understand how electrical energy is supplied by your electric company, you need to know how it is produced. A magnet and a conductor, such as a wire, can be used to induce a current in the conductor. The key is motion. **An electric current is induced in a conductor when the conductor moves through a magnetic field.** Generating an electric current from the motion of a conductor through a magnetic field is called **electromagnetic induction.** Current that is generated in this way is called induced current.

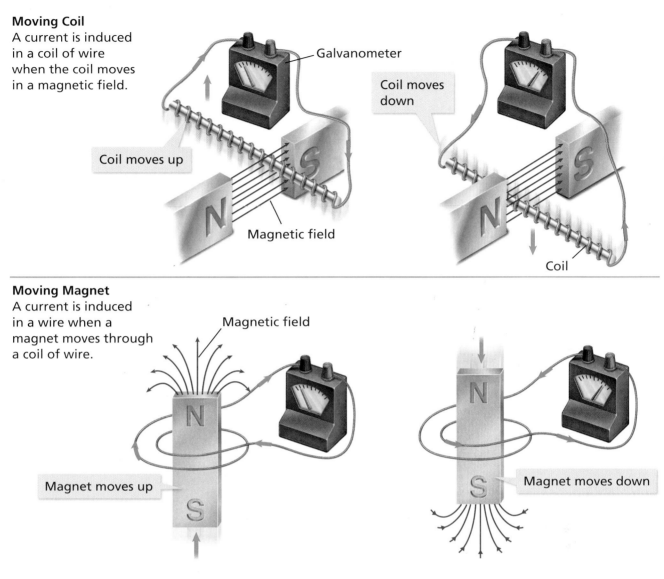

Moving Coil
A current is induced in a coil of wire when the coil moves in a magnetic field.

Galvanometer

Coil moves up

Coil moves down

Magnetic field

Coil

Moving Magnet
A current is induced in a wire when a magnet moves through a coil of wire.

Magnetic field

Magnet moves up

Magnet moves down

FIGURE 12

Inducing Current

When a coil of wire moves up or down in a magnetic field, a current is induced in the wire. If a magnet moves up or down through a coil of wire, a current is induced in the wire.
Interpreting Diagrams *How does the direction in which you move the wire and magnet affect the current?*

To induce a current in a conductor, either the conductor can move through the magnetic field or the magnet itself can move. In Figure 12, you can see what happens when a wire coil moves in a magnetic field. The coil of wire is connected to a galvanometer forming a closed circuit. If the wire coil is held still, the galvanometer will not register any current. But if the coil is moved up or down, the galvanometer shows an electric current is present. A current is induced without a battery or other voltage source by moving the coil! You saw this for yourself if you did the Discover Activity. In Figure 12, you can also see what happens when a magnet placed inside a wire coil is moved instead of the wire. The result is the same as moving the coil in the magnetic field. An electric current is induced in the coil.

Reading Checkpoint What happens when a wire coil moves in a magnetic field?

Direct Current In an induced current, charges may flow in one direction only, or they may alternate directions. The direction of an induced current depends on the direction in which the wire or magnet moves. You probably noticed in Figure 12 on the previous page that when the direction of the motion of the wire coil changed, the direction of the current reversed.

A current consisting of charges that flow in one direction only is called **direct current,** or DC. A direct current can be induced from a changing magnetic field or produced from an energy source such as a battery. When a battery is placed in a circuit, charges flow away from one end of the battery, around the circuit, and into the other end of the battery. Thomas Edison used direct current in his first electric generating plant.

Science and **History**

Generating Electrical Energy

Several scientists were responsible for bringing electricity from the laboratory into everyday use.

**1830–1831
Electric Induction**
Michael Faraday and Joseph Henry each discover that an electric current can be induced by a changing magnetic field. Understanding induction makes possible the development of motors and generators.

1820 Electromagnetism
Hans Christian Oersted discovers that an electric current creates a magnetic field. The relationship between electricity and magnetism is called electromagnetism.

1800	1820	1840

Alternating Current What would happen if a wire in a magnetic field were moved up and down repeatedly? The induced current in the wire would reverse direction repeatedly as well. This kind of current is called **alternating current,** or AC. An alternating current consists of charges that move back and forth in a circuit. The electric current in the circuits in homes, schools, and other buildings is alternating current.

Alternating current has a major advantage over direct current. An AC voltage can be easily raised or lowered to a higher or lower voltage. This means that a high voltage can be used to send electrical energy over great distances. Then the voltage can be reduced to a safer level for everyday use.

✓ **Reading Checkpoint** What is the advantage of using alternating current?

Writing in Science

Letter Find out more about the work of Michael Faraday, Joseph Henry, or Hans Christian Oersted. Write a letter to a friend in which you describe your work as a research assistant for the scientist you choose. Include descriptions of his experimental procedures and the equipment he uses. Tell how his work has led to surprising discoveries.

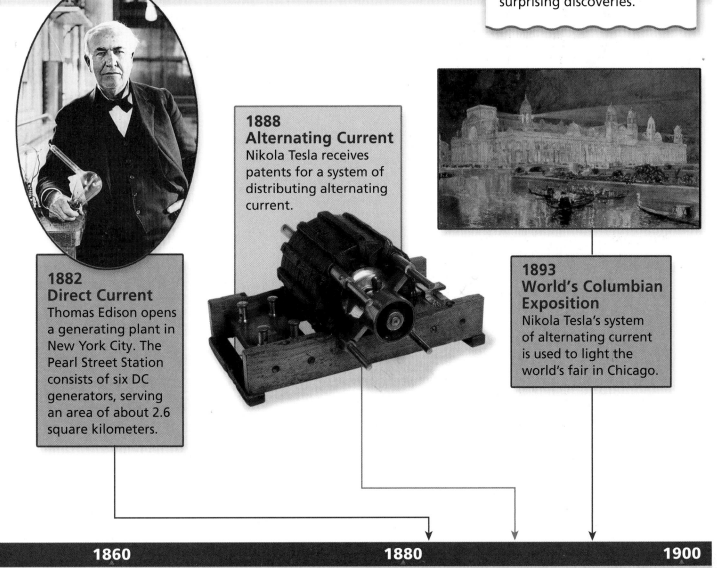

**1882
Direct Current**
Thomas Edison opens a generating plant in New York City. The Pearl Street Station consists of six DC generators, serving an area of about 2.6 square kilometers.

**1888
Alternating Current**
Nikola Tesla receives patents for a system of distributing alternating current.

**1893
World's Columbian Exposition**
Nikola Tesla's system of alternating current is used to light the world's fair in Chicago.

1860   1880   1900

Generators

An **electric generator** is a device that transforms mechanical energy into electrical energy. An electric generator is the opposite of an electric motor. An electric motor uses an electric current in a magnet field to produce motion. **A generator uses motion in a magnetic field to produce an electric current.**

AC Generators In Figure 13 you can see how a simple AC generator works. As the crank is turned, the armature rotates in the magnetic field. One side of the armature moves up, and the other side moves down. The up and down motion induces a current in the wire. The current is in opposite directions on the two sides of the armature.

After the armature turns halfway, each side of it reverses direction in the magnetic field. The side that moved up moves down, and vice versa. The current in the wire changes direction as well. The result is an alternating current is induced.

As the armature turns, slip rings turn with it. Slip rings may remind you of the commutator in a motor. They are attached to the ends of the armature. As they turn, they make contact with the brushes. The brushes can be connected to the rest of the circuit. In this way, a generator becomes an energy source.

DC Generators A DC generator is like an AC generator, except that it contains a commutator instead of slip rings. In fact, a DC generator and the motor you read about in Section 2 are the same thing. If you supply electrical energy to the motor, it will spin. But if you spin the motor, you will produce electrical energy. The motor becomes a DC generator.

Go Online
active art

For: Motors and Generators activity
Visit: PHSchool.com
Web Code: cgp-4033

FIGURE 13
How a Generator Works

In an AC generator, an armature is rotated in a magnetic field. This induces an electric current in the armature. **Applying Concepts** *How many times does the current reverse direction each time the armature rotates?*

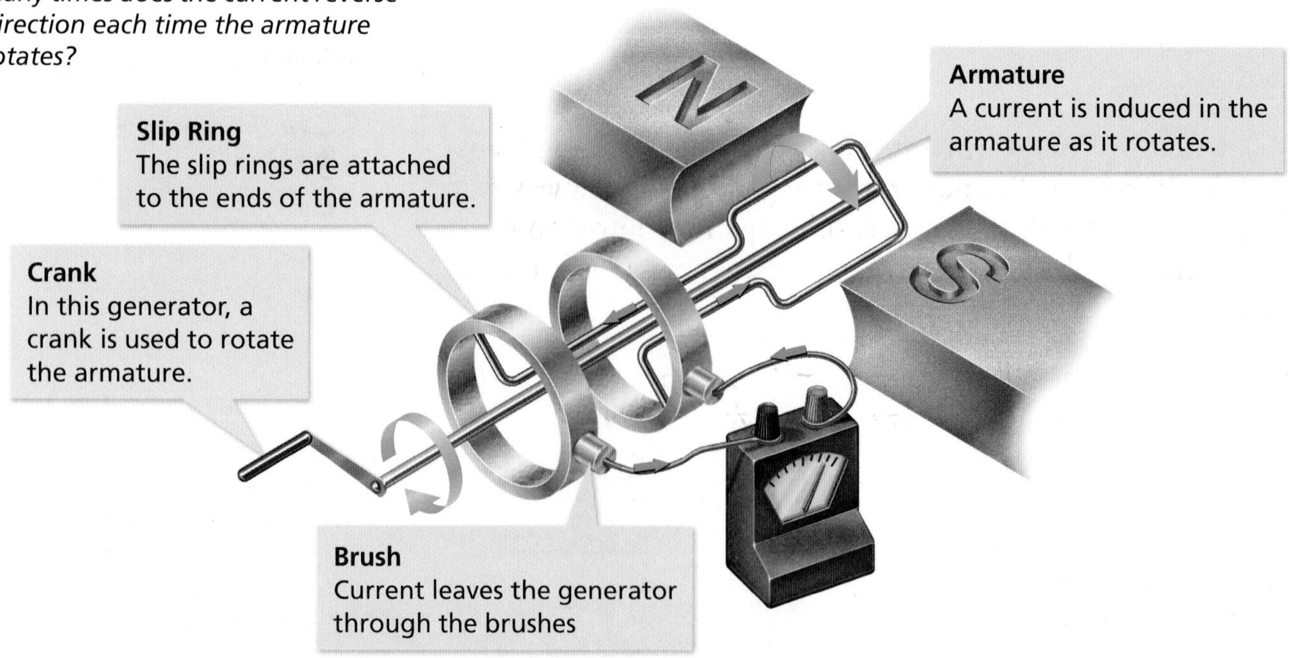

Slip Ring
The slip rings are attached to the ends of the armature.

Crank
In this generator, a crank is used to rotate the armature.

Armature
A current is induced in the armature as it rotates.

Brush
Current leaves the generator through the brushes

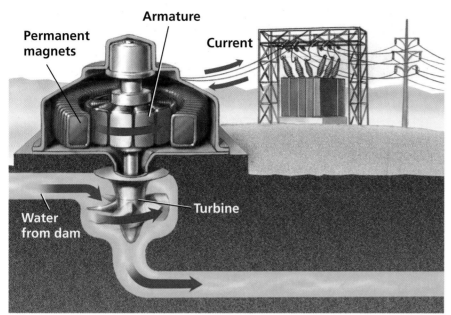

Permanent magnets

Armature

Current

Water from dam

Turbine

Using Generators The electric company uses giant generators to produce most of the electrical energy you use in your home and school. But, instead of using a crank to supply the mechanical energy to turn the armature, a turbine is used. Turbines are large circular devices made up of many blades. Figure 14 shows how a turbine is attached to the armature in a generator. The turbine spins as the water flows by it. As a result, the armature spins and generates electric current.

✓ Reading Checkpoint   What is a turbine?

Transformers

The electrical energy generated by electric companies is transmitted over long distance at very high voltages. However in your home, electrical energy is used at much lower voltages. What changes the voltage of the electrical energy? The answer is transformers.

What is a Transformer? **A transformer is a device that increases or decreases voltage.** A **transformer** consists of two separate coils of insulated wire wrapped around an iron core. One coil, called the primary coil, is connected to a circuit with a voltage source and alternating current. The other coil, the secondary coil, is connected to a separate circuit that does not contain a voltage source.

Primary coil   Secondary coil

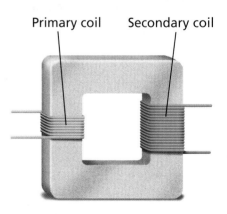

FIGURE 15
A Transformer
The primary coil of a transformer is connected to a voltage source. The secondary coil is not connected to a voltage source.

A Transformer at Work When a current is in the primary coil of the transformer, it produces a magnetic field. The magnetic field changes as the current alternates. This changing magnetic field is like a moving magnetic field. It induces a current in the secondary coil. A transformer works only if the current in the primary coil is changing. If the current does not change, the magnetic field does not change. No current will be induced in the secondary coil. So a transformer will not work with direct current.

Types of Transformers If the number of loops in the primary and secondary coils of a transformer is the same, the voltage of the induced current is the same as the original voltage. But if the secondary coil has more loops than the primary coil, the voltage in the secondary coil will be greater. A transformer that increases voltage is called a **step-up transformer.**

FIGURE 16
Changing Voltage
Transformers are involved in the transmission of electrical energy from an electric plant to a home. **Relating Cause and Effect** *How does the number of loops in the primary and secondary coils affect the voltage of the induced current?*

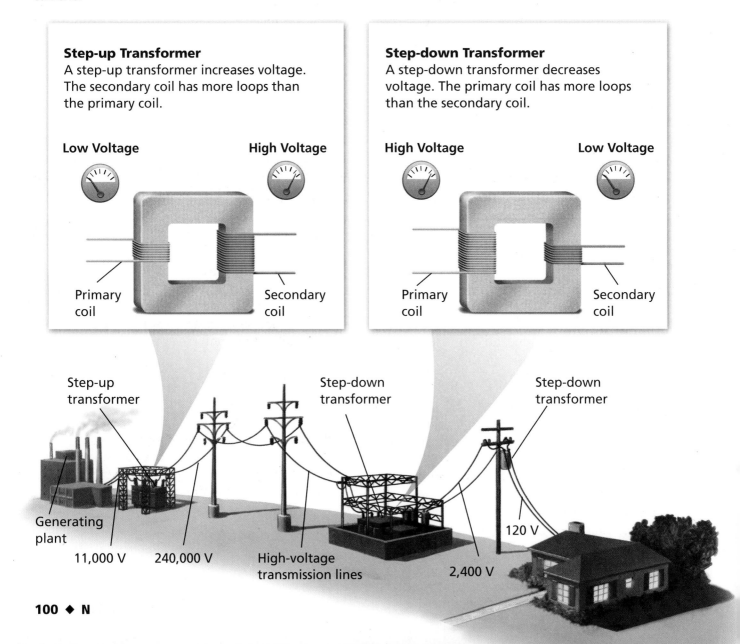

Step-up Transformer
A step-up transformer increases voltage. The secondary coil has more loops than the primary coil.

Low Voltage   High Voltage

Primary coil   Secondary coil

Step-down Transformer
A step-down transformer decreases voltage. The primary coil has more loops than the secondary coil.

High Voltage   Low Voltage

Primary coil   Secondary coil

Step-up transformer   Step-down transformer   Step-down transformer

Generating plant

11,000 V   240,000 V   High-voltage transmission lines   2,400 V   120 V

Suppose there are fewer loops in the secondary coil than in the primary coil. The voltage in the secondary coil will be less than in the primary coil. A transformer that decreases voltage is called a **step-down transformer.** Figure 16 shows both types of transformers.

Uses of Transformers An important use of transformers is in the transmission of electrical energy from generating plants. The most efficient way to transmit current over long distances is to maintain high voltages—about 11,000 volts to 765,000 volts. But the high voltage must be decreased to be used safely in your home. The use of step-up and step-down transformers allows safe transmission of electrical energy from generating plants to the consumer.

Transformers are also used in some electrical devices. Fluorescent lights, televisions, and X-ray machines require higher voltages than the current in your home, which is about 120 volts. These devices contain step-up transformers. Other devices, such as doorbells, electronic games, and portable CD players, require lower voltages, about 6 to 12 volts. They contain step-down transformers.

Using Electricity and Magnetism

Video Preview
▶ Video Field Trip
Video Assessment

 Reading Checkpoint) **What is the voltage in your house?**

Section 3 Assessment

Target Reading Skill **Previewing Visuals** Refer to your questions and answers about Figure 13 to help you answer Question 2 below.

Reviewing Key Concepts

1. **a. Defining** What is electromagnetic induction?
   b. Describing What are two ways to induce an electric current?
   c. Relating Cause and Effect What determines whether an induced current is a direct current or an alternating current?
2. **a. Reviewing** How is energy transformed by a generator?
   b. Summarizing How does a generator produce an alternating current?
   c. Comparing and Contrasting How are an AC generator and a DC generator the same? How are they different?

3. **a. Reviewing** What does a transformer do?
   b. Interpreting Diagrams Look at Figure 16. What is the difference between a step-up transformer and a step-down transformer?
   c. Applying Concepts Why do some appliances have step-down transformers built into them?

Lab zone At-Home **Activity**

Step-Up and Step-Down Draw a diagram that shows how electrical energy gets to your home from the place it is generated. Include in your diagram the likely locations of step-up and step-down transformers. Explain your diagram to a family member. Then with your family member, try to locate the step-down transformer that provides your home's electrical energy.

① What Is Electromagnetism?

Key Concepts

- An electric current produces a magnetic field.

- The magnetic field produced by a current has three characteristics. The field can be turned on or off, have its direction reversed, or have its strength changed.

- An electromagnet is a strong magnet that can be turned on and off.

Key Terms

electromagnetism
solenoid
electromagnet

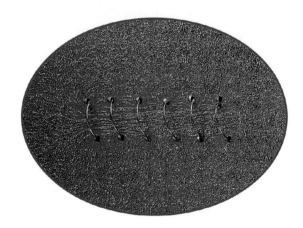

② Electricity, Magnetism, and Motion

Key Concepts

- When a wire with a current is placed in a magnetic field, electrical energy is transformed into mechanical energy.

- Electric current is used to turn the pointer of a galvanometer.

- An electric motor transforms electrical energy into mechanical energy.

Key Terms

energy	galvanometer
electrical energy	electric motor
mechanical energy	

③ Electricity From Magnetism

Key Concepts

- An electric current is induced in a conductor when the conductor moves through a magnetic field.

- A generator uses motion in a magnetic field to produce an electric current.

- A transformer is a device that increases or decreases voltage.

Key Terms

electromagnetic induction
direct current
alternating current
electric generator
transformer
step-up transformer
step-down transformer

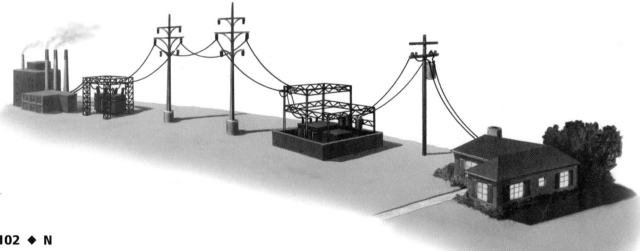

Review and Assessment

Go Online
PHSchool.com
For: Self-Assessment
Visit: PHSchool.com
Web Code: cga-4030

Organizing Information

Concept Mapping Copy the concept map about electromagnetism onto a separate sheet of paper. Then complete the concept map and add a title. (For more about concept maps, see the Skills Handbook.)

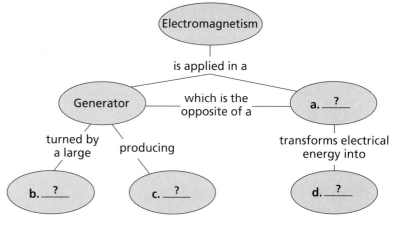

Reviewing Key Terms

Choose the letter of the best answer.

1. The relationship between electricity and magnetism is called
   a. electrical energy.
   b. an electromagnet.
   c. electromagnetism.
   d. induced current.

2. A coil of wire with a current is called a
   a. generator.
   b. motor.
   c. solenoid.
   d. transformer.

3. When a ferromagnetic material is placed within a solenoid, the resulting device is called a(n)
   a. galvanometer.   **b.** electromagnet.
   c. motor.   **d.** transformer.

4. Electrical energy is transformed into mechanical energy in a
   a. motor.   **b.** generator.
   c. transformer.   **d.** electromagnet.

5. A device that changes the voltage of alternating current is a
   a. transformer.   **b.** motor.
   c. generator.   **d.** galvanometer.

If the statement is true, write *true*. If it is false, change the underlined word or words to make the statement true.

6. The device that turns a needle in a galvanometer is called an <u>electromagnet</u>.

7. Several loops of wire wrapped around an iron core form the <u>armature</u> of a motor.

8. Generating a current by moving a conductor in a magnetic field is <u>induction</u>.

9. An <u>electric motor</u> transforms mechanical energy into electrical energy.

10. A <u>solenoid</u> increases or decreases voltage.

Writing in Science

News Report You are a television news reporter covering the opening of a new dam that generates electrical energy. Write a short news story describing how the dam transforms mechanical energy from the motion of the water into electrical energy.

Discovery CHANNEL SCHOOL

Using Electricity and Magnetism
Video Preview
Video Field Trip
▶ Video Assessment

Review and Assessment

Checking Concepts

11. How can the magnetic field produced by a current be changed?

12. How is a galvanometer similar to a motor? How is it different?

13. What are the roles of the commutator and the brushes in an electric motor?

14. How are alternating current and direct current the same? How are they different?

15. Describe how an AC generator operates.

16. What role does a turbine play in generating electricity?

17. Explain how transformers are used to efficiently transmit electrical energy from the electric company where it is produced to your home where it is used.

Thinking Critically

18. **Relating Cause and Effect** Why does a compass needle move when placed near a wire with an electric current? What do you think happens to the compass needle when the circuit is shut off?

19. **Inferring** How could you modify a solenoid to produce a stonger magnetic field?

20. **Applying Concepts** Make a diagram of a wire loop in a magnetic field. Show how the direction of a current in the wire is related to the direction of rotation of the loop.

21. **Predicting** Four electromagnets are illustrated in the diagram below. Will the electromagnet labeled **A** or **B** produce a stronger magnetic field? Will the electromagnet **B** or **C** produce a stronger field? Explain your choices.

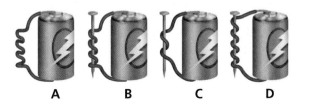

A   B   C   D

22. **Comparing and Contrasting** Compare a motor and a generator. Include information about the kind of energy conversion that takes place in each device.

23. **Applying Concepts** How are the uses of an electromagnet different from those of a permanent magnet?

Applying Skills

Use the illustration of a transformer to answer Questions 24–26.

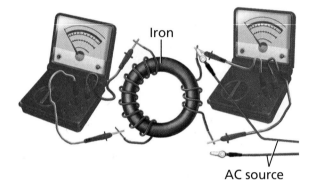

Iron

AC source

24. **Classifying** What type of transformer is shown in the illustration above? Explain how you know.

25. **Inferring** Which coil is the primary coil and which is the secondary coil?

26. **Predicting** What will the two voltmeters show when the circuit on the right side of the diagram is completed?

Lab zone Chapter Project

Performance Assessment Present the results of your energy audit to the class in a visual format. Make a bar, circle, or line graph showing the appliances and the energy they used. Identify the appliance that uses the most electrical energy in a week. Also discuss the way you calculated energy use. What problems did you have? What information couldn't you collect?

Standardized Test Prep

Test-Taking Tip

Interpreting a Graph

If you are asked to interpret a line graph, look at the labels of the horizontal and vertical axes. The labels inform you what relationship is plotted on the graph—in other words, what variables are being compared. Study the graph for Questions 4–5 and answer the sample question.

Sample Question

What variable is plotted on the *x*-axis?
  A the number of solenoids
  B the magnetic field strength
  C the number of loops in the solenoid
  D the length of solenoid

Answer

Choice **C** is correct. You can eliminate **A** and **D**, because neither axis mentions the number of solenoids or the length of the solenoid. **B** is incorrect because it is on the vertical axis, or *y*-axis.

A scientist measured the magnetic field strength of a solenoid after increasing the number of loops. Magnetic field strength is measured using a unit called a gauss. The graph below plots the results. Use the graph to answer Questions 4–5.

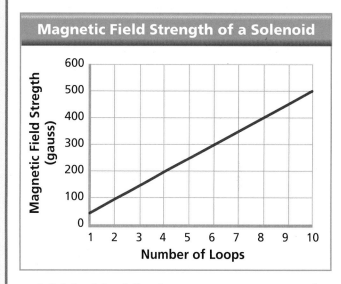

Choose the letter of the best answer.

1. If a step-up transformer is to increase voltage, it needs
   A a DC source connected to the primary coil.
   B a DC source connected to the secondary coil.
   C more turns in the primary coil than in the secondary coil.
   D more turns in the secondary coil than in the primary coil.

2. To measure the current induced from moving a wire through a magnetic field, which piece of equipment would a scientist need?
   F a galvanometer   **G** a flashlight bulb
   H an insulated wire   **J** an LED

3. What happens when a magnet moves through a coil of wire?
   A The magnet loses magnetism.
   B A current is induced in the magnet.
   C A current is induced in the wire.
   D Electrical energy is transformed into mechanical energy.

4. Which of the following statements expresses the relationship shown on the graph?
   F As the number of loops decreases, the magnetic field strength increases.
   G As the number of loops increases, the magnetic field strength decreases.
   H As the number of loops increases, the magnetic field strength increases.
   J The number of loops does not affect the magnetic field strength.

5. What would you expect the magnetic field strength of the solenoid with 12 loops to be?
   A 300 gauss
   B 600 gauss
   C 700 gauss
   D 1200 gauss

Constructed Response

6. Explain how a generator transforms mechanical energy into electrical energy.

This circuit board is made up of thousands of tiny electronic devices. ▶

Lab zone™ Chapter **Project**

Bits and Bytes

In this chapter, you will learn about the devices that make computers possible, how computers work, and how they are used. As you complete the chapter, you will identify a new computer use, or application.

Your Goal To study an existing computer application and then propose and detail a new application

Your project must

- show what the existing computer application does and explain its benefits
- explain how data are received and transformed by the computer as you use the application
- describe each step that occurs as your new application runs

Plan It! Brainstorm with your classmates about existing computer applications. Make a list of devices that use programmed information, such as clock radios, automated bank teller machines, and grocery store bar code scanners. Choose a new application and make a plan for your teacher's approval. Then present the existing application and your new one to the class.

Electronic Signals and Semiconductors

Reading Preview

Key Concepts
- What are two types of electronic signals?
- How are semiconductors used to make electronic components?

Key Terms
- electronics • electronic signal
- analog signal • digital signal
- semiconductor • diode
- transistor • integrated circuit

Target Reading Skill

Asking Questions Before you read, preview the red headings. In a graphic organizer like the one below, ask a *what* question for each heading. As you read, write the answers to your questions.

Electronic Signals and Devices

Question	Answer
What are analog and digital signals?	Analog signals are . . .

Lab zone · Discover **Activity**

Can You Send Information With a Flashlight?

1. Write a short sentence on a sheet of paper.
2. Morse code is a language that uses dots and dashes to convey information. Convert your sentence to dots and dashes using the International Morse Code chart at the right.
3. Turn a flashlight on and off quickly to represent dots. Leave the flashlight on a little longer to represent dashes. Practice using the flashlight for different letters.
4. Use the flashlight to transmit your sentence to a partner. Ask your partner to translate your message and write down your sentence.

Think It Over

Inferring Were you able to transmit information using light? How does your light message differ from the same message read aloud?

International Morse Code			
A .—	B —...	C —.—.	D —..
E .	F ..—.	G ——.	H ....
I ..	J .———	K —.—	L .—..
M ——	N —.	O ———	P .——.
Q ——.—	R .—.	S ...	T —
U ..—	V ...—	W .——	X —..—
Y —.——	Z ——..		

Every day, you use devices that run on electric current. But not all these devices are the same. Light bulbs and toasters are examples of *electrical* devices. An electrical device relies on a continuous supply of electric current.

When you watch television or talk on a cell phone, you are using *electronic* devices. The difference between electronic and electrical devices is in the way that they use electric current.

Electronics is the use of electric current to control, communicate, and process information. How do electronic devices work? Electronics is based on electronic signals. Any information that can be measured or numbered, whether it is electrical or not, can be converted to a signal. An **electronic signal** is a varying electric current that represents information.

◄ **Cameras can use electronic signals to take photographs.**

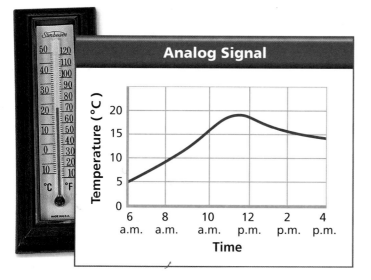

Analog Signal

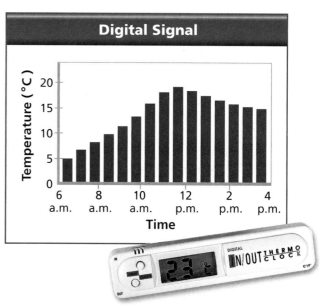

Digital Signal

Analog and Digital Signals

There are two basic kinds of electronic signals: analog signals and digital signals. The two types of signals represent information in different ways.

Analog Signals In **analog signals,** a current is varied smoothly to represent information. An analog signal varies in much the same way that temperature varies in a liquid-filled thermometer. This kind of thermometer shows temperature as the height of a liquid in a tube. The height of the liquid rises and falls smoothly with the temperature. The "analog signal" from the liquid-filled thermometer can be represented by a line graph like the one in Figure 1.

Digital Signals In **digital signals,** pulses of current are used to represent information. Rather than varying smoothly to represent information, a digital signal carries information in pulses, or steps. If you did the Discover activity, you used pulses of light to represent letters.

A digital signal varies much the same way the numbers on a digital thermometer vary. You have probably seen a digital thermometer in front of a bank. The number on the thermometer is constant for a while and then changes suddenly by a whole degree. Of course, the temperature doesn't really change so suddenly. But the thermometer can only show the temperature to the nearest degree, and so the temperature seems to jump. The digital signal from a digital thermometer can be represented by a bar graph, as shown in Figure 1.

Reading Checkpoint How is the changing temperature on a liquid-filled thermometer like an analog signal?

FIGURE 1
Analog and Digital
An analog signal varies smoothly. A digital signal varies in steps.
Predicting *How would the bar graph be different if it showed temperature measurements made every minute?*

Go **O**nline
*SCi*LINKS
For: Links on electronic signals
Visit: www.SciLinks.org
Web Code: scn-1441

FIGURE 2
Semiconductors
The electrical resistance of pure
silicon is reduced by adding
atoms of other elements to it.

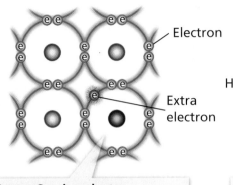

N-type Semiconductor
Adding an element with an
extra electron to silicon
creates a n-type semiconductor.

P-type Semiconductor
Adding an element with fewer
electrons, or holes, creates a
p-type semiconductor.

Semiconductor Devices

How can an electronic device transmit electronic signals? To
transmit an electronic signal, an electronic device must be able
to vary the current through a circuit. To vary current, electronic devices use semiconductors. A **semiconductor** is a
material that conducts current better than insulators but not as
well as conductors. A semiconductor conducts current only
under certain conditions.

How Semiconductors Work How can a material conduct
current only under certain conditions? Silicon and other semiconductors are elements that have extremely high resistance
in their pure forms. However, if atoms of other elements are
added to semiconductors, the resulting material can conduct
current much more easily.

By controlling the number and type of atoms added, scientists produce two types of semiconductors. In Figure 2, you
can see that adding atoms with extra electrons to silicon produces an n-type semiconductor. "N," for "negative," indicates
that the material can release, or give off, electrons. Look again
at Figure 2. Notice that adding atoms with fewer electrons, or
holes, to silicon produces a p-type semiconductor. "P," for
"positive," indicates that the material has room for and can
receive an electron.

Scientists combine n-type and p-type semiconductors in
layers. This layered structure allows for the delicate control of
current needed for many electronic devices. **The two types of
semiconductors can be combined in different ways to make
diodes, transistors, and integrated circuits.** These components control current in electronic devices.

Lab zone Skills Activity

Communicating

How do you make someone
understand how tiny a chip is
or how fast an electronic
signal travels? An analogy
can help communicate what
a measurement means. An
analogy uses a similarity
between two things that are
otherwise unlike each other.
For example, "a chip is as
small as a baby's fingernail"
is an analogy. So is "an
electronic signal moves as
fast as a bolt of lightning."
Write your own analogies to
describe how many diodes
there are in one integrated
circuit chip.

Diodes An electronic component that consists of an n-type and a p-type semiconductor joined together is a **diode.** A diode, shown in Figure 3, allows current in one direction only. If you connect a diode in a circuit in one direction, there will be a current. But if you turn the diode around, there will not be a current. Diodes can be used to change an alternating current to a direct current. Diodes can also be used as a switch.

Transistors When a layer of one type of semiconductor is sandwiched between two layers of the other type of semiconductor, a transistor is formed. Figure 3 shows the structure of a transistor. A **transistor** has two uses: it either amplifies an electronic signal or switches current on and off.

When electronic signals travel great distances, they gradually grow weak. When they are received, signals must be amplified, or made stronger, so that they can be used. Transistors revolutionized the electronics industry by making amplifiers much cheaper and more reliable.

When a transistor acts as a switch, it either allows a current or cuts it off. Millions of transistors that act as switches are what make computers work.

FIGURE 3
Diodes and Transistors
Diodes (top) allow current in only one direction. Transistors (bottom) can amplify electronic signals or act as switches. **Comparing and Contrasting** *How are diodes and transistors similar? How are they different?*

Diode A diode is a combination of an n-type and a p-type semiconductor.

Transistor A transistor is a combination of three layers of semiconductors.

FIGURE 4
Combining Electronic Components
Diodes and transistors can be combined to carry out specific tasks within electronic devices. The singing fish uses electronics to move and make sounds when a person walks by.

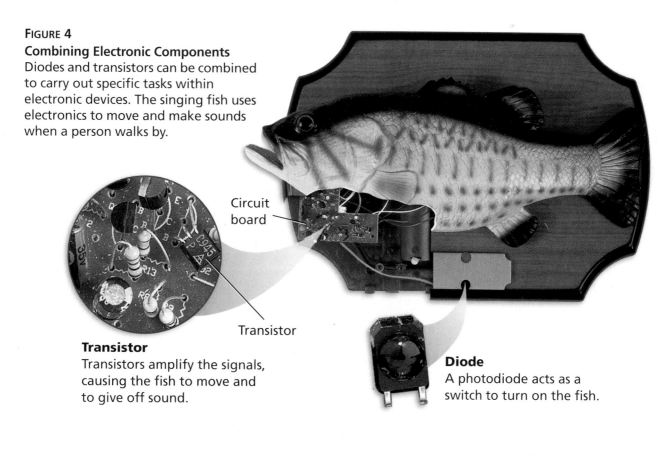

Circuit board

Transistor

Transistor
Transistors amplify the signals, causing the fish to move and to give off sound.

Diode
A photodiode acts as a switch to turn on the fish.

FIGURE 5
Integrated Circuits
An integrated circuit chip is smaller than an ant. Yet the integrated circuit contains hundreds of thousands of diodes and transistors.

Integrated Circuits Individual electronic components can be combined into larger groups, called integrated circuits, to increase their usefulness. An **integrated circuit** is a thin slice of semiconductor that contains many diodes, transistors, and other electronic components. Integrated circuits are also called chips. Figure 5 shows a magnified view of a chip from a computer. A chip smaller than one millimeter on each side can contain hundreds of thousands of components. Electronic signals flow through integrated circuits at tremendous speeds because the various components are so close together. On some chips, the space between two components can be one hundredth as thick as a human hair. The high-speed signals of integrated circuits make possible devices from video games to spacecraft. The small size of integrated circuits has allowed the size of electronic devices such as computers to be greatly reduced.

Reading Checkpoint What is a chip?

Section 1 Assessment

Target Reading Skill Asking Questions Use the answer to the questions you wrote about the section headings to help you answer the questions below.

Reviewing Key Concepts

1. a. **Listing** What are the two basic kinds of electronic signals?
   b. **Comparing and Contrasting** How are the two types of electronic signals similar? How are they different?
   c. **Classifying** A grandfather clock uses a pendulum that continuously swings to control the clock's hands. What type of signal does the swinging pendulum represent? Explain.

2. a. **Reviewing** How are semiconductors used in electronic devices?
   b. **Explaining** What is a transistor?
   c. **Relating Cause and Effect** A loudspeaker changes electronic signals into sounds. Why would transistors be useful parts of a loudspeaker?

Writing in Science

Directions Review the Morse code at the beginning of the section. Write directions a friend could use to send you messages using light or sound.

Technology Lab
• Tech & Design •

Design a Battery Sensor

Problem

How can an LED be used to tell if a battery is installed correctly?

Skills Focus

evaluating the design, redesigning, observing, drawing conclusions

Materials

- 2 D cells
- LED
- bicolor LED (optional)
- flashlight using 2 D-cells
- flashlight bulb and socket
- two insulated wires with alligator clips

Procedure

PART 1 LED Properties

1. Attach one wire to each terminal of the LED.

2. Tape the two cells together, positive terminal to negative terminal, to make a 3-volt battery.

3. Attach the other ends of the wires to the terminals of the battery and observe the LED.

4. Switch the wires connected to the battery terminals and observe the LED again.

5. Repeat Steps 1–4, but substitute a flashlight bulb in its socket for the LED.

PART 2 Sensor Design

6. Many electrical devices that run on batteries will not run if the batteries are installed backwards (positive where negative should be). Design a device that uses an LED to indicate if batteries are installed backwards.

7. Draw your design. Show how the LED, the device, and the battery are connected. (*Hint:* The LED can be connected either in series or in parallel with the battery and the device.)

8. Make a model of your sensor to see if it works with a flashlight.

Analyze and Conclude

1. **Observing** What did you observe in Part 1 when you connected the LED to the battery the first time? The second time?

2. **Drawing Conclusions** Based on your observations, is the LED a diode? How do you know?

3. **Evaluating the Design** How did your observations of the LED's properties affect your design in Part 2?

4. **Troubleshooting** Describe any problems you had while designing and building your sensor.

5. **Redesigning** In what ways could you improve your sensor?

Communicate

Write a product brochure for your battery sensor. Be sure to describe in detail how your sensor can be used to tell if batteries are installed correctly in electrical devices. Include other possible uses for your sensor. What practical application can you see for such an LED?

Electronic Communication

Reading Preview

Key Concepts
- How is sound transmitted by telephone?
- What are two ways that sounds can be reproduced?
- How are electromagnetic waves involved in the transmission of radio and television signals?

Key Terms
- electromagnetic wave
- amplitude • frequency
- amplitude modulation (AM)
- frequency modulation (FM)

Target Reading Skill
Building Vocabulary A definition states the meaning of a word or phrase by telling about its most important feature or function. After you read the section, reread the paragraphs that contain definitions of Key Terms. Use all the information you have learned to write a definition of each Key Term in your own words.

◄ **Talking on a cellular phone**

Discover **Activity**

Are You Seeing Spots?

1. Turn on a color television. Hold a hand lens at arm's length up to the television screen.
2. Move the lens closer to and farther from the screen until you can see a clear image through it. What do you see within the image?

Think It Over
Classifying What three colors make up the images on the television screen? How do you think these colors make up the wide range of colors you see on television?

Have you ever thought about the amazing technology that enables you to see and hear an event as it happens halfway around the globe? Since the first telegraph message was sent in 1844, people have become accustomed to long distance communication by telephone, radio, and television. Compared with the past, communication today is fast, dependable, and cheap. This is because of advancements in the field of electronics.

Telephones

In a telephone, sound is transformed into an electronic signal that is transmitted and then transformed back into sound. The first telephone was invented by Alexander Graham Bell in 1876. Modern telephones have some of the same main parts as the telephone patented by Bell: a transmitter, a receiver, and a dialing mechanism.

Transmitter Sound is transformed into an electronic signal in the transmitter of a telephone. Transforming sound into an electronic signal is possible because sound travels as a wave. These waves cause a metal disk in the microphone to vibrate, transforming the sound into an electronic signal. The signal can travel through a series of switches and wires to the receiving telephone. Modern telephone equipment can also transform the electronic signals to a pattern of light that travels through optical fibers.

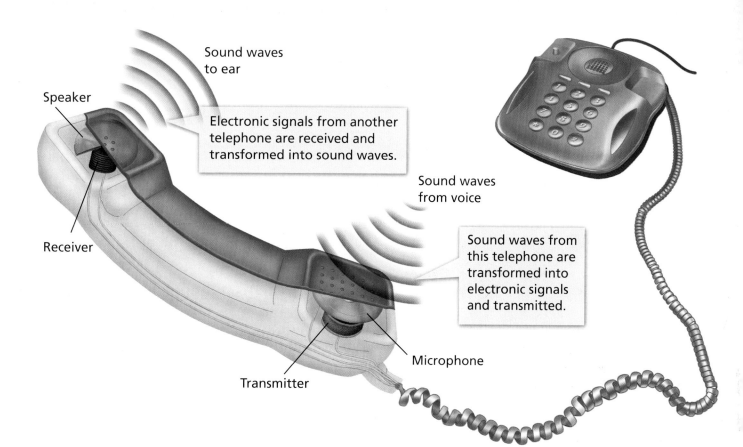

Speaker

Sound waves to ear

Electronic signals from another telephone are received and transformed into sound waves.

Receiver

Sound waves from voice

Sound waves from this telephone are transformed into electronic signals and transmitted.

Transmitter

Microphone

Receiver The receiver is located in the earpiece of a telephone. The receiver uses a speaker to transform the electronic signal back into sound. A speaker is made up of an electromagnet and a thin metal disk. During a conversation, the amount of electric current in the electromagnet varies with the signal strength. Therefore, the strength of the magnetic field around the electromagnet varies as well. This causes the disk to vibrate in a pattern that matches the electronic signal. These vibrations produce sound waves, which represent the voice on the other telephone. Many modern receivers now use semiconductors instead of electromagnets.

Dialing Mechanism Another part of the telephone is the dialing mechanism. When you dial a telephone number, you are telling the telephone company's switching system where you want the call to go. A dial telephone sends a series of pulses or clicks to the switching network. A push-button device sends different tones. The tones act as signals to the electronic circuits in the switching network. Today, push-button devices have become standard on almost all telephones.

FIGURE 6
How a Telephone Works
When you speak into a telephone, your voice is transformed into electronic signals. The signals are transmitted to the listener's phone, where they are transformed back into sound.
Applying Concepts *How does the dialing mechanism work?*

 Reading Checkpoint   **What does a telephone transmitter do?**

▲ Magnified view of a stylus in a record groove

FIGURE 7
Analog Sound: Phonograph The needle of a record player moves along the groove of a record. **Interpreting Photos** *Why does the smooth shape tell you that the groove represents an analog signal?*

Sound Recordings

Sound recordings also communicate information using electronic signals. **Sound can be reproduced using an analog device such as a phonograph or a digital device such as a CD player.**

Analog Sound Recording When a deejay spins a record by moving it back and forth, the sound varies smoothly. The music the deejay in Figure 7 is playing is stored as analog signals on a plastic record. But how does sound come from a piece of plastic? When you play a record, a needle, or stylus, runs along a spiral groove in the plastic. The wavy pattern of the groove varies in the same way that the sound waves from the musicians did. The needle in the groove follows the groove's wavy pattern. The needle's movement, in turn, moves a tiny magnet that induces an electric current in a coil of wire. This current matches the pattern of the groove in the record.

The current produced by the needle is an analog signal representing the original sounds played by the musicians. The signal varies continuously as it copies the information stored on the record. The analog signal is fed into an amplifier and then into a speaker, which changes the signal back into sound.

Digital Sound Recording As you can see in Figure 8, a CD, or compact disc, is very different from a plastic record. It contains microscopic holes, called pits. The level areas between the pits are called flats. Like the groove on a record, these pits and flats are arranged in a spiral. They allow sound to be stored in steps. Although you can't tell from the photograph, the spiral on a compact disc is divided into pieces of equal time. The arrangement of pits and flats within each piece of the spiral is a code. Each piece of this code represents the sound at one instant.

When the CD spins, a beam of light scans the pits and flats. The light reflects from the flats but not from the pits. This causes the reflected light to form a pattern of tiny flashes of light. The flashes are then transformed into pulses of electric current, or a digital signal. The digital signal is fed into an amplifier and then a speaker, where it is changed back into sound.

 Reading Checkpoint How do the pits and flats on a CD make a digital signal?

FIGURE 8
Digital Sound: CD Player
Each series of 3 pits or flats on this diagram of a CD represents the sound at one instant.

◀ Magnified view of CD surface

Pit
Flat

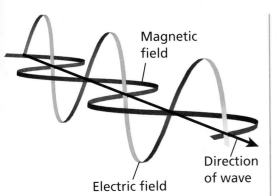

Magnetic field

Electric field

Direction of wave

FIGURE 9
Electromagnetic Waves
A changing electric field generates a changing magnetic field. In turn, a changing magnetic field generates a changing electric field.

Electromagnetic Waves

You learned in the last section that electronic signals are transmitted through semiconductors within electronic devices. But, in the case of radio and television, the electronic signal usually has to travel over a long distance from a radio or television station. **Electronic signals can be carried over long distances by electromagnetic waves.**

Electric and Magnetic Fields You already may be familiar with some types of waves, such as water waves or sound waves. Electromagnetic waves share some characteristics with these waves. However, electromagnetic waves do not need to travel through matter. An **electromagnetic wave** is a wave that consists of moving, or changing electric and magnetic fields.

The idea that a wave is made of electric and magnetic fields may sound a little strange at first. But you have already learned that electricity and magnetism are related. You know that a changing magnetic field produces an electric field. The reverse is also true—a changing electric field produces a magnetic field.

If a magnetic field is changing, like the up-and-down movements of a water wave, a changing electric field will form. The changing electric field that is formed then produces a changing magnetic field. The electric and magnetic fields will keep producing each other over and over again, as shown in Figure 9. The result is an electromagnetic wave. The light that you see, the microwaves that heat food in a microwave oven, and the X-rays that a dentist or doctor uses are all types of electromagnetic waves.

Math ▶ Analyzing Data

Communication Frequencies

The graph shows the frequency ranges, or bands, for some common communication devices. The top and bottom of each range is the maximum and minimum frequency for that device.

1. **Reading Graphs** What does the *y*-axis of the graph represent?

2. **Reading Graphs** What is the frequency range for a cordless phone? An FM radio?

3. **Interpreting Graphs** What pattern do you see for the frequency bands in the graph? Explain.

4. **Drawing Conclusions** What device might interfere with television reception? Explain.

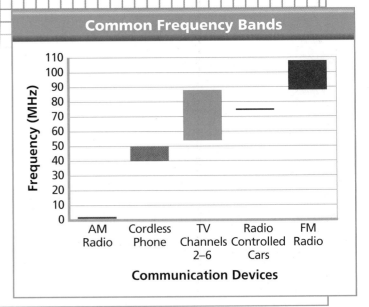

Common Frequency Bands

Frequency (MHz)

Communication Devices: AM Radio, Cordless Phone, TV Channels 2–6, Radio Controlled Cars, FM Radio

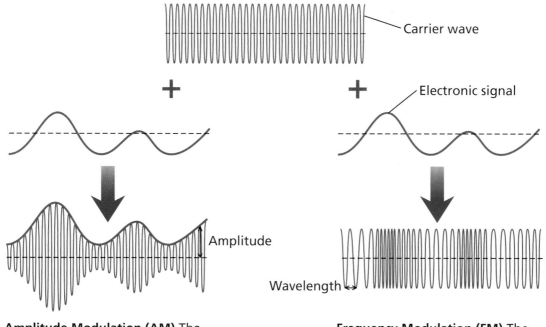

Carrier wave

Electronic signal

Amplitude

Wavelength

Amplitude Modulation (AM) The amplitude of the carrier wave varies with the strength of the electronic signal.

Frequency Modulation (FM) The frequency of the carrier wave varies with the strength of the electronic signal.

Amplitude and Frequency Modulation All waves have certain basic characteristics. Figure 10 shows a simple wave moving from left to right. The high points are called crests and the low points are called troughs. Waves are described in terms of two quantities, amplitude and frequency. The **amplitude** is the height from the center line to a crest or trough. The **frequency** of a wave is the number of waves passing a given point each second.

The amplitude and frequency of an electromagnetic wave can be changed, or modulated, to carry an electronic signal. The wave that is modulated, shown in red in Figure 10, is called the carrier wave. The electronic signal is shown in blue. In this case, the signal is an analog signal in which the strength, or amplitude, of an electric current changes.

The carrier wave can be modulated to match the electronic signal in two different ways, as shown in Figure 10. One way is to change the amplitude of the carrier wave to match that of the signal. This process is known as **amplitude modulation (AM).** The other way is to change the frequency of the carrier wave to match the amplitude of the signal. Then the space between the waves varies with the strength of the signal. This process is known as **frequency modulation (FM).**

FIGURE 10
Modulating Waves
A carrier wave's amplitude and frequency can be modulated to carry an electronic signal.
Interpreting Diagrams *How is a carrier wave modulated to transmit an AM radio signal?*

Go **O**nline
active art

For: Modulating Electromagnetic Waves activity
Visit: PHSchool.com
Web Code: cgp-4042

Reading Checkpoint What is amplitude?

Radio

Voices or music on an AM or FM radio station are electronic signals carried by an electromagnetic wave. But where do the sounds you hear come from?

Transmission The process begins at a radio station where sounds are generated and transformed into an electronic signal. When a musician plays into a microphone at a radio station, the sound waves produce a varying electric current. This current is an analog signal that represents the sound waves. It is sometimes called an audio signal.

The audio signal is then sent to a transmitter. The transmitter amplifies the audio signal and combines it with a carrier wave. The combined electromagnetic wave is then sent to an antenna, which sends it out in all directions.

Reception Your radio has its own antenna that receives electromagnetic waves from the radio station. The carrier wave has a specific frequency. You tune in to the wave by selecting that frequency on your radio. Your radio amplifies the audio signal and separates it from the carrier wave. The signal is then sent to the radio's speaker, which is the reverse of a microphone. The speaker transforms the audio signal back into sound.

✓ **Reading Checkpoint** What is an audio signal?

FIGURE 11
How Radios Work
At the radio station, voices and music are transformed into electronic signals and then broadcast. Individual radios pick up the electronic signals and change them back to sound.
Interpreting Photos *What is the role of the transmitter?*

❶ **Signal Generated** A person generates sound waves that are transformed into an audio signal.

❷ **Transmission** The audio signal is sent to a transmitter and combined with a carrier wave that is broadcast at a specific frequency.

❸ **Reception** A radio receives the wave at a specific frequency and separates the audio signal. Speakers transform the audio signal into sound.

① Signal Generated At a television station, video and audio signals are recorded and generated by cameras and microphones. The transmitter sends out the signals.

② Transmission Video and audio signals are carried on electromagnetic waves. The waves travel to a satellite and then to a local cable station.

③ Reception Your television receives the signals from a wire connected to the cable station. You tune into a specific frequency by selecting a television channel.

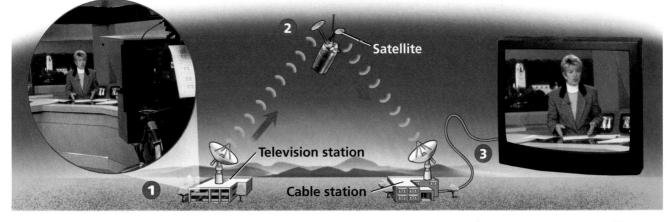

Satellite

Television station

Cable station

Television

Electromagnetic waves can be used to carry images as well as sound. The transmission of the images and sounds on television is very similar to that of radio sounds.

Transmission The audio and video signals that make up the image on your television screen are generated at a television station. Both signals are carried by electromagnetic waves. The signals are usually sent from transmitting antennas on the ground. But sometimes the signal is blocked by land features or by nearby buildings. Or sometimes a transmitter cannot reach homes that are too far away. To solve these problems, local cable television networks have been developed. These networks distribute television signals through cables from a central receiver to homes.

Communications satellites are also used to relay television signals. A communications satellite orbits Earth, always staying above the same point on the ground. These satellites receive signals from one part of the planet and transmit them to another almost instantly. This enables you to watch events from around the world as they occur.

Reception Each television contains a receiver that accepts video and audio signals. As in a radio, the carrier wave for each television station is at a specific frequency. You tune in the frequency by selecting a channel. Your television amplifies the signal and separates it from the carrier wave. The audio signal is transformed back into sound by the television's speakers.

FIGURE 12
How Televisions Work
Televisions transmit images as well as sound, but they transmit and receive electronic signals in a way similar to radios.
Interpreting Data *What role do satellites play in the transmission of television signals?*

DISCOVERY CHANNEL
SCHOOL

Electronics

Video Preview
▶ Video Field Trip
Video Assessment

FIGURE 13
Types of Televisions
Traditional televisions use bulky cathode-ray tubes to produce images. Newer technologies permit televisions to be thinner and lighter.

Cathode-ray tube television

Thin screen television

Television Screens How does a television set change a video signal into the picture on a television screen? Today there are several technologies that can do this.

Most televisions use cathode-ray tubes. A cathode-ray tube contains solid fluorescent materials that transform beams of electrons into tiny, colored dots of light. The dots are in the primary colors of light—red, blue, and green. Your eyes combine these three colors to form all of the colors in the images you see.

Newer televisions produce images in other ways. Video signals can be sent to a liquid crystal or to a mixture of gases called a plasma. Both of these technologies can be used to produce a thin screen television like the one shown in Figure 13. A liquid crystal display television produces images in the same way a laptop computer does. In a plasma television, the video signal heats tiny pockets of gases, causing them to glow in different colors.

✓ **Reading Checkpoint** How are television images produced?

Section 2 Assessment

🎯 **Target Reading Skill** Building Vocabulary Use your definitions to help you answer the questions.

Reviewing Key Concepts

1. a. **Identifying** What are the three main parts of a telephone?
   b. **Summarizing** How is sound transmitted and received during a telephone call?
   c. **Relating Cause and Effect** In telephones, what causes electric current to vary in the transmitter, producing an electronic signal?
2. a. **Defining** What are electromagnetic waves?
   b. **Describing** What are two characteristics of an electromagnetic wave?
   c. **Comparing and Contrasting** How is an electromagnetic wave changed to produce AM and FM waves?

3. a. **Reviewing** How is information transmitted to radios and televisions?
   b. **Sequencing** What happens to an electronic signal when it reaches your television?

Lab zone ▸ At-Home **Activity**

What's a Remote? A remote control uses electromagnetic waves to operate an electronic device—for instance, a television, VCR, radio, or toy—from a distance. Find a device with a remote control. Ask your family members to help you locate the receiver for the remote control on the device. Find out how far away from the device you can stand and still operate it. Find out what objects the waves will travel through. Will they bounce off mirrors? Off walls? Off your hand?

Computers

Reading Preview

Key Concepts
- How is information stored and processed in a computer?
- What are the functions of computer hardware and software?

Key Terms
- computer
- binary system
- hardware
- central processing unit (CPU)
- input device
- output device
- software
- computer programmer

🎯 Target Reading Skill

Outlining As you read, make an outline about computers. Use the red headings for the main topics and the blue headings for the subtopics.

Computers
I. What Is a Computer?
A. The Binary System
B.
C.
II. Computer Hardware
A.

Lab zone — Discover **Activity**

How Fast Are You?

1. Write out ten math problems involving the addition or subtraction of two two-digit numbers.
2. Switch lists with a friend.
3. Take turns timing how long it takes each of you to solve the ten problems by hand.
4. Then time how long it takes each of you to solve the ten problems using a calculator. What is the time difference? Is there a difference in accuracy?

Think It Over
Inferring What are the advantages of using an electronic device to complete calculations?

Over two thousand years ago, the first calculator was invented. This calculating device is called an abacus. For centuries, people in many parts of the world have used the abacus to count by sliding beads along strings. During the twentieth century, mechanical adding machines were developed. Then, in the 1960s, electronic calculators and computers began to be widely used. In just a few decades, these electronic devices changed the way people around the world perform calculations.

What Is a Computer?

A **computer** is an electronic device that stores, processes, and retrieves information. One of the reasons that computers can process and store so much information is that they do not store information in the same form that you see it—numbers, letters, and pictures. **Computer information is represented in the binary system.** The **binary system** uses combinations of just two digits, 0 and 1. Although computers can use analog signals, almost all modern computers are digital.

◀ **Calculating with an abacus**

FIGURE 14
Binary Switches
To store information, a computer translates binary numbers into electronic switch positions. The background photo shows electronic switches in an enlarged view.
Interpreting Diagrams *What is the base-10 number 5 in the binary system?*

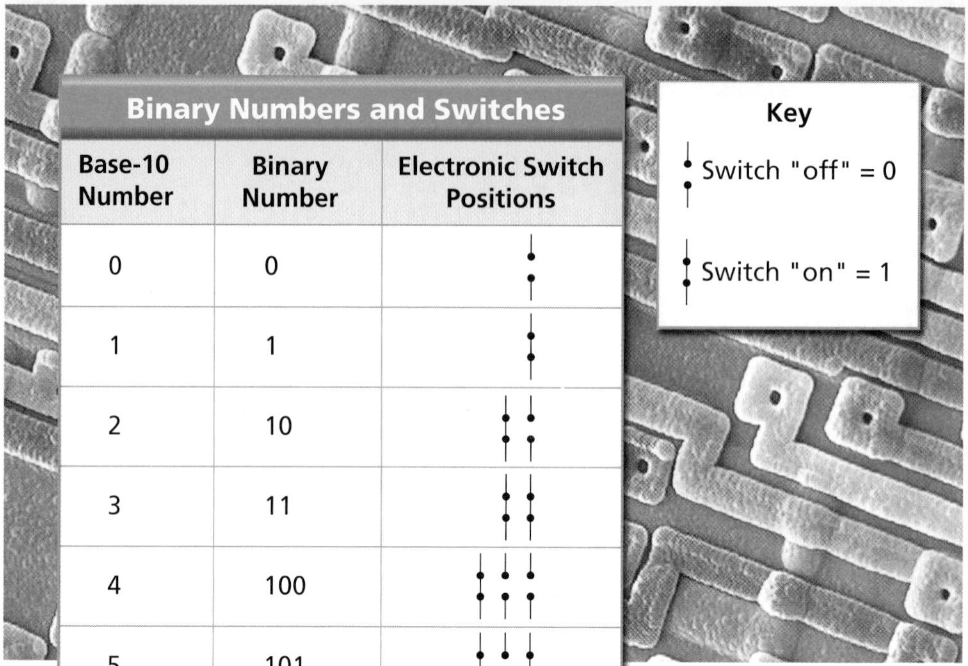

Binary Numbers and Switches				Key	
Base-10 Number	Binary Number	Electronic Switch Positions		Switch "off" = 0	
0	0			Switch "on" = 1	
1	1				
2	10				
3	11				
4	100				
5	101				
10	1010				

The Binary System How can large numbers be represented using only series of 1's and 0's? Begin by thinking about the numbers with which you are more familiar. You are used to using the base-10 number system. Each place value in a number represents the number 10 raised to some power. The digits 0 through 9 are then multiplied by the place value in each position. For example, the number 327 means 3×100 plus 2×10 plus 7×1.

Using the Binary System The binary system is similar to the base-10 number system, except that the base number is 2. A binary number's place value begins with 1, 2, 4, and 8 instead of 1, 10, 100, and 1,000. In the binary system, only 0 and 1 are multiplied by each place value.

Computers use the binary system because electronic signals can represent the 0's and 1's. Computer chips contain thousands of tiny circuits with transistors that act as switches. A switch in the off position represents a 0 and a switch in the on position represents a 1. Look at Figure 14 to see how switches can represent binary numbers.

Bits and Bytes Each 1 or 0 in the binary system is called a bit, short for binary digit. Arrangements of eight bits are called bytes. Computer memories are rated in kilobytes (one thousand bytes), megabytes (one million bytes), gigabytes (one billion bytes) or even terabytes (one trillion bytes).

Reading Checkpoint What two digits are used in the binary system?

Lab zone Skills Activity

Calculating
A set of encyclopedias contains 25 volumes with an average of 400 pages per book. Each page contains 1,200 words and the average word is 6 letters long. Suppose each letter requires 1 byte. Could the entire set fit on a single gigabyte chip?

Computer Hardware

The physical parts that allow a computer to receive, store, and present information make up the computer's **hardware.** Computer hardware refers to the permanent components of the computer. **Computer hardware includes a central processing unit, input devices, output devices, and memory storage devices.** You can identify the different devices in Figure 15.

Central Processing Unit (CPU) The central processing unit serves as the brain of a computer. The **central processing unit,** or CPU, directs the operation of the computer, performs logical operations and calculations, and directs the storage and retrieval of information.

Input and Output Devices Data are fed to the CPU by an **input device.** There are several different types of input devices. The one most familiar to you is probably the keyboard. A mouse, joystick, light pen, scanner, microphone, and touch-sensitive screen are also input devices.

Data from a computer are presented on an **output device.** A computer monitor, on which you view information, is the most familiar output device. Other output devices are printers and speakers. Some devices, such as modems, may serve as both input and output devices. A modem allows a computer to exchange information with other computers.

FIGURE 15
Computer Hardware
Here are a number of common computer components. The different devices that make up a computer are called hardware.

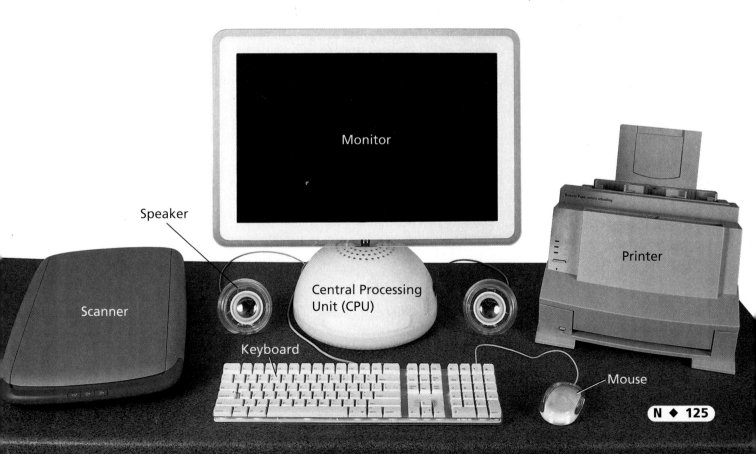

Speaker

Scanner

Monitor

Central Processing Unit (CPU)

Keyboard

Printer

Mouse

Internal Memory Computers store information in their memory. There are two general types of computer memory, internal and external. Chips on the main circuit board within the CPU are referred to as internal memory. Random Access Memory (RAM) is the temporary storage area for data while the computer is operating. Information stored in RAM is lost when the computer is turned off.

Information the computer needs to operate properly is stored in Read Only Memory (ROM). The CPU can read these data but cannot change them. Information in ROM is permanently stored and is not lost when the computer is turned off.

• Tech & Design in History •

Development of Computers
Although some modern computers can fit in the palm of your hand, this wasn't always the case. Computers have come a long way in a relatively short period of time.

1823
The Difference Engine
British mathematician Charles Babbage designed the first computer, called the Difference Engine. It was a mechanical computing device that had more than 50,000 moving parts. For a later computer of Babbage's, Ada Lovelace wrote what is considered the first computer program.

1890
Census Counting Machine
Herman Hollerith constructed a machine that processed information by allowing electric current to pass through holes in punch cards. With Hollerith's machine, the United States census of 1890 was completed in one fourth the time needed for the 1880 census.

1800	1825	1850	1875

External Memory Neither RAM nor ROM allows you to save information when you turn your computer off. For that reason, devices outside the main CPU circuit are used to store information. They are called external memory. The most widely used form of external storage is the disk. Information is read from a disk or entered onto a disk by a disk drive. Hard disks are rigid magnetic metal disks that stay inside the computer. Information on a hard disk remains in the computer and can be accessed whenever you use the computer. Floppy disks and optical discs can be removed from the computer.

 Reading Checkpoint What is read-only memory (ROM)?

Writing in Science

Newspaper Article In 1953 there were only about 100 computers in the entire world. Today, there are hundreds of millions of computers in businesses, homes, government offices, schools, and stores. Select one of the early forms of the computer. Write a newspaper article introducing it and its applications to the public.

1946 ENIAC
The first American-built computer was developed by the United States Army. The Electronic Numerical Integrator and Calculator, or ENIAC, consisted of thousands of vacuum tubes and filled an entire warehouse. To change the program, programmers had to rewire the entire machine.

1974 Personal Computers
The first personal computer (PC) went on the market. Today's personal computer is 400 times faster than the ENIAC, 3,000 times lighter, and several million dollars cheaper.

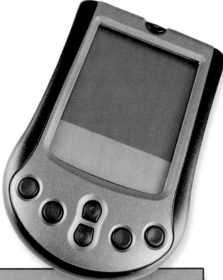

2000 Personal Data Assistant
Electronic devices have become smaller, and wireless communication has become more common. Hand-held computers can store personal data, send e-mails, and even share images.

| 1925 | 1950 | 1975 | 2000 |

Computer Software

A computer needs **software,** or instructions, to tell it what to do. **Software is a set of instructions that directs the computer hardware to perform operations on stored information.** The software is also called a computer program. Whenever you use a word processor, solve mathematical problems, or play a computer game, a computer program is instructing the computer to perform in a certain way.

Two Kinds of Software One category of computer software is called the operating system of the computer. An operating system is a set of basic instructions that keep a computer running. Perhaps you have heard of the operating software known as DOS, or disk operating system. Unix is another example of operating software.

A second category of software is usually called applications software. Applications are particular tasks that a computer may carry out. These programs are grouped by their function, such as word processing, graphics, games, or simulations.

FIGURE 16
Computer Software
The electrodes attached to this person's body enable a computer to track the person's movements. Later, artists will used the stored information to create animated game sequences. The instructions for doing this task are contained in a software program.

Computer Programming The people who program computers are called computer programmers. **Computer programmers** use computer languages that convert input information into instructions that the CPU can understand. You may have heard the names of some computer languages, such as Basic, C++, and Java. Each language is designed for a specific purpose. For example, some languages allow users to complete complex calculations. But a program written in such a language may not be practical for word processing.

Programmers create software by using a step-by-step development process. First, they outline exactly what the program will do. Second, they develop a flowchart. A flowchart is a diagram showing the order of computer actions and data flow. Third, they write the instructions for the computer in a particular language. Complicated programs may contain millions of instructions. And finally, they test the program.

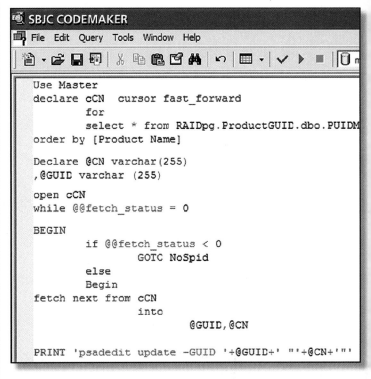

FIGURE 17
Programming a Computer
Programmers use computer languages to write instructions for the CPU.

Reading Checkpoint What is a computer language?

Section 3 Assessment

Target Reading Skill Outlining Use the information in your outline about computers to help you answer the questions below.

Reviewing Key Concepts

1. a. **Defining** What is a computer?
   b. **Explaining** How do computers store and process information?
   c. **Applying Concepts** How can electrical off and on switches be combined with numbers to store information?
2. a. **Reviewing** What is the function of computer hardware? Software?
   b. **Comparing and Contrasting** Describe the roles of input and output devices.

c. **Sequencing** Place the following parts in the correct order for entering, correcting, saving, and then printing a message: CPU, output device, input device, memory storage.

Writing in Science

Software Advertisement Write an advertisement for a new software application. The application should be for word processing, graphics, or simulations. In your ad, give your software application's name, explain what the software does, and describe features that will appeal to customers.

Computer Programming

Problem

Can you create a model of a computer program?

Skills

observing, forming operational definitions, making models

Materials

- 2 identical sets of 10 interlocking bricks per student
- newspaper
- pencil and paper

Procedure

1. Obtain 2 sets of bricks, a piece of newspaper, and a pencil and paper. Ask your lab partner to do the same.

2. You and your partner should do Steps 3–6 without communicating with each other.

3. Place one brick on a table. On a piece of paper, write the number "1." Next to the number write instructions that someone can follow to place the brick exactly as you did. What you wrote is called a line of instruction. See the example above.

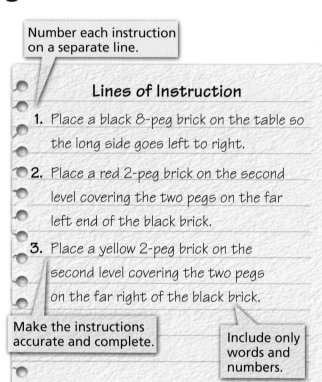

Number each instruction on a separate line.

Lines of Instruction

1. Place a black 8-peg brick on the table so the long side goes left to right.

2. Place a red 2-peg brick on the second level covering the two pegs on the far left end of the black brick.

3. Place a yellow 2-peg brick on the second level covering the two pegs on the far right of the black brick.

Make the instructions accurate and complete.

Include only words and numbers.

4. Select another brick from the same set and attach it to the previous brick. Write a number "2" on your paper and another line of instruction next to the number.

5. Repeat Step 4 eight more times, using the numbers 3 through 10 in front of your instruction lines. You should have one line of instruction for each brick you placed.

6. Cover your structure with the newspaper. Then, trade your second set of bricks and your instruction sheet with your lab partner.

7. Using your partner's instructions and brick set, build the same structure your partner built. Your partner should do the same using your instructions and brick set.

8. When you both are finished, uncover your partner's structure. Compare the structure with the one you built using your partner's instructions. Note any places where your structure is not identical to your partner's.

9. Together, review Line 1 of your partner's instructions. Determine whether the brick was placed exactly as in the original structure. Identify any problems in the line of instruction. (*Hint:* A line of instruction is a problem if it resulted in a brick being placed incorrectly, or if there is more than one way to carry out the instruction.)

10. If the line of instruction has a problem, work with your partner to rewrite it.

11. Review all the remaining lines of instruction one at a time, following the procedures in Steps 9 and 10.

12. Now review the structure you built using your partner's instructions. Repeat the procedures in Steps 8 –11.

13. When you are finished, discuss what you learned about writing lines of instruction.

14. Take apart your brick structures and place the bricks in their containers. Be careful not to mix up your set of bricks with your partner's set.

Analyze and Conclude

1. **Observing** Did you have to rewrite any of your instructions in Step 10? If so, explain why.

2. **Forming Operational Definitions** Write an operational definition of a well-written computer program.

3. **Making Models** During which steps of the lab were you modeling the actions of a computer programmer? In which steps were you modeling the actions of a computer?

4. **Making Models** "Debugging" means examining a computer program to identify instructions that might be a problem. Which steps of this lab modeled debugging?

5. **Communicating** Suppose you are the owner of a small software programming company. Write a newspaper employment advertisement that describes the characteristics of a good programmer.

More to Explore

Build and write instructions for a structure using more than 10 bricks. Create a "computer language" that keeps your instructions as short as possible. For example, replace the word "connect" with a "+" symbol. Use one numbered line of instruction for each brick. With you teacher's permission, plan and carry out a test of your computer language.

The Information Superhighway

Reading Preview

Key Concepts
- What is the purpose of a computer network?
- How can people protect themselves and their property as they use computer networks?

Key Terms
- computer network
- Internet
- World Wide Web
- encryption
- computer virus
- chat room
- intellectual property

Target Reading Skill
Identifying Main Ideas As you read the Using Computers Safely section, write the main idea in a graphic organizer like the one below. Then write three supporting details that further explain the main idea.

Main Idea

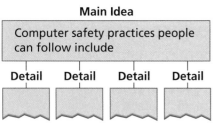

Computer safety practices people can follow include

Detail	Detail	Detail	Detail

Lab zone Discover Activity

How Important Are Computers?

1. Obtain a local or national newspaper.
2. Look through the newspaper for articles that refer to computers, the Internet, the World Wide Web, or the information superhighway.
3. Write down the topics of the articles. For example, was the article about politics, painting, money, or computers?
4. Create a data table to show your results.

Think It Over
Inferring What can you infer about the kinds of information available through the computer? How much do you think people use computers to obtain information?

Because of the Internet, the world is at your fingertips! You can send an e-mail message to someone on the other side of the planet. Through the World Wide Web, information is yours for the searching as you prepare a school report. The news, sports scores, travel information, and weather reports are all available at any time. How is this possible? The answer is through the use of a computer connected to a network.

Computer Networks

You have traveled on a network of roads and highways that connects cities and towns. A **computer network** is a group of computers connected by cables or telephone lines. **A computer network allows people in different locations to share information and software.**

A global network ▶

There are two types of networks. A set of computers connected in one classroom or office building is known as a local area network (LAN). Computers connected across larger distances form a wide area network (WAN). In wide area networks, very powerful computers serve as a support connection for hundreds of less powerful computers.

The Internet The most significant wide area network is the Internet. The **Internet** is a global network that links millions of computers in businesses, schools, and research organizations. The Internet is a network of host computers that extends around the world. You might say that the Internet is a network of networks. The Internet, along with other smaller networks, sometimes is called the information superhighway.

The Internet began in 1969 as a military communications system. Colleges and universities were later added to the Internet so that scientists could exchange data. Beginning in 1993, businesses were allowed to sell Internet connections to individuals. These businesses are known as Internet service providers (ISPs). With easy access available, use of the Internet has grown at an incredible rate.

World Wide Web The World Wide Web (www) was developed in 1989. The **World Wide Web** is a system that allows you to display and view files, called pages, on the Internet. A Web page can include text, pictures, video, or sound. Prior to the development of the World Wide Web, Internet users could only view information in the form of words and numbers. Through the World Wide Web, users can look at images similar to those you might see on television or videos. Software programs called search engines allow people to search through the Web for information.

Reading Checkpoint How has the World Wide Web changed the Internet?

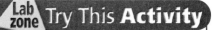
Lab zone Try This **Activity**

What a Web You Weave

Many businesses and individuals have home pages on the World Wide Web. Such pages usually describe the characteristics of the business or person.

Communicating Design your own home page that describes your interests, hobbies, and achievements. A home page usually allows a user to click on certain words to find out more information about a particular topic. Be sure to include text, photographs, and art in your design.

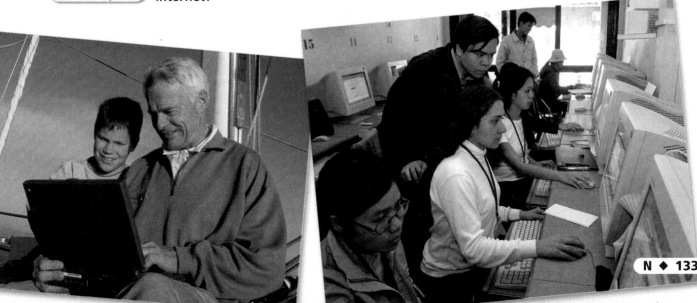

FIGURE 18
Safety First
People can protect themselves and their property by using computer networks properly.
Interpreting Diagrams *How does encryption protect communications within a network?*

Using Computers Safely

Computer networks provide great benefits. But they also pose potential problems. By following careful practices, people can protect themselves and their property as they use computer networks. Here are four issues to consider.

Protect Private Data People may use networks to share personal information such as financial records, credit card numbers, medical data, and business records. It is essential to guard that kind of information from misuse. **Share personal information only on networks that require authorization and use security software to keep out unwanted users.** Look for networks that encrypt information. **Encryption** is a mathematical process of coding information so that only the intended user can read it.

Avoid Viruses Computer viruses are a form of vandalism. **Computer viruses** are programs that interfere with the normal operation of a computer. Like a living virus, a computer virus enters a computer and reproduces itself. It can destroy stored data or even disable a computer. **Use software to detect viruses before they cause damage.** When you download a file, run virus-checking software. Store downloaded programs on a floppy disk or CD.

Go Online
SciLINKS NSTA

For: Links on computer networks
Visit: www.SciLinks.org
Web Code: scn-1444

Protect Personal Safety Many people enjoy chat rooms. **Chat rooms** allow multiple users to exchange messages simultaneously. However, users are not screened, so you do not know who is using the chat room with you. **Never give your name, address, or telephone number.** Do not respond to offensive messages, and do not accept files from strangers.

Respect Intellectual Property A computer program is a piece of intellectual property. **Intellectual property** can be an idea or creative work, such as a book or musical performance. Governments protect intellectual property by granting copyrights and patents. When you buy a copyrighted program, you buy a license for your own use. **Do not make copies for friends to use.** Violating copyrights or patents can result in fines or other penalties.

 What kind of information does encryption protect?

FIGURE 19
Intellectual Property
The copyright symbol on this CD protects the intellectual property rights of the company that produced it. **Predicting** *What might happen to the software and music industries if too many people copy CDs rather than buy them?*

Section 4 Assessment

Target Reading Skill **Using Prior Knowledge** Review your graphic organizer about computer networks and revise it based on what you just learned in the section.

Reviewing Key Concepts

1. a. **Reviewing** What is a computer network?
   b. **Describing** Give an example of a computer network.
   c. **Making Judgments** What are the advantages of computer networks?
2. a. **Identifying** What are three kinds of personal information that might be shared on a computer network?
   b. **Explaining** What is one way to protect personal information when using a network?
   c. **Summarizing** Write three simple rules that would help protect your family and your family's property when using computer networks.

Lab zone **At-Home Activity**

Conduct an Interview Although computers are commonplace today, this was not always the case. Interview a family member who grew up before computers were common. Prepare a list of questions for the interview. Find out whether that person has used a computer, what he or she thinks about computers, and how computers might have changed his or her life. Ask if the large number of applications for computers has come as a surprise.

When Seeing ISN'T Believing

Combining photography and computers can produce visual magic. A computer can turn a photo's objects and colors into a code. Then, using a computer to change the codes, a person can change a photo in amazing ways. Changing photos with computers is called digital manipulation.

The Issues

Advantages of Photo Manipulation

Computers allow people to greatly improve a photograph. Images of objects or people can be added, removed, or moved around. Fuzzy pictures can become sharper. Colors can be brightened. Unclear or tiny details can be made easy to see. Old or damaged photos can be made to look like new.

▲ Original image

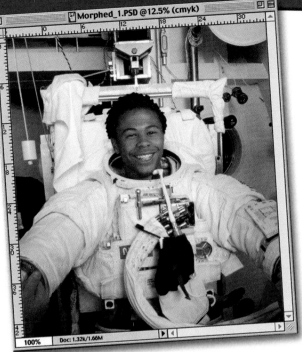

▲ Photos can be combined using digital manipulation.

▲ Digital manipulation can change your image in realistic ways.

Disadvantages of Photo Manipulation

It's nearly impossible to tell the difference between a changed and unchanged photo. Some people worry that digital manipulation could be used to harm or cheat people. Personal or family photos could be changed to a person's disadvantage. Newspapers, magazines, and TV stations could mislead the public about individuals and stories. Faked photos might be presented as evidence in court cases.

What Safeguards Are Needed?

Should governments pass laws against changing photographs? Such laws would be hard to enforce, and they might make it difficult to use digital manipulation for useful purposes. Such laws might also violate the right of free speech, since the courts consider photos a kind of speech, or expression. Should photographers or organizations police themselves? They could write codes of conduct. For example, it could be considered acceptable to make photos clearer digitally, but not to add, take away, or move around parts of a photo. Some photographers who work for newspapers have suggested such a code. Another safeguard might be to put a symbol on any digitally manipulated photo.

You Decide

1. Identify the Problem
Summarize the problems created by digital manipulation of photos.

2. Analyze the Options
Research this topic further at the library or on the Internet. List additional arguments for and against manipulating photos, and explain possible remedies.

3. Find a Solution
You run a TV station. Your assistants want to use two digitally changed photos, one in a commercial and one in a news story about an individual. Will you let them use one, or both, or neither? Explain.

Go Online
PHSchool.com

For: More on photo manipulation
Visit: PHSchool.com
Web Code: cgh-4040

① Electronic Signals and Semiconductors

Key Concepts

- There are two basic kinds of electronic signals: analog signals and digital signals.
- The two types of semiconductors can be combined in different ways to make diodes, transistors, and integrated circuits.

Key Terms

electronics
electronic signal
analog signal
digital signal
semiconductor
diode
transistor
integrated circuit

② Electronic Communication

Key Concepts

- In a telephone, sound is transformed into an electronic signal that is transmitted and then transformed back into sound.
- Sound can be reproduced using an analog device such as a phonograph or a digital device such as a CD player.
- Electronic signals can be carried over long distances by electromagnetic waves.
- Voices and music on an AM or FM radio station are electronic signals carried by an electromagnetic wave.
- Electromagnetic waves can be used to carry images as well as sound.

Key Terms

electromagnetic wave
amplitude
frequency
amplitude modulation (AM)
frequency modulation (FM)

③ Computers

Key Concepts

- Computer information is represented in the binary system.
- Computer hardware includes a central processing unit, input devices, output devices, and memory storage devices.
- Software is a set of instructions that directs the computer hardware to perform operations on stored information.

Key Terms

computer
binary system
hardware
central processing unit
  (CPU)

input device
output device
software
computer
  programmer

④ The Information Superhighway

Key Concepts

- A computer network allows people in different locations to share information and software.
- Share personal information only on networks that require authorization and use security software to keep out unwanted users.
- Use software to detect viruses before they cause damage.
- Never give your name, address, or telephone number in chat rooms.
- Do not make copies of intellectual property or copyrighted material for friends to use.

Key Terms

computer network
World Wide Web
computer virus
intellectual property

Internet
encryption
chat room

Review and Assessment

Organizing Information

Flowcharts Copy the flowchart about telephone communication onto a separate sheet of paper. Then complete it and add a title. (For more on flowcharts, see the Skills Handbook.)

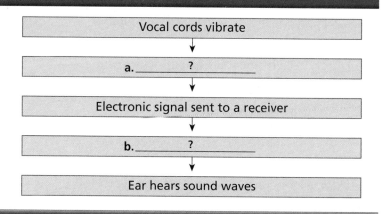

Vocal cords vibrate
↓
a. _____ ?
↓
Electronic signal sent to a receiver
↓
b. _____ ?
↓
Ear hears sound waves

Reviewing Key Terms

Choose the letter of the best answer.

1. The use of electric current to communicate information is
   a. encryption.
   b. amplitude modulation.
   c. electrical communication.
   d. electronics.

2. A sandwich of three layers of semiconductor that is used to amplify an electric signal is known as a(n)
   a. diode.
   b. modem.
   c. transistor.
   d. integrated circuit.

3. An electromagnetic wave consists of
   a. changing electric and magnetic fields.
   b. AM and FM waves.
   c. electrons and protons.
   d. beams of electrons.

4. An example of an output device is a
   a. transistor.
   b. printer.
   c. hard disk.
   d. diskette.

5. A group of computers connected by cables or telephone lines is a
   a. microprocessor.
   b. CPU.
   c. modem.
   d. network.

If the statement is true, write *true*. If it is false, change the underlined word or words to make the statement true.

6. A <u>transistor</u> changes alternating current into direct current.

7. Before <u>computers</u>, electronic devices used vacuum tubes to control electric current.

8. <u>Input</u> devices feed data into a computer.

9. Computer programs are also called <u>hardware</u>.

10. A(n) <u>virus</u> is a program that interferes with the normal operation of a computer.

Writing in Science

Sequence of Events Imagine that you are a director in charge of televising a live music concert. Describe the sequence of events through which the images will be transmitted from a camera on stage to the television screens in people's homes.

DISCOVERY CHANNEL SCHOOL

Electronics

Video Preview
Video Field Trip
▶ Video Assessment

Review and Assessment

Checking Concepts

11. Compare an analog signal with a digital signal.

12. Define each of the following in your own words: diode, transistor, and integrated circuit.

13. Draw an illustration of an electromagnetic wave. Explain how an electromagnetic wave is generated.

14. How is a radio show broadcast and received?

15. How is the World Wide Web different from the Internet?

Thinking Critically

16. **Relating Cause and Effect** What are some advantages of semiconductors and the electronic components made from semiconductors?

17. **Calculating** The television pictures people enjoy are composed of images shown very quickly. Each image on a traditional television screen lasts for $\frac{1}{30}$ of a second. How many images appear on the screen during a 30-minute program?

18. **Applying Concepts** A computer program is a list of instructions that tells a computer exactly how to perform a task. Write a program that describes the steps involved in some small task, such as walking your dog, taking out the trash, setting the table, or playing a game. Reread and revise your description so that a person could use it to correctly perform the task.

19. **Making Judgments** Why does a government protect a computer program as the intellectual property of the author?

20. **Classifying** What type of semiconductor device is shown in the diagram below? How can you tell?

Applying Skills

Use the illustrations below to answer Questions 21–24.

Examine the waves diagrammed below. The diagrams may not all show a variation of the same wave.

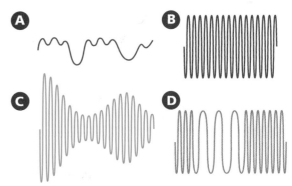

21. **Predicting** Diagram A represents an audio signal. What would that signal look like if it were converted to an AM radio signal? Draw a sketch to illustrate your answer.

22. **Interpreting Diagrams** Which of these waves might be a carrier wave? Describe the role of a carrier wave in electronic communication.

23. **Classifying** Two radio transmitters send out electronic signals shown as diagram C and diagram D. Which represents an AM wave? Which represents an FM wave? How can you tell?

24. **Comparing and Contrasting** Could the wave in diagram C be a modulated version of the wave in diagram A? Explain how you know.

Lab zone Chapter **Project**

Performance Assessment Present both the existing computer application and the new one you invented to the class. Provide diagrams of each and describe their operation. You might want to pretend to sell your new invention to the class. Prepare a poster describing the task that your new application will accomplish. Show yourself enjoying the benefits!

Standardized Test Prep

Choose the letter of the best answer.

1. Each of the events listed below happens in the process of producing an image and sound in a television set. Which event happens last?
   A A communication satellite receives electromagnetic signals.
   B Electronic signals are converted into sound and light.
   C Electromagnetic signals are sent out from an antenna.
   D Light and sound are converted into electronic signals.

2. In the binary number system, the number 8 would be written as
   F 2.
   G 8.
   H 100.
   J 1000.

Use the graphs and your knowledge of science to answer Question 3.

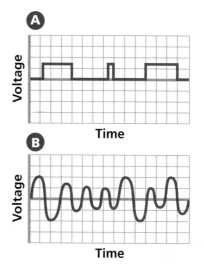

3. Which of the following statements about graphs A and B is correct?
   A Graph A shows an analog signal and graph B shows a digital signal.
   B Graph A shows a digital signal and graph B shows an analog signal.
   C Both graphs show analog signals.
   D Neither graph shows an analog signal.

4. Which of the following is not a good way to protect yourself and your property while using a computer network?
   F Use computer software that detects viruses.
   G Store downloaded programs on floppy disks or CDs.
   H Use your real name when you visit a chat room.
   J Do not accept electronic files from strangers.

5. Which of the following items is an input device?
   A computer monitor
   B hard disk
   C mouse
   D central processing unit

Constructed Response

6. Explain what an integrated circuit is. Also explain why integrated circuits are useful devices.

Edison— Genius of Invention

What inventor gave us
- sound recording?
- motion pictures?
- electric lighting?

The First Light Bulb
This is a model of Edison's first successful lamp. The light bulb is made of a carbon filament inside a glass bulb. Electricity flowing through the filament makes the filament white hot, so that it glows. Below, a drawing of the light bulb appears in a Menlo Park notebook.

In 1881, the electric light was a novelty. City streets and some homes were lit with gas. Most homes used oil lamps or candles. Thomas Edison was still developing his system of indoor electric lighting.

Electric lights brought with them a system of power distribution, which made other uses of electricity possible. Imagine living without any electrical appliances, and you'll understand the changes in everyday life that Edison started.

Thomas Edison (1847–1931) had almost no schooling. Yet his mind bubbled with ideas. At the time of his death, Edison held 1,093 patents. A patent is a government license protecting an inventor's right to make and sell a product. One of Edison's most important ideas was never patented. He created the first laboratory for industrial research.

Thomas Edison at 14
Edison worked as a telegrapher for about six years.

The Wizard of Menlo Park

Before 1900, most inventors worked alone. Edison, in contrast, depended on a strong team of research co-workers to carry out his ideas. Edison had an unusual ability to inspire those who worked for him. Some of his original team stayed with him for years. A very hard worker himself, Edison demanded that everyone on his team also work long hours.

By 1876, Edison had enough money to set up an "invention factory." He chose the small town of Menlo Park, New Jersey. His Menlo Park laboratory became the world's first industrial research laboratory.

Edison's team often made improvements on other people's inventions. The light bulb is an example. Other scientists had invented electric lamps, but their light bulbs burned rapidly. The problem was to find a material for the filament that would not overheat or burn out quickly.

The Menlo Park team spent months testing hundreds of materials. First, they rolled each material into a long, thin strand. Then, they carbonized it, which meant baking it until it turned to charcoal. Finally, they tested it in a vacuum, or in the absence of air. Most materials failed in only a few minutes or a few hours. The breakthrough came in 1879. The first successful filament was a length of ordinary cotton thread, carefully carbonized. The newspapers carried the headlines "Success in a Cotton Thread" and "It Makes a Light, Without Gas or Flame."

Edison's Lab
Edison set up his research laboratory in Menlo Park.

Science Activity

Work together as a team to invent a new electrical device.

- What could a new electrical device help you do? How could it make your life easier?

- Brainstorm for possible products that would help you in some way. Write down all possible ideas.

- Evaluate each solution and agree on the best one.

- Plan your design and make a labeled drawing. List the supplies you will need. Note any new skills you should learn.

- Write down the steps you will use to build your device.

Lighting Manhattan

Edison recognized the value of publicity. Besides being a productive inventor, he knew how to promote himself. He made glowing predictions about his new electric system. Electrical energy would soon be so cheap, he said, that "only the rich would be able to afford candles."

When he built his first neighborhood generating station, Edison made a shrewd choice of location. The Pearl Street power station brought light and power to about 2.6 square kilometers of downtown Manhattan. It supplied businesses and factories, as well as private homes. The circuits could light 400 light bulbs. Some of those lights were in the offices of J. P. Morgan, the leading banker and financier of the time. Other lights were located in the offices of *The New York Times*. Here's what the *Times* reporter wrote on September 5, 1882.

New York City
This photo shows Broadway in the 1880s.

SEPTEMBER 5, 1882—Yesterday for the first time The Times Building was illuminated by electricity. Mr. Edison had at last perfected his incandescent light, had put his machinery in order, and had started up his engines, and last evening his company lighted up about one-third of the lower City district in which The Times Building stands.

It was not until about seven o'clock, when it began to grow dark, that the electric light really made itself known and showed how bright and steady it is. It was a light that a man could sit down under and write for hours without the consciousness of having any artificial light about him. There was a very slight amount of heat from each lamp, but not nearly as much as from a gas-burner—one-fifteenth as much as from gas, the inventor says. The light was soft, mellow, and grateful to the eye, and it seemed almost like writing by daylight to have a light without a particle of flicker and with scarcely any heat to make the head ache. The decision was unanimously in favor of the Edison electric lamp as against gas.

————Excerpted with permission from *The New York Times*.

Language Arts Activity

The reporter who wrote the newspaper story observed details carefully and used them to write about an event—the first lights in his office. Look back at the story. Now write about the event as Edison would have told it to convince people to buy light bulbs and install electric generating systems. You could make an advertisement. Inform your readers about the product and persuade them to buy it.

Solving Practical Problems

As he grew older, Edison worried that American students were not learning mathematics well enough. To motivate students, he suggested using problems that related to real-life situations. In 1925, when he was 78, he proposed these problems below as recorded in his notebooks. Note that light bulbs were called lamps. Tungsten is a metal used in light bulbs.

Edison Lamp
This advertisement promotes reading by Edison's Mazda lamp.

Problem 1
American electric plants now serve 9,500,000 homes. The estimated number of homes in the United States is 21,000,000. What percentage receives electrical energy?

Problem 2
It needs about 280,000,000 tungsten lamps [bulbs] each year to supply the market today. And yet the first lamp factory in the world—the Edison Lamp Works. . .—was not started until 1880, and I was told it would never pay. The output for our first year was about 25,000 globes [bulbs]. How many times that figure would be required for the present market?

Problem 3
A household using 21 lamps requires about 7 new lamps each year. What percentage is this?

Problem 4
If these lamps had been bought at the retail prices of the first year of the lamp factory, they would have cost $1.25 each. How much would the family save by the decreased prices of today?

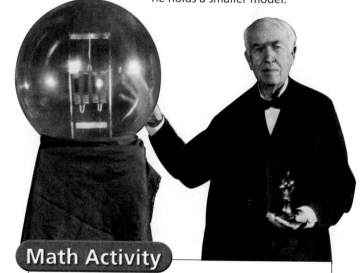

Inventor Thomas Edison
Edison stands next to his original light bulb invention. In his hand, he holds a smaller model.

Math Activity

Solve the four math problems that Edison wrote. To solve Problem 4, use 1925 prices. That year, incandescent light bulbs (or lamps) cost $.30 each.

Daily Life Transformed

Edison's inventions in the late 1800s helped spark a technological and social revolution. Some of these inventions forever transformed the way people live, play, and work.

Edison's light bulb made indoor lighting practical. Along with the light bulb, he developed the idea of a central electric generating system to distribute electricity to homes and businesses. That system included generators, underground cables, junction boxes, and meters. Other inventors improved on Edison's ideas for lights and electricity.

Other Edison inventions influenced ways that people entertain themselves. Edison created the phonograph, a rotating disk that could record and play back sounds. About that same time, Edison invented the first movie camera, a device that could store pictures. These inventions spurred the development of the recording and film industries.

Edison Movie
This poster advertises one of Edison's early movies.

Improved Phonograph
A later version of Edison's phonograph included a horn to project the sound.

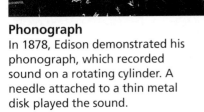

Phonograph
In 1878, Edison demonstrated his phonograph, which recorded sound on a rotating cylinder. A needle attached to a thin metal disk played the sound.

Electric lights now light up the country from coast to coast. This map, based on population data, shows what the United States might look like from space at night. Using a map of the United States, identify the regions that are the brightest.

What cities are located there? Which states have the most urban areas? Which have the least? Use an almanac to find out the population of five of the largest cities. Compare these data with the total United States population.

Tie It Together

Modern Times

Many of the inventions that came out of Menlo Park still affect things we do today. Work in pairs to research one of Edison's inventions. Or research another scientist's inventions. Find out how the device changed and improved in the 1900s. Write up your research and present it to the class. If the device is no longer used, explain what has replaced it. Here are a few inventions from which to choose. (Not all of them were Edison's.)

- stock ticker
- telegraph
- phonograph
- disk record
- voting machine
- electric pen and press
- radio transmitter
- linotype
- typewriter
- telephone
- automobile
- vacuum tube
- mechanical music

Cassette Player
Is this device related to Edison's invention?

Think Like a Scientist

Scientists have a particular way of looking at the world, or scientific habits of mind. Whenever you ask a question and explore possible answers, you use many of the same skills that scientists do. Some of these skills are described on this page.

Observing

When you use one or more of your five senses to gather information about the world, you are **observing.** Hearing a dog bark, counting twelve green seeds, and smelling smoke are all observations. To increase the power of their senses, scientists sometimes use microscopes, telescopes, or other instruments that help them make more detailed observations.

An observation must be an accurate report of what your senses detect. It is important to keep careful records of your observations in science class by writing or drawing in a notebook. The information collected through observations is called evidence, or data.

Inferring

When you interpret an observation, you are **inferring,** or making an inference. For example, if you hear your dog barking, you may infer that someone is at your front door. To make this inference, you combine the evidence—the barking dog—and your experience or knowledge—you know that your dog barks when strangers approach—to reach a logical conclusion.

Notice that an inference is not a fact; it is only one of many possible interpretations for an observation. For example, your dog may be barking because it wants to go for a walk. An inference may turn out to be incorrect even if it is based on accurate observations and logical reasoning. The only way to find out if an inference is correct is to investigate further.

Predicting

When you listen to the weather forecast, you hear many predictions about the next day's weather—what the temperature will be, whether it will rain, and how windy it will be. Weather forecasters use observations and knowledge of weather patterns to predict the weather. The skill of **predicting** involves making an inference about a future event based on current evidence or past experience.

Because a prediction is an inference, it may prove to be false. In science class, you can test some of your predictions by doing experiments. For example, suppose you predict that larger paper airplanes can fly farther than smaller airplanes. How could you test your prediction?

Activity

Use the photograph to answer the questions below.

Observing Look closely at the photograph. List at least three observations.

Inferring Use your observations to make an inference about what has happened. What experience or knowledge did you use to make the inference?

Predicting Predict what will happen next. On what evidence or experience do you base your prediction?

Classifying

Could you imagine searching for a book in the library if the books were shelved in no particular order? Your trip to the library would be an all-day event! Luckily, librarians group together books on similar topics or by the same author. Grouping together items that are alike in some way is called **classifying.** You can classify items in many ways: by size, by shape, by use, and by other important characteristics.

Like librarians, scientists use the skill of classifying to organize information and objects. When things are sorted into groups, the relationships among them become easier to understand.

Activity

Classify the objects in the photograph into two groups based on any characteristic you choose. Then use another characteristic to classify the objects into three groups.

Making Models

Have you ever drawn a picture to help someone understand what you were saying? Such a drawing is one type of model. A model is a picture, diagram, computer image, or other representation of a complex object or process. **Making models** helps people understand things that they cannot observe directly.

Scientists often use models to represent things that are either very large or very small, such as the planets in the solar system, or the parts of a cell. Such models are physical models—drawings or three-dimensional structures that look like the real thing. Other models are mental models—mathematical equations or words that describe how something works.

Activity

This student is using a model to demonstrate what causes day and night on Earth. What do the flashlight and the tennis ball in the model represent?

Communicating

Whenever you talk on the phone, write a report, or listen to your teacher at school, you are communicating. **Communicating** is the process of sharing ideas and information with other people. Communicating effectively requires many skills, including writing, reading, speaking, listening, and making models.

Scientists communicate to share results, information, and opinions. Scientists often communicate about their work in journals, over the telephone, in letters, and on the Internet.

They also attend scientific meetings where they share their ideas with one another in person.

Activity

On a sheet of paper, write out clear, detailed directions for tying your shoe. Then exchange directions with a partner. Follow your partner's directions exactly. How successful were you at tying your shoe? How could your partner have communicated more clearly?

Skills Handbook ◆ 149

Making Measurements

By measuring, scientists can express their observations more precisely and communicate more information about what they observe.

Measuring in SI

The standard system of measurement used by scientists around the world is known as the International System of Units, which is abbreviated as SI (**Système International d'Unités,** in French). SI units are easy to use because they are based on multiples of 10. Each unit is ten times larger than the next smallest unit and one tenth the size of the next largest unit. The table lists the prefixes used to name the most common SI units.

Common SI Prefixes		
Prefix	Symbol	Meaning
kilo-	k	1,000
hecto-	h	100
deka-	da	10
deci-	d	0.1 (one tenth)
centi-	c	0.01 (one hundredth)
milli-	m	0.001 (one thousandth)

Length To measure length, or the distance between two points, the unit of measure is the **meter (m).** The distance from the floor to a doorknob is approximately one meter. Long distances, such as the distance between two cities, are measured in kilometers (km). Small lengths are measured in centimeters (cm) or millimeters (mm). Scientists use metric rulers and meter sticks to measure length.

Common Conversions	
1 km	=	1,000 m
1 m	=	100 cm
1 m	=	1,000 mm
1 cm	=	10 mm

Liquid Volume To measure the volume of a liquid, or the amount of space it takes up, you will use a unit of measure known as the **liter (L).** One liter is the approximate volume of a medium-size carton of milk. Smaller volumes are measured in milliliters (mL). Scientists use graduated cylinders to measure liquid volume.

Activity

The larger lines on the metric ruler in the picture show centimeter divisions, while the smaller, unnumbered lines show millimeter divisions. How many centimeters long is the shell? How many millimeters long is it?

Activity

The graduated cylinder in the picture is marked in milliliter divisions. Notice that the water in the cylinder has a curved surface. This curved surface is called the *meniscus.* To measure the volume, you must read the level at the lowest point of the meniscus. What is the volume of water in this graduated cylinder?

Common Conversion
1 L = 1,000 mL

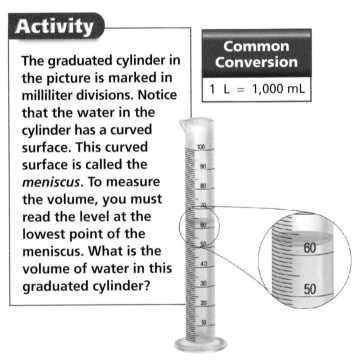

Mass To measure mass, or the amount of matter in an object, you will use a unit of measure known as the **gram (g).** One gram is approximately the mass of a paper clip. Larger masses are measured in kilograms (kg). Scientists use a balance to find the mass of an object.

Common Conversion

1 kg = 1,000 g

Activity

The mass of the potato in the picture is measured in kilograms. What is the mass of the potato? Suppose a recipe for potato salad called for one kilogram of potatoes. About how many potatoes would you need?

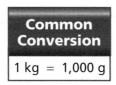

0.25 KG

Temperature To measure the temperature of a substance, you will use the **Celsius scale.** Temperature is measured in degrees Celsius (°C) using a Celsius thermometer. Water freezes at 0°C and boils at 100°C.

Time The unit scientists use to measure time is the **second (s).**

Activity

What is the temperature of the liquid in degrees Celsius?

Converting SI Units

To use the SI system, you must know how to convert between units. Converting from one unit to another involves the skill of **calculating,** or using mathematical operations. Converting between SI units is similar to converting between dollars and dimes because both systems are based on multiples of ten.

Suppose you want to convert a length of 80 centimeters to meters. Follow these steps to convert between units.

1. Begin by writing down the measurement you want to convert—in this example, 80 centimeters.

2. Write a conversion factor that represents the relationship between the two units you are converting. In this example, the relationship is 1 meter = 100 centimeters. Write this conversion factor as a fraction, making sure to place the units you are converting from (centimeters, in this example) in the denominator.

3. Multiply the measurement you want to convert by the fraction. When you do this, the units in the first measurement will cancel out with the units in the denominator. Your answer will be in the units you are converting to (meters, in this example).

Example

80 centimeters = ▨ meters

$$80 \text{ centimeters} \times \frac{1 \text{ meter}}{100 \text{ centimeters}} = \frac{80 \text{ meters}}{100}$$

$$= 0.8 \text{ meters}$$

Activity

Convert between the following units.

1. 600 millimeters = ▨ meters
2. 0.35 liters = ▨ milliliters
3. 1,050 grams = ▨ kilograms

Conducting a Scientific Investigation

In some ways, scientists are like detectives, piecing together clues to learn about a process or event. One way that scientists gather clues is by carrying out experiments. An experiment tests an idea in a careful, orderly manner. Although experiments do not all follow the same steps in the same order, many follow a pattern similar to the one described here.

Posing Questions

Experiments begin by asking a scientific question. A scientific question is one that can be answered by gathering evidence. For example, the question "Which freezes faster—fresh water or salt water?" is a scientific question because you can carry out an investigation and gather information to answer the question.

Developing a Hypothesis

The next step is to form a hypothesis. A **hypothesis** is a possible explanation for a set of observations or answer to a scientific question. In science, a hypothesis must be something that can be tested. A hypothesis can be worded as an *If . . . then . . .* statement. For example, a hypothesis might be *"If I add salt to fresh water, then the water will take longer to freeze."* A hypothesis worded this way serves as a rough outline of the experiment you should perform.

Designing an Experiment

Next you need to plan a way to test your hypothesis. Your plan should be written out as a step-by-step procedure and should describe the observations or measurements you will make.

Two important steps involved in designing an experiment are controlling variables and forming operational definitions.

Controlling Variables In a well-designed experiment, you need to keep all variables the same except for one. A **variable** is any factor that can change in an experiment. The factor that you change is called the **manipulated variable**. In this experiment, the manipulated variable is the amount of salt added to the water. Other factors, such as the amount of water or the starting temperature, are kept constant.

The factor that changes as a result of the manipulated variable is called the **responding variable.** The responding variable is what you measure or observe to obtain your results. In this experiment, the responding variable is how long the water takes to freeze.

An experiment in which all factors except one are kept constant is called a **controlled experiment.** Most controlled experiments include a test called the control. In this experiment, Container 3 is the control. Because no salt is added to Container 3, you can compare the results from the other containers to it. Any difference in results must be due to the addition of salt alone.

Forming Operational Definitions Another important aspect of a well-designed experiment is having clear operational definitions. An **operational definition** is a statement that describes how a particular variable is to be measured or how a term is to be defined. For example, in this experiment, how will you determine if the water has frozen? You might decide to insert a stick in each container at the start of the experiment. Your operational definition of "frozen" would be the time at which the stick can no longer move.

Experimental Procedure
1. Fill 3 containers with 300 milliliters of cold tap water.
2. Add 10 grams of salt to Container 1; stir. Add 20 grams of salt to Container 2; stir. Add no salt to Container 3.
3. Place the 3 containers in a freezer.
4. Check the containers every 15 minutes. Record your observations.

Interpreting Data

The observations and measurements you make in an experiment are called **data.** At the end of an experiment, you need to analyze the data to look for any patterns or trends. Patterns often become clear if you organize your data in a data table or graph. Then think through what the data reveal. Do they support your hypothesis? Do they point out a flaw in your experiment? Do you need to collect more data?

Drawing Conclusions

A **conclusion** is a statement that sums up what you have learned from an experiment. When you draw a conclusion, you need to decide whether the data you collected support your hypothesis or not. You may need to repeat an experiment several times before you can draw any conclusions from it. Conclusions often lead you to pose new questions and plan new experiments to answer them.

Activity

Is a ball's bounce affected by the height from which it is dropped? Using the steps just described, plan a controlled experiment to investigate this problem.

Technology Design Skills

Engineers are people who use scientific and technological knowledge to solve practical problems. To design new products, engineers usually follow the process described here, even though they may not follow these steps in the exact order. As you read the steps, think about how you might apply them in technology labs.

Identify a Need

Before engineers begin designing a new product, they must first identify the need they are trying to meet. For example, suppose you are a member of a design team in a company that makes toys. Your team has identified a need: a toy boat that is inexpensive and easy to assemble.

Research the Problem

Engineers often begin by gathering information that will help them with their new design. This research may include finding articles in books, magazines, or on the Internet. It may also include talking to other engineers who have solved similar problems. Engineers often perform experiments related to the product they want to design.

For your toy boat, you could look at toys that are similar to the one you want to design. You might do research on the Internet. You could also test some materials to see whether they will work well in a toy boat.

Drawing for a boat design ▼

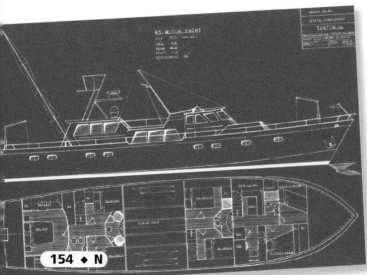

Design a Solution

Research gives engineers information that helps them design a product. When engineers design new products, they usually work in teams.

Generating Ideas Often design teams hold brainstorming meetings in which any team member can contribute ideas. **Brainstorming** is a creative process in which one team member's suggestions often spark ideas in other group members. Brainstorming can lead to new approaches to solving a design problem.

Evaluating Constraints During brainstorming, a design team will often come up with several possible designs. The team must then evaluate each one.

As part of their evaluation, engineers consider constraints. **Constraints** are factors that limit or restrict a product design. Physical characteristics, such as the properties of materials used to make your toy boat, are constraints. Money and time are also constraints. If the materials in a product cost a lot, or if the product takes a long time to make, the design may be impractical.

Making Trade-offs Design teams usually need to make trade-offs. In a **trade-off,** engineers give up one benefit of a proposed design in order to obtain another. In designing your toy boat, you will have to make trade-offs. For example, suppose one material is sturdy but not fully waterproof. Another material is more waterproof, but breakable. You may decide to give up the benefit of sturdiness in order to obtain the benefit of waterproofing.

Build and Evaluate a Prototype

Once the team has chosen a design plan, the engineers build a prototype of the product. A **prototype** is a working model used to test a design. Engineers evaluate the prototype to see whether it works well, is easy to operate, is safe to use, and holds up to repeated use.

Think of your toy boat. What would the prototype be like? Of what materials would it be made? How would you test it?

Troubleshoot and Redesign

Few prototypes work perfectly, which is why they need to be tested. Once a design team has tested a prototype, the members analyze the results and identify any problems. The team then tries to **troubleshoot,** or fix the design problems. For example, if your toy boat leaks or wobbles, the boat should be redesigned to eliminate those problems.

Communicate the Solution

A team needs to communicate the final design to the people who will manufacture and use the product. To do this, teams may use sketches, detailed drawings, computer simulations, and word descriptions.

Activity

You can use the technology design process to design and build a toy boat.

Research and Investigate

1. Visit the library or go online to research toy boats.

2. Investigate how a toy boat can be powered, including wind, rubber bands, or baking soda and vinegar.

3. Brainstorm materials, shapes, and steering for your boat.

Design and Build

4. Based on your research, design a toy boat that
   • is made of readily available materials
   • is no larger than 15 cm long and 10 cm wide
   • includes a power system, a rudder, and an area for cargo
   • travels 2 meters in a straight line carrying a load of 20 pennies

5. Sketch your design and write a step-by-step plan for building your boat. After your teacher approves your plan, build your boat.

Evaluate and Redesign

6. Test your boat, evaluate the results, and troubleshoot any problems.

7. Based on your evaluation, redesign your toy boat so it performs better.

Creating Data Tables and Graphs

**How can you make sense of the data in a science experiment?
The first step is to organize the data to help you understand them.
Data tables and graphs are helpful tools for organizing data.**

Data Tables

You have gathered your materials and set up your experiment. But before you start, you need to plan a way to record what happens during the experiment. By creating a data table, you can record your observations and measurements in an orderly way.

Suppose, for example, that a scientist conducted an experiment to find out how many Calories people of different body masses burn while doing various activities. The data table shows the results.

Notice in this data table that the manipulated variable (body mass) is the heading of one column. The responding variable (for

Calories Burned in 30 Minutes			
Body Mass	Experiment 1: Bicycling	Experiment 2: Playing Basketball	Experiment 3: Watching Television
30 kg	60 Calories	120 Calories	21 Calories
40 kg	77 Calories	164 Calories	27 Calories
50 kg	95 Calories	206 Calories	33 Calories
60 kg	114 Calories	248 Calories	38 Calories

Experiment 1, the number of Calories burned while bicycling) is the heading of the next column. Additional columns were added for related experiments.

Bar Graphs

To compare how many Calories a person burns doing various activities, you could create a bar graph. A bar graph is used to display data in a number of separate, or distinct, categories. In this example, bicycling, playing basketball, and watching television are the three categories.

To create a bar graph, follow these steps.

1. On graph paper, draw a horizontal, or *x*-, axis and a vertical, or *y*-, axis.

2. Write the names of the categories to be graphed along the horizontal axis. Include an overall label for the axis as well.

3. Label the vertical axis with the name of the responding variable. Include units of measurement. Then create a scale along the axis by marking off equally spaced numbers that cover the range of the data collected.

4. For each category, draw a solid bar using the scale on the vertical axis to determine the height. Make all the bars the same width.

5. Add a title that describes the graph.

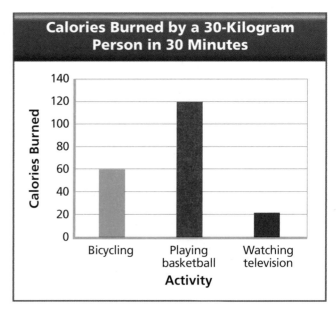

Line Graphs

To see whether a relationship exists between body mass and the number of Calories burned while bicycling, you could create a line graph. A line graph is used to display data that show how one variable (the responding variable) changes in response to another variable (the manipulated variable). You can use a line graph when your manipulated variable is **continuous,** that is, when there are other points between the ones that you tested. In this example, body mass is a continuous variable because there are other body masses between 30 and 40 kilograms (for example, 31 kilograms). Time is another example of a continuous variable.

Line graphs are powerful tools because they allow you to estimate values for conditions that you did not test in the experiment. For example, you can use the line graph to estimate that a 35-kilogram person would burn 68 Calories while bicycling.

To create a line graph, follow these steps.

1. On graph paper, draw a horizontal, or *x*-, axis and a vertical, or *y*-, axis.

2. Label the horizontal axis with the name of the manipulated variable. Label the vertical axis with the name of the responding variable. Include units of measurement.

3. Create a scale on each axis by marking off equally spaced numbers that cover the range of the data collected.

4. Plot a point on the graph for each piece of data. In the line graph above, the dotted lines show how to plot the first data point (30 kilograms and 60 Calories). Follow an imaginary vertical line extending up from the horizontal axis at the 30-kilogram mark. Then follow an imaginary horizontal line extending across from the vertical axis at the 60-Calorie mark. Plot the point where the two lines intersect.

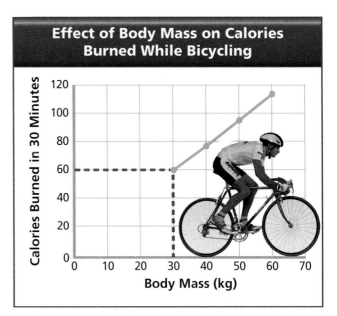

Effect of Body Mass on Calories Burned While Bicycling

5. Connect the plotted points with a solid line. (In some cases, it may be more appropriate to draw a line that shows the general trend of the plotted points. In those cases, some of the points may fall above or below the line. Also, not all graphs are linear. It may be more appropriate to draw a curve to connect the points.)

6. Add a title that identifies the variables or relationship in the graph.

Activity

Create line graphs to display the data from Experiment 2 and Experiment 3 in the data table.

Activity

You read in the newspaper that a total of 4 centimeters of rain fell in your area in June, 2.5 centimeters fell in July, and 1.5 centimeters fell in August. What type of graph would you use to display these data? Use graph paper to create the graph.

Circle Graphs

Like bar graphs, circle graphs can be used to display data in a number of separate categories. Unlike bar graphs, however, circle graphs can only be used when you have data for *all* the categories that make up a given topic. A circle graph is sometimes called a pie chart. The pie represents the entire topic, while the slices represent the individual categories. The size of a slice indicates what percentage of the whole a particular category makes up.

The data table below shows the results of a survey in which 24 teenagers were asked to identify their favorite sport. The data were then used to create the circle graph at the right.

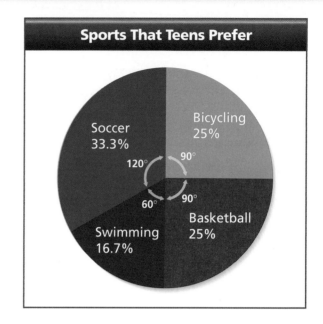
Sports That Teens Prefer

Soccer 33.3% — 120°
Bicycling 25% — 90°
Swimming 16.7% — 60°
Basketball 25% — 90°

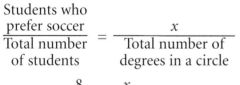

Favorite Sports

Sport	Students
Soccer	8
Basketball	6
Bicycling	6
Swimming	4

To create a circle graph, follow these steps.

1. Use a compass to draw a circle. Mark the center with a point. Then draw a line from the center point to the top of the circle.

2. Determine the size of each "slice" by setting up a proportion where *x* equals the number of degrees in a slice. (*Note:* A circle contains 360 degrees.) For example, to find the number of degrees in the "soccer" slice, set up the following proportion:

$$\frac{\text{Students who prefer soccer}}{\text{Total number of students}} = \frac{x}{\text{Total number of degrees in a circle}}$$

$$\frac{8}{24} = \frac{x}{360}$$

Cross-multiply and solve for x.

$$24x = 8 \times 360$$
$$x = 120$$

The "soccer" slice should contain 120 degrees.

3. Use a protractor to measure the angle of the first slice, using the line you drew to the top of the circle as the 0° line. Draw a line from the center of the circle to the edge for the angle you measured.

4. Continue around the circle by measuring the size of each slice with the protractor. Start measuring from the edge of the previous slice so the wedges do not overlap. When you are done, the entire circle should be filled in.

5. Determine the percentage of the whole circle that each slice represents. To do this, divide the number of degrees in a slice by the total number of degrees in a circle (360), and multiply by 100%. For the "soccer" slice, you can find the percentage as follows:

$$\frac{120}{360} \times 100\% = 33.3\%$$

6. Use a different color for each slice. Label each slice with the category and with the percentage of the whole it represents.

7. Add a title to the circle graph.

Activity

In a class of 28 students, 12 students take the bus to school, 10 students walk, and 6 students ride their bicycles. Create a circle graph to display these data.

Math Review

Scientists use math to organize, analyze, and present data.
This appendix will help you review some basic math skills.

Mean, Median, and Mode

The **mean** is the average, or the sum of the data divided by the number of data items. The middle number in a set of ordered data is called the **median.** The **mode** is the number that appears most often in a set of data.

> **Example**
>
> A scientist counted the number of distinct songs sung by seven different male birds and collected the data shown below.
>
> | Male Bird Songs | | | | | | | |
> |---|---|---|---|---|---|---|---|
> | Bird | A | B | C | D | E | F | G |
> | Number of Songs | 36 | 29 | 40 | 35 | 28 | 36 | 27 |
>
> To determine the mean number of songs, add the total number of songs and divide by the number of data items—in this case, the number of male birds.
>
> $$\text{Mean} = \frac{231}{7} = 33 \text{ songs}$$
>
> To find the median number of songs, arrange the data in numerical order and find the number in the middle of the series.
>
> **27 28 29 35 36 36 40**
>
> The number in the middle is 35, so the median number of songs is 35.
> The mode is the value that appears most frequently. In the data, 36 appears twice, while each other item appears only once. Therefore, 36 songs is the mode.

> **Practice**
>
> Find out how many minutes it takes each student in your class to get to school. Then find the mean, median, and mode for the data.

Probability

Probability is the chance that an event will occur. Probability can be expressed as a ratio, a fraction, or a percentage. For example, when you flip a coin, the probability that the coin will land heads up is 1 in 2, or $\frac{1}{2}$, or 50 percent.

The probability that an event will happen can be expressed in the following formula.

$$P(\text{event}) = \frac{\text{Number of times the event can occur}}{\text{Total number of possible events}}$$

> **Example**
>
> A paper bag contains 25 blue marbles, 5 green marbles, 5 orange marbles, and 15 yellow marbles. If you close your eyes and pick a marble from the bag, what is the probability that it will be yellow?
>
> $$P(\text{yellow marbles}) = \frac{15 \text{ yellow marbles}}{50 \text{ marbles total}}$$
>
> $$P = \frac{15}{50}, \text{ or } \frac{3}{10}, \text{ or } 30\%$$

> **Practice**
>
> Each side of a cube has a letter on it. Two sides have *A*, three sides have *B*, and one side has *C*. If you roll the cube, what is the probability that *A* will land on top?

Area

The **area** of a surface is the number of square units that cover it. The front cover of your text-book has an area of about 600 cm^2.

Area of a Rectangle and a Square To find the area of a rectangle, multiply its length times its width. The formula for the area of a rectangle is

$$A = \ell \times w, \text{ or } A = \ell w$$

Since all four sides of a square have the same length, the area of a square is the length of one side multiplied by itself, or squared.

$$A = s \times s, \text{ or } A = s^2$$

Example

A scientist is studying the plants in a field that measures 75 m × 45 m. What is the area of the field?

$$A = \ell \times w$$
$$A = 75 \text{ m} \times 45 \text{ m}$$
$$A = 3{,}375 \text{ m}^2$$

Area of a Circle The formula for the area of a circle is

$$A = \pi \times r \times r, \text{ or } A = \pi r^2$$

The length of the radius is represented by r, and the value of π is approximately $\frac{22}{7}$.

Example

Find the area of a circle with a radius of 14 cm.

$$A = \pi r^2$$
$$A = 14 \times 14 \times \tfrac{22}{7}$$
$$A = 616 \text{ cm}^2$$

Practice

Find the area of a circle that has a radius of 21 m.

Circumference

The distance around a circle is called the circumference. The formula for finding the circumference of a circle is

$$C = 2 \times \pi \times r, \text{ or } C = 2\pi r$$

Example

The radius of a circle is 35 cm. What is its circumference?

$$C = 2\pi r$$
$$C = 2 \times 35 \times \tfrac{22}{7}$$
$$C = 220 \text{ cm}$$

Practice

What is the circumference of a circle with a radius of 28 m?

Volume

The volume of an object is the number of cubic units it contains. The volume of a wastebasket, for example, might be about 26,000 cm^3.

Volume of a Rectangular Object To find the volume of a rectangular object, multiply the object's length times its width times its height.

$$V = \ell \times w \times h, \text{ or } V = \ell w h$$

Example

Find the volume of a box with length 24 cm, width 12 cm, and height 9 cm.

$$V = \ell w h$$
$$V = 24 \text{ cm} \times 12 \text{ cm} \times 9 \text{ cm}$$
$$V = 2{,}592 \text{ cm}^3$$

Practice

What is the volume of a rectangular object with length 17 cm, width 11 cm, and height 6 cm?

Fractions

A **fraction** is a way to express a part of a whole. In the fraction $\frac{4}{7}$, 4 is the numerator and 7 is the denominator.

Adding and Subtracting Fractions To add or subtract two or more fractions that have a common denominator, first add or subtract the numerators. Then write the sum or difference over the common denominator.

To find the sum or difference of fractions with different denominators, first find the least common multiple of the denominators. This is known as the least common denominator. Then convert each fraction to equivalent fractions with the least common denominator. Add or subtract the numerators. Then write the sum or difference over the common denominator.

> **Example**
>
> $$\frac{5}{6} - \frac{3}{4} = \frac{10}{12} - \frac{9}{12} = \frac{10 - 9}{12} = \frac{1}{12}$$

Multiplying Fractions To multiply two fractions, first multiply the two numerators, then multiply the two denominators.

> **Example**
>
> $$\frac{5}{6} \times \frac{2}{3} = \frac{5 \times 2}{6 \times 3} = \frac{10}{18} = \frac{5}{9}$$

Dividing Fractions Dividing by a fraction is the same as multiplying by its reciprocal. Reciprocals are numbers whose numerators and denominators have been switched. To divide one fraction by another, first invert the fraction you are dividing by—in other words, turn it upside down. Then multiply the two fractions.

> **Example**
>
> $$\frac{2}{5} \div \frac{7}{8} = \frac{2}{5} \times \frac{8}{7} = \frac{2 \times 8}{5 \times 7} = \frac{16}{35}$$

> **Practice**
>
> Solve the following: $\frac{3}{7} \div \frac{4}{5}$.

Decimals

Fractions whose denominators are 10, 100, or some other power of 10 are often expressed as decimals. For example, the fraction $\frac{9}{10}$ can be expressed as the decimal 0.9, and the fraction $\frac{7}{100}$ can be written as 0.07.

Adding and Subtracting With Decimals To add or subtract decimals, line up the decimal points before you carry out the operation.

> **Example**
>
> $$\begin{array}{r} 27.4 \\ + \ 6.19 \\ \hline 33.59 \end{array} \qquad \begin{array}{r} 278.635 \\ - \ 191.4 \\ \hline 87.235 \end{array}$$

Multiplying With Decimals When you multiply two numbers with decimals, the number of decimal places in the product is equal to the total number of decimal places in each number being multiplied.

> **Example**
>
> $$\begin{array}{r} 46.2 \ \text{(one decimal place)} \\ \times \ 2.37 \ \text{(two decimal places)} \\ \hline 109.494 \ \text{(three decimal places)} \end{array}$$

Dividing With Decimals To divide a decimal by a whole number, put the decimal point in the quotient above the decimal point in the dividend.

> **Example**
>
> $$15.5 \div 5$$
> $$\begin{array}{r} 3.1 \\ 5\overline{)15.5} \end{array}$$

To divide a decimal by a decimal, you need to rewrite the divisor as a whole number. Do this by multiplying both the divisor and dividend by the same multiple of 10.

> **Example**
>
> $$1.68 \div 4.2 = 16.8 \div 42$$
> $$\begin{array}{r} 0.4 \\ 42\overline{)16.8} \end{array}$$

> **Practice**
>
> Multiply 6.21 by 8.5.

Ratio and Proportion

A **ratio** compares two numbers by division. For example, suppose a scientist counts 800 wolves and 1,200 moose on an island. The ratio of wolves to moose can be written as a fraction, $\frac{800}{1,200}$, which can be reduced to $\frac{2}{3}$. The same ratio can also be expressed as 2 to 3 or 2 : 3.

A **proportion** is a mathematical sentence saying that two ratios are equivalent. For example, a proportion could state that $\frac{800 \text{ wolves}}{1,200 \text{ moose}} = \frac{2 \text{ wolves}}{3 \text{ moose}}$. You can sometimes set up a proportion to determine or estimate an unknown quantity. For example, suppose a scientist counts 25 beetles in an area of 10 square meters. The scientist wants to estimate the number of beetles in 100 square meters.

Example

1. Express the relationship between beetles and area as a ratio: $\frac{25}{10}$, simplified to $\frac{5}{2}$.

2. Set up a proportion, with x representing the number of beetles. The proportion can be stated as $\frac{5}{2} = \frac{x}{100}$.

3. Begin by cross-multiplying. In other words, multiply each fraction's numerator by the other fraction's denominator.

   $5 \times 100 = 2 \times x$, or $500 = 2x$

4. To find the value of x, divide both sides by 2. The result is 250, or 250 beetles in 100 square meters.

Practice

Find the value of x in the following proportion: $\frac{6}{7} = \frac{x}{49}$.

Percentage

A **percentage** is a ratio that compares a number to 100. For example, there are 37 granite rocks in a collection that consists of 100 rocks. The ratio $\frac{37}{100}$ can be written as 37%. Granite rocks make up 37% of the rock collection.

You can calculate percentages of numbers other than 100 by setting up a proportion.

Example

Rain falls on 9 days out of 30 in June. What percentage of the days in June were rainy?

$$\frac{9 \text{ days}}{30 \text{ days}} = \frac{d\%}{100\%}$$

To find the value of d, begin by cross-multiplying, as for any proportion:

$9 \times 100 = 30 \times d \qquad d = \frac{900}{30} \qquad d = 30$

Practice

There are 300 marbles in a jar, and 42 of those marbles are blue. What percentage of the marbles are blue?

Significant Figures

The **precision** of a measurement depends on the instrument you use to take the measurement. For example, if the smallest unit on the ruler is millimeters, then the most precise measurement you can make will be in millimeters.

The sum or difference of measurements can only be as precise as the least precise measurement being added or subtracted. Round your answer so that it has the same number of digits after the decimal as the least precise measurement. Round up if the last digit is 5 or more, and round down if the last digit is 4 or less.

> **Example**
>
> Subtract a temperature of 5.2°C from the temperature 75.46°C.
>
> **75.46 − 5.2 = 70.26**
>
> 5.2 has the fewest digits after the decimal, so it is the least precise measurement. Since the last digit of the answer is 6, round up to 3. The most precise difference between the measurements is 70.3°C.

> **Practice**
>
> Add 26.4 m to 8.37 m. Round your answer according to the precision of the measurements.

Significant figures are the number of nonzero digits in a measurement. Zeroes between nonzero digits are also significant. For example, the measurements 12,500 L, 0.125 cm, and 2.05 kg all have three significant figures. When you multiply and divide measurements, the one with the fewest significant figures determines the number of significant figures in your answer.

> **Example**
>
> Multiply 110 g by 5.75 g.
>
> **110 × 5.75 = 632.5**
>
> Because 110 has only two significant figures, round the answer to 630 g.

Scientific Notation

A **factor** is a number that divides into another number with no remainder. In the example, the number 3 is used as a factor four times.

An **exponent** tells how many times a number is used as a factor. For example, $3 \times 3 \times 3 \times 3$ can be written as 3^4. The exponent 4 indicates that the number 3 is used as a factor four times. Another way of expressing this is to say that 81 is equal to 3 to the fourth power.

> **Example**
>
> $3^4 = 3 \times 3 \times 3 \times 3 = 81$

Scientific notation uses exponents and powers of ten to write very large or very small numbers in shorter form. When you write a number in scientific notation, you write the number as two factors. The first factor is any number between 1 and 10. The second factor is a power of 10, such as 10^3 or 10^6.

> **Example**
>
> The average distance between the planet Mercury and the sun is 58,000,000 km. To write the first factor in scientific notation, insert a decimal point in the original number so that you have a number between 1 and 10. In the case of 58,000,000, the number is 5.8.
>
> To determine the power of 10, count the number of places that the decimal point moved. In this case, it moved 7 places.
>
> **58,000,000 km = 5.8 × 10^7 km**

> **Practice**
>
> Express 6,590,000 in scientific notation.

Reading Comprehension Skills

Each section in your textbook introduces a Target Reading Skill.
You will improve your reading comprehension by using the
Target Reading Skills described below.

Using Prior Knowledge

Your prior knowledge is what you already know before you begin to read about a topic. Building on what you already know gives you a head start on learning new information. Before you begin a new assignment, think about what you know. You might look at the headings and the visuals to spark your memory. You can list what you know. Then, as you read, consider questions like these.

• How does what you learn relate to what you know?

• How did something you already know help you learn something new?

• Did your original ideas agree with what you have just learned?

Asking Questions

Asking yourself questions is an excellent way to focus on and remember new information in your textbook. For example, you can turn the text headings into questions. Then your questions can guide you to identify the important information as you read. Look at these examples:

Heading: Using Seismographic Data
Question: How are seismographic data used?
Heading: Kinds of Faults
Question: What are the kinds of faults?

You do not have to limit your questions to text headings. Ask questions about anything that you need to clarify or that will help you understand the content. *What* and *how* are probably the most common question words, but you may also ask *why*, *who*, *when*, or *where* questions.

Previewing Visuals

Visuals are photographs, graphs, tables, diagrams, and illustrations. Visuals contain important information. Before you read, look at visuals and their labels and captions. This preview will help you prepare for what you will be reading.

Often you will be asked what you want to learn about a visual. For example, after you look at the normal fault diagram below, you might ask: What is the movement along a normal fault? Questions about visuals give you a purpose for reading—to answer your questions.

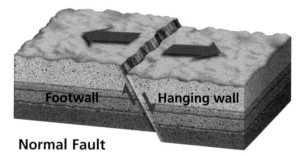

Footwall   Hanging wall

Normal Fault

Outlining

An outline shows the relationship between main ideas and supporting ideas. An outline has a formal structure. You write the main ideas, called topics, next to Roman numerals. The supporting ideas, called subtopics, are written under the main ideas and labeled A, B, C, and so on. An outline looks like this:

Technology and Society
I. Technology through history
II. The impact of technology on society
A.
B.

Identifying Main Ideas

When you are reading science material, it is important to try to understand the ideas and concepts that are in a passage. Each paragraph has a lot of information and detail. Good readers try to identify the most important—or biggest—idea in every paragraph or section. That's the main idea. The other information in the paragraph supports or further explains the main idea.

Sometimes main ideas are stated directly. In this book, some main ideas are identified for you as key concepts. These are printed in boldface type. However, you must identify other main ideas yourself. In order to do this, you must identify all the ideas within a paragraph or section. Then ask yourself which idea is big enough to include all the other ideas.

Comparing and Contrasting

When you compare and contrast, you examine the similarities and differences between things. You can compare and contrast in a Venn diagram or in a table.

Venn Diagram A Venn diagram consists of two overlapping circles. In the space where the circles overlap, you write the characteristics that the two items have in common. In one of the circles outside the area of overlap, you write the differing features or characteristics of one of the items. In the other circle outside the area of overlap, you write the differing characteristics of the other item.

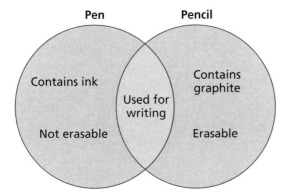

Table In a compare/contrast table, you list the characteristics or features to be compared across the top of the table. Then list the items to be compared in the left column. Complete the table by filling in information about each characteristic or feature.

Blood Vessel	Function	Structure of Wall
Artery	Carries blood away from heart	
Capillary		
Vein		

Identifying Supporting Evidence

A hypothesis is a possible explanation for observations made by scientists or an answer to a scientific question. Scientists must carry out investigations and gather evidence that either supports or disproves the hypothesis.

Identifying the supporting evidence for a hypothesis or theory can help you understand the hypothesis or theory. Evidence consists of facts—information whose accuracy can be confirmed by testing or observation.

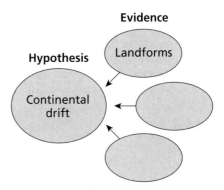

Sequencing

A sequence is the order in which a series of events occurs. A flowchart or a cycle diagram can help you visualize a sequence.

Flowchart To make a flowchart, write a brief description of each step or event in a box. Place the boxes in order, with the first event at the top of the page. Then draw an arrow to connect each step or event to the next.

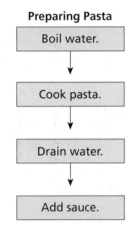

Preparing Pasta

Boil water.

↓

Cook pasta.

↓

Drain water.

↓

Add sauce.

Cycle Diagram A cycle diagram shows a sequence that is continuous, or cyclical. A continuous sequence does not have an end because when the final event is over, the first event begins again. To create a cycle diagram, write the starting event in a box placed at the top of a page in the center. Then, moving in a clockwise direction, write each event in a box in its proper sequence. Draw arrows that connect each event to the one that occurs next.

Seasons of the Year

Relating Cause and Effect

Science involves many cause-and-effect relationships. A cause makes something happen. An effect is what happens. When you recognize that one event causes another, you are relating cause and effect.

Words like *cause, because, effect, affect,* and *result* often signal a cause or an effect. Sometimes an effect can have more than one cause, or a cause can produce several effects.

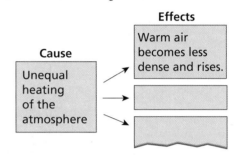

Cause

Unequal heating of the atmosphere

Effects

Warm air becomes less dense and rises.

Concept Mapping

Concept maps are useful tools for organizing information on any topic. A concept map begins with a main idea or core concept and shows how the idea can be subdivided into related subconcepts or smaller ideas.

You construct a concept map by placing concepts (usually nouns) in ovals and connecting them with linking words (usually verbs). The biggest concept or idea is placed in an oval at the top of the map. Related concepts are arranged in ovals below the big idea. The linking words connect the ovals.

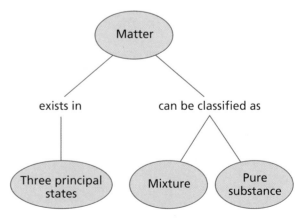

Matter

exists in — can be classified as

Three principal states

Mixture

Pure substance

Building Vocabulary

Knowing the meaning of these prefixes, suffixes, and roots will help you understand the meaning of words you do not recognize.

Word Origins Many science words come to English from other languages, such as Greek and Latin. By learning the meaning of a few common Greek and Latin roots, you can determine the meaning of unfamiliar science words.

Prefixes A prefix is a word part that is added at the beginning of a root or base word to change its meaning.

Suffixes A suffix is a word part that is added at the end of a root word to change the meaning.

Greek and Latin Roots		
Greek Roots	**Meaning**	**Example**
ast-	star	astronaut
geo-	Earth	geology
metron-	measure	kilometer
opt-	eye	optician
photo-	light	photograph
scop-	see	microscope
therm-	heat	thermostat
Latin Roots	**Meaning**	**Example**
aqua-	water	aquarium
aud-	hear	auditorium
duc-, duct-	lead	conduct
flect-	bend	reflect
fract-, frag-	break	fracture
ject-	throw	reject
luc-	light	lucid
spec-	see	inspect

Prefixes and Suffixes		
Prefix	**Meaning**	**Example**
com-, con-	with	communicate, concert
de-	from; down	decay
di-	two	divide
ex-, exo-	out	exhaust
in-, im-	in, into; not	inject, impossible
re-	again; back	reflect, recall
trans-	across	transfer
Suffix	**Meaning**	**Example**
-al	relating to	natural
-er, -or	one who	teacher, doctor
-ist	one who practices	scientist
-ity	state of	equality
-ology	study of	biology
-tion, -sion	state or quality of	reaction, tension

Safety Symbols

These symbols warn of possible dangers in the laboratory and remind you to work carefully.

 Safety Goggles Wear safety goggles to protect your eyes in any activity involving chemicals, flames or heating, or glassware.

 Lab Apron Wear a laboratory apron to protect your skin and clothing from damage.

 Breakage Handle breakable materials, such as glassware, with care. Do not touch broken glassware.

 Heat-Resistant Gloves Use an oven mitt or other hand protection when handling hot materials such as hot plates or hot glassware.

 Plastic Gloves Wear disposable plastic gloves when working with harmful chemicals and organisms. Keep your hands away from your face, and dispose of the gloves according to your teacher's instructions.

 Heating Use a clamp or tongs to pick up hot glassware. Do not touch hot objects with your bare hands.

 Flames Before you work with flames, tie back loose hair and clothing. Follow instructions from your teacher about lighting and extinguishing flames.

 No Flames When using flammable materials, make sure there are no flames, sparks, or other exposed heat sources present.

 Corrosive Chemical Avoid getting acid or other corrosive chemicals on your skin or clothing or in your eyes. Do not inhale the vapors. Wash your hands after the activity.

 Poison Do not let any poisonous chemical come into contact with your skin, and do not inhale its vapors. Wash your hands when you are finished with the activity.

 Fumes Work in a ventilated area when harmful vapors may be involved. Avoid inhaling vapors directly. Only test an odor when directed to do so by your teacher, and use a wafting motion to direct the vapor toward your nose.

 Sharp Object Scissors, scalpels, knives, needles, pins, and tacks can cut your skin. Always direct a sharp edge or point away from yourself and others.

 Animal Safety Treat live or preserved animals or animal parts with care to avoid harming the animals or yourself. Wash your hands when you are finished with the activity.

 Plant Safety Handle plants only as directed by your teacher. If you are allergic to certain plants, tell your teacher; do not do an activity involving those plants. Avoid touching harmful plants such as poison ivy. Wash your hands when you are finished with the activity.

 Electric Shock To avoid electric shock, never use electrical equipment around water, or when the equipment is wet or your hands are wet. Be sure cords are untangled and cannot trip anyone. Unplug equipment not in use.

 Physical Safety When an experiment involves physical activity, avoid injuring yourself or others. Alert your teacher if there is any reason you should not participate.

 Disposal Dispose of chemicals and other laboratory materials safely. Follow the instructions from your teacher.

 Hand Washing Wash your hands thoroughly when finished with the activity. Use antibacterial soap and warm water. Rinse well.

 General Safety Awareness When this symbol appears, follow the instructions provided. When you are asked to develop your own procedure in a lab, have your teacher approve your plan before you go further.

Science Safety Rules

General Precautions

Follow all instructions. Never perform activities without the approval and supervision of your teacher. Do not engage in horseplay. Never eat or drink in the laboratory. Keep work areas clean and uncluttered.

Dress Code

Wear safety goggles whenever you work with chemicals, glassware, heat sources such as burners, or any substance that might get into your eyes. If you wear contact lenses, notify your teacher.

Wear a lab apron or coat whenever you work with corrosive chemicals or substances that can stain. Wear disposable plastic gloves when working with organisms and harmful chemicals. Tie back long hair. Remove or tie back any article of clothing or jewelry that can hang down and touch chemicals, flames, or equipment. Roll up long sleeves. Never wear open shoes or sandals.

First Aid

Report all accidents, injuries, or fires to your teacher, no matter how minor. Be aware of the location of the first-aid kit, emergency equipment such as the fire extinguisher and fire blanket, and the nearest telephone. Know whom to contact in an emergency.

Heating and Fire Safety

Keep all combustible materials away from flames. When heating a substance in a test tube, make sure that the mouth of the tube is not pointed at you or anyone else. Never heat a liquid in a closed container. Use an oven mitt to pick up a container that has been heated.

Using Chemicals Safely

Never put your face near the mouth of a container that holds chemicals. Never touch, taste, or smell a chemical unless your teacher tells you to.

Use only those chemicals needed in the activity. Keep all containers closed when chemicals are not being used. Pour all chemicals over the sink or a container, not over your work surface. Dispose of excess chemicals as instructed by your teacher.

Be extra careful when working with acids or bases. When mixing an acid and water, always pour the water into the container first and then add the acid to the water. Never pour water into an acid. Wash chemical spills and splashes immediately with plenty of water.

Using Glassware Safely

If glassware is broken or chipped, notify your teacher immediately. Never handle broken or chipped glass with your bare hands.

Never force glass tubing or thermometers into a rubber stopper or rubber tubing. Have your teacher insert the glass tubing or thermometer if required for an activity.

Using Sharp Instruments

Handle sharp instruments with extreme care. Never cut material toward you; cut away from you.

Animal and Plant Safety

Never perform experiments that cause pain, discomfort, or harm to animals. Only handle animals if absolutely necessary. If you know that you are allergic to certain plants, molds, or animals, tell your teacher before doing an activity in which these are used. Wash your hands thoroughly after any activity involving animals, animal parts, plants, plant parts, or soil.

During field work, wear long pants, long sleeves, socks, and closed shoes. Avoid poisonous plants and fungi as well as plants with thorns.

End-of-Experiment Rules

Unplug all electrical equipment. Clean up your work area. Dispose of waste materials as instructed by your teacher. Wash your hands after every experiment.

English and Spanish Glossary

alternating current Current consisting of charges that move back and forth in a circuit. (p. 97)
corriente alterna Corriente que consiste en cargas eléctricas que se mueven hacia adelante y hacia atrás en un circuito.

ammeter A device used to measure current in a circuit. (p. 64)
amperímetro Aparato usado para medir la corriente en un circuito.

amplitude The height of a wave from the center to a crest or trough. (p. 119)
amplitud Altura de una onda desde su parte media a la cresta o al valle.

amplitude modulation (AM) A change in the amplitude of a carrier wave to match the amplitude of a signal. (p. 119)
amplitud modulada (AM) Cambio en la amplitud de una onda portadora para que corresponda con la amplitud de la señal.

analog signal An electric current that is varied smoothly to represent information. (p. 109)
señal analógica Corriente eléctrica que varía levemente para representar información.

atom The smallest particle of an element that has the properties of that element. (p. 15)
átomo La partícula más pequeña de un elemento, que tiene las propiedades de ese elemento.

aurora A glowing region produced by the interaction of charged particles from the sun and atoms in the atmosphere. (p. 27)
aurora polar Área resplandeciente en la atmósfera de la Tierra producida por la interacción de partículas cargadas del Sol y los átomos de la atmósfera.

battery A combination of two or more electrochemical cells in series. (p. 56)
pila Combinación de dos o más celdas electroquímicas en serie.

binary system A number system using combinations of only two digits, 0 and 1. (p. 123)
sistema binario Sistema de números que usa combinaciones de sólo dos dígitos, 0 y 1.

central processing unit (CPU) Directs the operation of a computer, performs logical operations and calculations. (p. 125)
unidad central de procesamiento (CPU) Dirige la operación de una computadora, realiza operaciones y cálculos lógicos.

chat room A network feature that allows two or more users to exchange messages. (p. 135)
salón de charla Característica de una red que permite que dos o más usuarios intercambien mensajes.

chemical energy The energy stored in chemical compounds. (p. 55)
energía química Energía almacenada en los compuestos químicos.

chemical reaction A process in which substances change into new substances with different properties. (p. 55)
reacción química Proceso por el cual las sustancias químicas se convierten en nuevas sustancias químicas con propiedades diferentes.

circuit breaker A reusable safety switch that breaks the circuit when the current becomes too high. (p. 73)
interruptor de circuito Interruptor de seguridad que se puede volver a usar, que se usa para cortar el circuito cuando la corriente es demasiado alta.

compass A device with a magnetized needle that can spin freely. (p. 22)
brújula Instrumento con una aguja imantada que puede girar libremente.

computer An electronic device that stores, processes, and retrieves information. (p. 123)
computadora Aparato electrónico que almacena, procesa y obtiene información.

computer network A group of computers connected by cables or telephone lines that allows people to share information. (p. 132)
red de computadoras Grupo de computadoras conectadas por cables o líneas telefónicas que permite que la gente comparta información.

computer programmer A person who uses computer languages to write programs, or sets of operation instructions, for computers. (p. 129)
programador de computadoras Persona que usa los lenguajes de computación para escribir programas o conjuntos de instrucciones de operaciones para computadoras.

computer virus A program that can enter a computer, destroy files, and disable the computer. (p. 134)
virus de computadoras Programa que puede entrar en una computadora, destruir documentos y estropearla.

conduction A method of charging an object by allowing electrons to flow by direct contact from one object to another object. (p. 38)
conducción Método para cargar un objeto que consiste en permitir que los electrones fluyan por contacto directo de un objeto a otro.

conductor A material through which charges can easily flow. (p. 47)
conductor Material a través del cual pueden fluir las cargas eléctricas fácilmente.

conservation of charge The law that states that charges are neither created nor destroyed but only transferred from one material to another. (p. 38)
conservación de la carga eléctrica Ley que enuncia que las cargas no se crean ni se destruyen, sino que sólo se transfieren de un material a otro.

D

digital signal Pulses of current used to represent information. (p. 109)
señal digital Pulsaciones de corriente que se usan para representar información.

diode An electronic component that consists of layers of two types of semiconductors. (p. 111)
diodo Componente electrónico que consiste en capas de dos tipos de semiconductores.

direct current Current consisting of charges that flow in only one direction in a circuit. (p. 96)
corriente directa Corriente que consiste en cargas eléctricas que fluyen en una sola dirección en un circuito.

dry cell An electrochemical cell in which the electrolyte is a paste. (p. 57)
celda seca Celda electroquímica en la que el electrolito es una pasta.

E

electrical energy The energy of moving electrical charges. (p. 86)
energía eléctrica Energía de cargas eléctricas que se mueven.

electric circuit A complete, unbroken path through which electric charges can flow. (p. 46)
circuito eléctrico Camino completo y continuo a través del cual pueden fluir las cargas eléctricas.

electric current The continuous flow of electric charges through a material. (p. 45)
corriente eléctrica Flujo continuo de cargas eléctricas a través de un material.

electric field The region around a charged object where the object's electric force interacts with other charged objects. (p. 36)
campo eléctrico Región alrededor de un objeto cargado en donde su fuerza eléctrica interactúa con otros objetos con carga eléctrica.

electric force The attraction or repulsion between electric charges. (p. 36)
fuerza eléctrica Atracción o repulsión entre cargas eléctricas.

electric generator A device that transforms mechanical energy into electrical energy. (p. 98)
generador eléctrico Instrumento que convierte la energía mecánica en energía eléctrica.

electric motor A device that transforms electrical energy to mechanical energy. (p. 88)
motor eléctrico Instrumento que convierte la energía eléctrica en energía mecánica.

electrochemical cell A device that transforms chemical energy into electrical energy. (p. 56)
celda electroquímica Instrumento que convierte la energía química en energía eléctrica.

electrode A metal part of an electrochemical cell, which gains or loses electrons. (p. 56)
electrodo Parte metálica de una celda electroquímica que gana o pierde electrones.

electrolyte A liquid or paste that conducts electric current. (p. 56)
electrolito Líquido o pasta que conduce la corriente eléctrica.

electromagnet A magnet created by wrapping a coil of wire with a current around a ferromagnetic core. (p. 83)
electroimán Imán creado al enrollar una espiral de alambre con corriente alrededor de un núcleo ferromagnético.

electromagnetic induction The process of generating an electric current from the motion of a conductor through a magnetic field. (p. 94)
inducción electromagnética Proceso por el cual se genera una corriente eléctrica a partir del movimiento de un conductor a través de un campo magnético.

electromagnetic wave A wave made up of a combination of a changing electric field and changing magnetic field. (p. 118)
onda electromagnética Onda formada por una combinación de un campo eléctrico cambiante y un campo magnético cambiante.

electromagnetism The relationship between electricity and magnetism. (p. 81)
electromagnetismo Relación entre la electricidad y el magnetismo.

electron A negatively charged particle that is found outside the nucleus of an atom. (p. 15)
electrón Partícula con carga negativa que se halla fuera del núcleo de un átomo.

electronic signal A varying electric current that represents information. (p. 108)
señal electrónica Corriente eléctrica variable que representa información.

electronics The use of electric current to control, communicate, and process information. (p. 108)
electrónica Uso de la corriente eléctrica para controlar, comunicar y procesar información.

element One of about 100 basic materials that make up all matter. (p. 15)
elemento Uno de aproximadamente 100 materiales básicos que componen toda la materia.

encryption A process of coding information so that only the intended user can read it. (p. 134)
encriptación Proceso de codificación de la información para que sólo la pueda leer el usuario deseado.

energy The ability to move an object some distance. (p. 86)
energía Capacidad para mover un objeto a una determinada distancia.

F

ferromagnetic material A material that is strongly attracted to a magnet, and which can be made into a magnet. (p. 17)
material ferromagnético Material que es atraído fuertemente a un imán y el cual puede transformarse en un imán.

frequency The number of waves passing a given point each second. (p. 119)
frecuencia Número de ondas que pasan por un punto dado en un segundo.

frequency modulation (FM) A change in the frequency of a carrier wave to match the amplitude of a signal. (p. 119)
frecuencia modulada (FM) Cambio en la frecuencia de una onda portadora para que corresponda con la amplitud de la señal.

friction A method of charging an object by rubbing it against another object; the force that one object exerts on another when the two rub against each other. (p. 38)
fricción Método para cargar con electricidad un objeto que consiste en frotarlo contra otro objeto; fuerza que ejerce un objeto sobre otro cuando se frotan mutuamente.

fuse A safety device with a thin metal strip that will melt if too much current passes through a circuit. (p. 73)
fusible Elemento de seguridad que tiene una tira metálica delgada que se derrite si pasa demasiada corriente a través de un circuito.

G

galvanometer A device that uses an electromagnet to detect small amounts of current. (p. 87)
galvanómetro Instrumento que usa un electroimán para detectar pequeñas cantidades de corriente.

grounded Allowing charges to flow directly from the circuit into Earth in the event of a short circuit. (p. 72)
conectado a tierra Permitir que la carga fluya directamente del circuito a la Tierra en el caso de un cortocircuito.

H

hardware The permanent components of a computer, including the central processing unit and input, output, and memory storage devices. (p. 125)
hardware Componentes permanentes de una computadora, incluyendo la unidad central de procesamiento, dispositivos de entrada y salida, y dispositivos de registro de memoria.

I

induction A method of charging an object by means of the electric field of another object; the objects have no direct contact. (p. 38)
inducción Método para cargar un objeto mediante el campo eléctrico de otro objeto; objetos que no están en contacto directo.

input device A device that feeds data to a CPU; a keyboard is an input device. (p. 125)
dispositivo de entrada Dispositivo que envía información a una CPU; un teclado es un dispositivo de entrada.

insulator A material through which charges cannot easily flow. (p. 47)
aislante Material a través del cual las cargas eléctricas no pueden fluir con facilidad.

integrated circuit A circuit that has been manufactured on a chip (a tiny slice of semiconductor), which can contain thousands of diodes, transistors, and resistors. (p. 112)
circuito integrado Circuito que ha sido fabricado en un chip (una diminuta placa de un semiconductor), que puede contener miles de diodos, transistores y resistores.

intellectual property A story, poem, computer program, or similar product owned by the author. (p. 135)
propiedad intelectual Cuento, poema, programa de computadoras o producto similar que pertenece al autor.

Internet An international computer network that shares data, information, and news; the Internet links millions of businesses, schools, research organizations, and individual users. (p. 133)
Internet Red de computadoras internacional que comparte datos, información y noticias; la Internet conecta millones de negocios, escuelas, organizaciones de investigación y usuarios individuales.

magnet Any material that attracts iron and materials that contain iron. (p. 7)
imán Material que atrae hierro y materiales que contienen hierro.

magnetic declination The angle between geographic north and the north to which a compass needle points. (p. 24)
declinación magnética Ángulo entre el norte geográfico y el norte hacia donde apunta la alguja de una brújula.

magnetic domain A region in which the magnetic fields of all atoms are lined up in the same direction. (p. 16)
dominio magnético Área en la que los campos magnéticos de todos los átomos están alineados en la misma dirección.

magnetic field The region around a magnet where the magnetic force is exerted. (p. 9)
campo magnético Área alrededor de un imán en la cual se ejerce la fuerza magnética.

magnetic field lines Invisible lines that map out the magnetic field around a magnet. (p. 9)
líneas del campo magnético Líneas invisibles que representan el campo magnético alrededor de un imán.

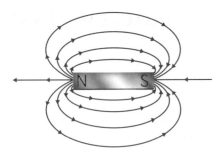

magnetic force A force produced when magnetic poles interact. (p. 8)
fuerza magnética Fuerza que se produce cuando interactúan los polos magnéticos.

magnetic pole The ends of a magnetic object, where the magnetic force is strongest. (p. 8)
polo magnético Extremo de un objeto magnético, donde la fuerza magnética es mayor.

magnetism The force of attraction or repulsion of magnetic materials. (p. 7)
magnetismo Atracción o repulsión de materiales magnéticos.

magnetosphere The region of Earth's magnetic field shaped by the solar wind. (p. 26)
magnetosfera Área del campo magnético de la Tierra formada por el viento solar.

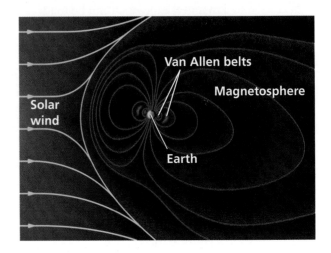

mechanical energy The energy an object has due to its movement or position. (p. 86)
energía mecánica Energía que tiene un objeto debido a su movimiento o posición.

neutron The small uncharged particle that is found in the nucleus of an atom. (p. 15)
neutrón Partícula pequeña sin carga que se haya en el núcleo de un átomo.

nucleus The core at the center of every atom. (p. 15)
núcleo Centro de un átomo.

Ohm's law The law that states that resistance is equal to voltage divided by current. (p. 61)
ley de Ohm Ley que enuncia que la resistencia es igual al voltaje dividido por la corriente.

output device A device that presents data from a computer; a monitor is an output device. (p. 125)
dispositivo de salida Dispositivo que presenta información de una computadora; un monitor es un dispositivo de salida.

parallel circuit An electric circuit with multiple paths. (p. 65)
 circuito paralelo Circuito eléctrico con caminos múltiples.

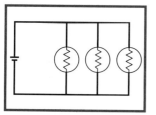

permanent magnet A magnet made of material that keeps its magnetism. (p. 18)
 imán permanente Imán hecho de un material que mantiene su magnetismo.

power The rate at which one form of energy is transformed into another; the unit of power is the watt. (p. 68)
 potencia Razón a la cual una forma de energía se convierte en otra; la unidad de potencia es el vatio.

proton A positively charged particle that is part of an atom's nucleus. (p. 15)
 protón Partícula con carga positiva ubicada en el núcleo de un átomo.

R

resistance The measurement of how difficult it is for charges to flow through a material. (p. 50)
 resistencia Medida de lo difícil que es para las cargas eléctricas fluir a través de un material.

S

semiconductor A material that conducts current under certain conditions. (p. 110)
 semiconductor Material que conduce la corriente bajo ciertas condiciones.

series circuit An electric circuit with a single path. (p. 64)
 circuito en serie Circuito eléctrico con un solo camino.

short circuit A connection that allows current to take an unintended path. (p. 71)
 cortocircuito Conexión que permite que la corriente tome un camino no establecido.

software A detailed set of instructions that directs the computer hardware to perform operations on stored information. (p. 128)
 software Conjunto de instrucciones detalladas que dirige el hardware de una computadora para que realice operaciones con la información almacenada.

solar wind Streams of electrically charged particles flowing at high speeds from the sun; solar wind pushes against Earth's magnetic field and surrounds it. (p. 26)
 viento solar Corrientes de partículas con carga eléctrica que fluyen a gran velocidad desde el Sol; el viento solar empuja el campo magnético de la Tierra y lo rodea

solenoid A coil of wire with a current that acts as a bar magnet. (p. 82)
 solenoide Espiral de alambre con una corriente que actúa como un imán de barra.

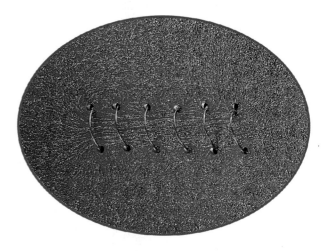

static discharge The loss of static electricity as electric charges transfer from one object to another. (p. 40)
 descarga estática Pérdida de la electricidad estática cuando las cargas eléctricas se transfieren de un objeto a otro.

static electricity A buildup of charges on an object. (p. 37)
 electricidad estática Acumulación de cargas eléctricas en un objeto.

step-down transformer A transformer that decreases voltage. (p. 101)
 transformador reductor Transformador que disminuye el voltaje.

step-up transformer A transformer that increases voltage. (p. 100)
 transformador elevador Transformador que aumenta el voltaje.

T

temporary magnet A magnet made from a material that easily loses its magnetism. (p. 18)
imán temporal Imán hecho de un material que pierde fácilmente su magnetismo.

terminal A convenient attachment point used to connect a cell or battery to a circuit. (p. 56)
terminal Punto de conexión conveniente que se usa para conectar una celda o batería a un circuito.

third prong The round prong of a plug that connects any metal pieces in an appliance to the safety grounding wire of a building. (p. 72)
tercer terminal Terminal redondeado de un enchufe que conecta cualquier parte de metal de un artefacto con el alambre a tierra de un edificio.

transformer A device that increases or decreases voltage. (p. 99)
transformador Instrumento que aumenta o disminuye el voltaje.

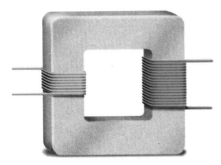

transistor An electronic component used to amplify an electronic signal or to switch current on and off. (p. 111)
transistor Componente electrónico que se usa para amplificar una señal electrónica o apagar y encender la corriente.

V

Van Allen belts Two doughnut-shaped regions 1,000–25,000 kilometers above Earth that contain electrons and protons traveling at high speed. (p. 26)
cinturones de Van Allen Par de regiones circulares ubicadas de 1,000 a 25,000 kilómetros de la Tierra; están formadas de electrones y protones que viajan a alta velocidad.

voltage The difference in electrical potential energy between two places in a circuit. (p. 49)
voltaje Diferencia en la energía potencial eléctrica entre dos lugares en un circuito.

voltage source A device that creates an electrical potential energy difference in an electric circuit; batteries and generators are voltage sources. (p. 49)
fuente de voltaje Instrumento que crea una diferencia en la energía potencial eléctrica en un circuito eléctrico; las pilas y los generadores son fuentes de voltaje.

voltmeter A device used to measure voltage, or electrical potential energy difference. (p. 66)
voltímetro Aparato usado para medir el voltaje o la diferencia de energía eléctrica potencial.

W

wet cell An electrochemical cell in which the electrolyte is a liquid. (p. 57)
celda húmeda Celda electroquímica en la que el electrolito es un líquido.

World Wide Web A part of the Internet that allows the displaying and viewing of text, pictures, video, and sound. (p. 133)
World Wide Web (WWW) Parte de la Internet que permite la presentación y visión de texto, fotos, video y sonido

Page numbers for key terms are printed in **boldface** type.
Page numbers for illustrations, maps, and charts are printed in *italics*.

Index

A

abacus 123
AC 97
AC generators 98
alloy, magnetic 17
alnico (magnetic alloy) 17
alternating current **97**
  AC generator 98
  diodes and change to direct current *111*
ammeter **64**
Ampère, André Marie 45
ampere (amp or A) 45
amplifier, transistor as 111
amplitude **119**
amplitude modulation (AM) **119**
analog signals *109*
analog sound recording 116
antenna 120, 121
appliances
  energy used by, calculating 70
  power rating for 68
applications software 128
area **160**
armature
  in electric motor *88*, 89
  in generator 98
atom *15*
  electron spin and magnetic properties of 15
  structure of 15
attraction of unlike magnetic poles 8
audio signal
  on radio 120
  on television 121
aurora australis 27
aurora borealis 27
auroras *27*
axle in electric motor 88

B

Babbage, Charles *126*
bar graph, digital signal represented by 109
base-10 number system 124
batteries 49, 54–55, **56**, 57
  development of first 55
  direct current from **96**
  electrochemical cells **56–57**
Bell, Alexander Graham 114
binary system **123**–124

bits 124
brainstorming **154**
bytes 124

C

cable television networks 121
calculating, skill of **151**
calculator 123
carrier wave 119, 120, 121
cathode-ray tubes 122
CD or compact disc 117
Celsius scale **151**
census counting machine *126*
central processing unit (CPU) **125**
charges, electric. *See* electric charge(s)
chat rooms **135**
chemical energy **55**
  transformation into electrical energy 56–57
chemical reaction **55**
  between electrolyte and electrodes in electrochemical cell 56
chip, integrated circuit 112
  in computers 124
circuit, integrated *112*, 124. *See also* electric circuit
circuit breaker *73*
classifying, skill of **149**
cobalt 17
Columbus, Christopher 22
combined magnetic fields *10*, *11*
communicating, skill of **149**
communication, electronic. *See* electronic communication
communications satellites 121
commutator 89, 98
compact disc (CD) 117
compass *22*
  observing electromagnetism with 80, 81
computer(s) **123–129**
  binary system used by **123**–124
  development of *126–127*
  hardware **125**–127
  magnetic resonance imaging and 90–91
  photography and 136–137
  safe use of 134–135
  software *128*–129, 133, 134
computer languages 129

computer networks *132*–133
  computer safety and 134–135
  types of 133
computer program. *See* **software, computer**
computer programmers 129
computer viruses 134
conclusion **153**
conduction **38**
  charging by 38, *39*, 41
conduction electrons 47
conductors *47*
  low resistance of 50
  motion through magnetic field, induced current from 94–97
conservation of charge 38
constraints **154**
controlled experiment **153**
copyrights, respecting 135
core, Earth's 23
CPU 125
crests of waves 119
Current, electric. *See* **Electric current**

D

data **153**
DC 96
DC generator/motor 98
dialing mechanism of telephone 115
diameter, resistance and 51
Difference Engine *126*
digital manipulation 136–137
digital signals *109*
  computers' use of 124
digital sound recording 117
diodes *111*
direct current (DC) **96**
  advantage of AC over 97
  DC generator 98
  diodes to change alternating current to *111*
disk 127
disk drive 127
disk operating system (DOS) 128
dry cell 56, **57**

E

Earth, magnetic 22–27
  Earth as magnet maker 25
  Earth's core and 23
  magnetic declination and *24*

Index

Page numbers for key terms are printed in **boldface** type.
Page numbers for illustrations, maps, and charts are printed in *italics*.

Index

Page numbers for key terms are printed in **boldface** type.
Page numbers for illustrations, maps, and charts are printed in *italics*.

Acknowledgments

Staff Credits

Diane Alimena, Scott Andrews, Jennifer Angel, Michele Angelucci, Laura Baselice, Carolyn Belanger, Barbara A. Bertell, Suzanne Biron, Peggy Bliss, Stephanie Bradley, James Brady, Anne M. Bray, Sarah M. Carroll, Kerry Cashman, Jonathan Cheney, Joshua D. Clapper, Lisa J. Clark, Bob Craton, Patricia Cully, Patricia M. Dambry, Kathy Dempsey, Leanne Esterly, Emily Ellen, Thomas Ferreira, Jonathan Fisher, Patricia Fromkin, Paul Gagnon, Kathy Gavilanes, Holly Gordon, Robert Graham, Ellen Granter, Diane Grossman, Barbara Hollingdale, Linda Johnson, Anne Jones, John Judge, Kevin Keane, Kelly Kelliher, Toby Klang, Sue Langan, Russ Lappa, Carolyn Lock, Rebecca Loveys, Constance J. McCarty, Carolyn B. McGuire, Ranida Touranont McKneally, Anne McLaughlin, Eve Melnechuk, Natania Mlawer, Janet Morris, Karyl Murray, Francine Neumann, Baljit Nijjar, Marie Opera, Jill Ort, Kim Ortell, Joan Paley, Dorothy Preston, Maureen Raymond, Laura Ross, Rashid Ross, Siri Schwartzman, Melissa Shustyk, Laurel Smith, Emily Soltanoff, Jennifer A. Teece, Elizabeth Torjussen, Amanda M. Watters, Merce Wilczek, Amy Winchester, Char Lyn Yeakley. **Additional Credits:** Tara Alamilla, Louise Gachet, Allen Gold, Andrea Golden, Terence Hegarty, Etta Jacobs, Meg Montgomery, Stephanie Rogers, Kim Schmidt, Adam Teller, Joan Tobin.

Illustration

Kerry Cashman: 108; **David Corrente:** 16, 23, 84, 98, 100t, 104, 111, 118, 120, 122; **John Edwards:** 90–91, 100b, 121; **Ray Goudey:** 45, 48–49; **J/B Woolsey Associates:** 64–65, 76, 115, 119; **Richard McMahon:** 36, 50, 63, 86–87, 92, 95–97, 99b, 126–127, 136–137; **Morgan Cain & Associates:** 9–11, 19, 25, 30–31, 35, 40, 82–83; **Precision Graphics:** 55–57, 88, 99t, 119, 140; **Ted Smykel:** 15, 17, 24, 46, 59, 110. **All charts and graphs by Matt Mayerchak.**

Photography

Photo Research John Judge
Cover Image top, Tom Ives/Corbis; **bottom,** Thom Lang/Corbis

Page vi, Manfred Kage/Peter Arnold; **vii, viii,** Richard Haynes; **x, 1,** Tom Trower/Ames Research Center/NASA; **2 all,** Ames Research Center/NASA; **3b,** Tom Trower/Ames Research Center/NASA; **3t,** Ames Research Center/NASA.

Chapter 1
Pages 4–5, Wayne R. Bilenduke/Getty Images, Inc.; **5 inset,** Richard Haynes; **6b,** Marcello Bertinetti/Photo Researcher, Inc; **6t,** Richard Haynes; **7b,** Richard Haynes; **7t,** Russ Lappa; **8 both,** Richard Megna/Fundamental Photographs; **10,** Richard Megna/Fundamental Photographs; **11 both,** Richard Megna/Fundamental Photographs; **12b,** Richard Haynes; **12t,** Aaron Rezny/The Stock Market; **13,** Richard Haynes; **14 both,** Richard Haynes; **17 both,** Richard Haynes; **18, 20, 21,** Richard Haynes; **22b,** Sisse Brimberg/National Geographic Image; **22t,** Russ Lappa; **27,** Kennan Ward/Corbis; **28b,** Richard Haynes; **28t,** Sisse Brimberg/National Geographic Image.

Chapter 2
Pages 32–33, Owaki-Kulla/Corbis; **33 inset,** Richard Haynes; **34 both,** Richard Haynes; **37 all,** Richard Haynes; **38, 39,** Richard Haynes; **41,** Jeff Hunter/Getty Images, Inc.; **42, 43,** Richard Haynes; **44b,** Larry Lefever/Grant Heilman Photography, Inc.; **44t,** Russ Lappa; **46, 47, 48,** Richard Haynes; **49,** Peter Anderson/Dorling Kindersley; **49 inset,** Adrian Weinbrecht/Photo Library.com; **51,** Johan van Jaarsveld/Gallo Images/Corbis; **52,** Mark Burnett/Stock Boston; **53,** Richard Haynes; **54b,** Patitucci Photo/Raw Talent Photo; **54t,** Russ Lappa; **55,** J-L Charmet/Science Photo Library/Photo Researcher, Inc; **58,** Kevin Cruff/FPG International; **59,** Richard Haynes; **60,** Chris Rawlings/Getty Images, Inc.; **61,** Richard Haynes; **62,** Ron Kimball/Ron Kimball Stock; **63, 64, 65, 66,** Russ Lappa; **67b,** Justin Pumfrey/Getty Images, Inc.; **67t,** Russ Lappa; **68l,** Getty Images, Inc.; **68ml,** Getty Images, Inc.; **68mr,** Gamma Ray Studio Inc/Getty Images, Inc.; **68r,** Whirlpool; **70b,** Toni Micheals; **70t,** B. Daemmrich/Stock Market; **71b,** Joel Page/AP Wide World; **71t,** Russ Lappa; **73,** Richard Haynes.

Chapter 3
Pages 78–79, Justin Sullivan/Getty Images, Inc.; **79 inset,** Jon Chomitz; **80,** Russ Lappa; **81b,** Richard Megna/Fundamental Photographs; **81t,** Richard Haynes; **82,** Richard Megna/Fundamental Photographs; **84,** Dick Durrance II/The Stock Market; **85b,** Prentice Hall School Division; **85t,** Russ Lappa; **87,** Richard Haynes; **89,** Tim Ridley/Dorling Kindersley; **91l,** UHB Trust/Getty Images, Inc.; **91m,** CNRI/SPL/Photo Researchers, Inc.; **91r,** Alfred Pasieka/SPL/Photo Researchers, Inc.; **92l,** Russ Lappa; **92r,** Richard Haynes; **93b,** Zoran Milich/Masterfile; **93t,** Russ Lappa; **94,** Richard Haynes; **96 both,** Clive Streeter; **97l,** Corbis-Bettman; **97m,** Clive Streeter; **97r,** The Granger Collection; **102,** Richard Megna/Fundamental Photographs.

Chapter 4
Pages 106–107, Klaus Lahnstein/Getty Images, Inc.; **107 inset,** Richard Haynes; **108, 109,** Russ Lappa; **111b,** Richard Haynes; **111 all the rest,** Russ Lappa; **112 both,** Manfred Kage/Peter Arnold; **113, 114,** Richard Haynes; **116 inset,** Andrew Syred/Photo Researchers, Inc.; **116l,** Russ Lappa; **116r,** Chuck Savage/Corbis; **117l,** Russ Lappa; **117r,** Michael Newman/PhotoEdit; **120l,** Mark Richards/PhotoEdit; **120m,** Getty Images; **120r,** Sky Bonillo/PhotoEdit; **1221l,** David R. Frazier/Photo Library/Photo Researchers, Inc.; **122b,** Getty Images, Inc.; **122 inset,** Joe McDonald/McDonald Wildlife Photography, Inc.; **122t,** David Young-Wolff/Photo Edit; **123b,** L. Dematteis/The Image Works; **123t,** Richard Haynes; **124,** Andrew Syred/Science Photo Library/Photo Researchers; **125,** Russ Lappa; **126l,** The Granger Collection, NY; **126r,** Corbis-Bettman; **127l,** A/P Wide World Photos; **127m,** Camilla Smith/Rainbow; **127r,** Ryan McVay/Getty Images, Inc.; **128,** Peter Menzel Photography; **129,** Zach Holmes; **130, 131,** Richard Haynes **132,** Gurinder Osan/AP/Wide World Photos; **133l,** Ronnie Kaufman/Corbis; **133r,** Richard Vogel/AP/Wide World Photos; **134,** David Young-Wolff/Photo Edit; **135,** Sarah Swersey, artwork on CD by Rachel Swersey; **136–37 portraits of a boy,** Getty Images, Inc.; **137 image of space suit,** Roger Ressmeyer/Corbis; **138b,** David Young-Wolff/PhotoEdit; **138t,** Manfred Kage/Peter Arnold.

Pages 142b, Library of Congress; **142m,** U.S. Dept. of the Interior, National Park Service, Edison National Historic Site; **142t,** Dave King/Dorling Kindersley; **143,** U.S. Dept. of the Interior, National Park Service, Edison National Historic Site; **144–45,** AP/Wide World Photos; **145b,** Bettman/Corbis; **145t,** Smithsonian Institution, EMP-LAR-BB1, Courtesy of the General Electric Lighting Co.; **146b,** Brooks/Brown/Photo Researchers, Inc.; **146m,** U.S. Dept. of the Interior, National Park Service, Edison National Historic Site; **146t,** Everett Collection; **147b,** Tom McCarthy/PhotoEdit; **147t,** U.S. Geological Survey/Science Photo Library/Photo Researchers, Inc.; **148,** Tony Freeman/PhotoEdit; **149b,** Russ Lappa; **149m,** Richard Haynes; **149t,** Russ Lappa; **150,** Richard Haynes; **152,** Richard Haynes; **154,** Tanton Yachts; **155,** Richard Haynes; **157b,** Richard Haynes; **157t,** Dorling Kindersley; **159,** ImageStop/Phototake; **162,** Richard Haynes; **169,** Richard Haynes; **170,** Kennan Ward/Corbis; **171,** Richard Haynes; **175,** Richard Megna/Fundamental Photographs.

All Metals